Kingship, Rebellion and Political Culture

Medieval Culture and Society

General Editor: Miri Rubin

Advisors: Jean Dunbabin and Robert Stacey

Medieval Culture and Society provides a framework for the study of an array of themes in the history of medieval Europe, including some which are looked at comparatively, and approaches them in the light of the new theoretical reflections.

The books in this series will be useful to students, to a wide range of scholars and to the general reader. Written in clear and elegant prose, they concisely present new sources and their interpretation and also highlight underlying method and theory.

Published titles

Jean Dunbabin
CAPTIVITY AND IMPRISONMENT IN MEDIEVAL EUROPE, 1000–1300

Yitzhak Hen
ROMAN BARBARIANS

Elisabeth van Houts
MEMORY AND GENDER IN MEDIEVAL EUROPE

Phillipp Schofield
PEASANT AND COMMUNITY IN MEDIEVAL ENGLAND, 1200–1500

Björn Weiler
KINGSHIP, REBELLION AND POLITICAL CULTURE
England and Germany, c. 1215–c. 1250

Medieval Culture and Society Series
Series Standing Order ISBN 978–0–333–75058–2 (Hardback)
978–0–333–80324–0 (Paperback)
(*outside North America only*)

You can receive future titles in this series as they are published by placing a standing order. Please contact your bookseller or, in case of difficulty, write to us at the address below with your name and address, the title of the series and the ISBN quoted above.

Customer Services Department, Macmillan Distribution Ltd, Houndmills, Basingstoke, Hampshire RG21 6XS, England

Kingship, Rebellion and Political Culture

England and Germany, c. 1215–c. 1250

Björn Weiler

Senior Lecturer in History, University of Wales, Aberystwyth

First published in hardback 2007 and in paperback 2011 by
PALGRAVE MACMILLAN

Palgrave Macmillan in the UK is an imprint of Macmillan Publishers Limited, registered in England, company number 785998, of Houndmills, Basingstoke, Hampshire RG21 6XS.

Palgrave Macmillan in the US is a division of St Martin's Press LLC, 175 Fifth Avenue, New York, NY 10010.

Palgrave Macmillan is the global academic imprint of the above companies and has companies and representatives throughout the world.

Palgrave® and Macmillan® are registered trademarks in the United States, the United Kingdom, Europe and other countries.

ISBN 978–1–4039–1167–4 hardback
ISBN 978–0–230–30236–5 paperback

This book is printed on paper suitable for recycling and made from fully managed and sustained forest sources. Logging, pulping and manufacturing processes are expected to conform to the environmental regulations of the country of origin.

A catalogue record for this book is available from the British Library.

A catalog record for this book is available from the Library of Congress.

10   9   8   7   6   5   4   3   2   1
20   19   18   17   16   15   14   13   12   11

Printed and bound in Great Britain by
CPI Antony Rowe, Chippenham and Eastbourne

Contents

Acknowledgements

This book was begun at the suggestion of Timothy Reuter, and his advice, counsel and criticism have been sorely missed. Michael Clanchy and Nick Vincent have been most encouraging and supportive throughout the various stages of this project; Miri Rubin and Bob Stacey exemplary editors; and Michael Strang at Palgrave a most patient publisher. Haki Antonsson, Len Scales and Nicholas Vincent have read all or part of the manuscript, and I am grateful for their encouraging comments. Parts of this book were presented to conferences and seminars at Bamberg, Bergen, Cambridge, Durham, Leeds, London, Paris, and St Andrews, and I am thankful for the many criticisms and suggestions received on these occasions. Bill Aird, Haki Antonsson, Sverre Bagge, Martin Brett, Philippe Buc, David Carpenter, Stephen Church, David d'Avray, Christoph Egger, Patrick Geary, Deborah Gerish, Piotr Gorecki, Sarah Hamilton, Frédérique Lachaud, Peter Lambert, Sarah Lambert, Simon MacLean, Leidulf Melve, Huw Pryce, Frank Rexroth, Theo Riches, Len Scales and Nicholas Vincent made for an at times repeat, but always instructive, critical and stimulating audience. Without their advice, collective wisdom and common sense, errors would have been even more numerous, misreadings wilder and interpretations more far-fetched. For what weaknesses remain, I alone take responsibility.

This book would still be unfinished without a year's research leave, funded by the University of Wales Aberystwyth, and the Arts and Humanities Research Council, and I am grateful for the opportunity to work in so concentrated and uninterrupted a fashion. Research for this book was made easier by the patient forbearance of Jeff Davies; the indefatigable services of Steve Mahoney and his colleagues; a generous supply of photocopies from Frank Rexroth and Christoph Egger; and a period of prolonged access to the holdings of Cambridge University Library. The latter came about through a Visiting Fellowship at the *Centre for Research in the Arts, Social Sciences and Humanities*, and I would like to thank Ludmilla Jordanova and the staff at Wolfson College and CRASSH for their support and hospitality, and for what proved to be an intellectually stimulating and academically most productive period. While the book was completed at Cambridge, a Visiting Fellowship at the *Centre for Medieval Studies* at the Universitet i Bergen allowed for final revisions to be made and an opportunity to test out some of the book's ideas.

Stephan Schmuck, Peter Lambert, Richard Rathbone, Gerry Hughes, James Vaughan, Martyn Powell, Jeff Davies, Robert Harrison, Phillipp Schofield, Andrew Priest and Roger Price provided much needed intellectual and social routes of escape, mostly to the Champion on the Thames in Cambridge or the Glengower Hotel closer to home (with an honourable mention to Haki Antonsson and the 'Office' in Bergen), but all the more fruitful ones for it. Last but by no means least, mention must be made of the British Academy funded research network on 'Political Culture in Norman and Angevin England (1066–272) in Comparative Perspective'. Its meetings, with their easy and free-flowing exchange of ideas, and atmosphere of friendly yet rigorous discussion, provided a much-appreciated (and eagerly anticipated) opportunity to debate, argue, think and explore. That all this could be done without needing to worry about output and output evaluation criteria, made this a project in which to have been involved has been both a pleasure and a privilege.

The cover illustration, from Matthew Paris' *Chronica Majora*, has been reprinted with kind permission of the Master and Fellows of Corpus Christi College, Cambridge (Parker Library Ms 16, fol. 56v).

Abbreviations

RW   *Rogeri de Wendover Chronica sive Flores Historiarum*, ed.
      H.O. Coxe, 5 vols, English Historical Society (London,
      1841–4)
TCE   *Thirteenth Century England*, ed. P. Coss and S.D. Lloyd
      (1983–95); R.H. Britnell, R. Frame and M.C. Prestwich
      (1997–2005); J. Burton, P.R. Schofield and B. Weiler (2007–)
TRHS *Transactions of the Royal Historical Society*

Introduction

This book seeks to offer both more and less than its title suggests. It will not cover thirteenth-century English and German politics as such, but will instead offer a snapshot centring on two pivotal events in the 1230s: the uprising of Richard Marshal against King Henry III of England (1233–4) and the rebellion of Henry (VII) against his father,[1] Emperor Frederick II (1234–5). These events have been chosen for a number of reasons: they are particularly well documented, were central to the political development of the two realms, and thus reveal structures, debates and movements which otherwise often remain hidden. In the German case, we have access to letters by the main actors themselves, a plethora of chronicles and annals, and vernacular sources (poetry as well as history); in England, several very detailed narratives survive, often with information that probably derived from immediate contact with some or all of the main parties. They thus enable us to offer a depth of analysis not normally possible in this period, and to trace a remarkable variety of viewpoints and perspectives. Second, these rebellions were important events: the Marshal's foreshadowed the problems which continued to beset Henry III for the remainder of his reign, and it set a precedent on which many subsequent challenges to royal authority in England were to be based. In Germany, it was not so much Henry (VII)'s rebellion that mattered, as how it was handled by his father. The legal, political and ideological framework that came to the fore in the response to Henry's challenge was to form the basis for subsequent reforms of imperial politics well into the fourteenth century. One of the key documents to emerge from Henry's revolt – the *Reichslandfrieden*, or imperial land peace, of Mainz (1235) – thus became one of the key constitutional documents of the medieval Empire, issued another seven times in the thirteenth century alone.[2] Looking back from the 1250s and later, after the demise of the Staufen dynasty, the rivalries over the imperial throne first between Richard of Cornwall and Alfonso of Castile, and then Ottokar of Bohemia and Rudolf of Habsburg, 1235 was thus perceived as the high point of imperial lordship, and an ideal status quo ante which ought to be restored.[3] This leads to the third and final point: because of their significance, and because they were so well documented, Henry (VII)'s and Richard Marshal's rebellion allow us to explore some of the underlying structures and movements that defined German and English politics in this period, and which make it thus possible to ask a series of more wide ranging questions, significant well beyond the immediate geographical and chronological focus of this book. This is a book about the culture of politics in medieval Europe, not the Marshal's or King Henry's revolts.

Another reason those two rebellions have been chosen is because they juxtapose two political systems which, the *communis opinio* of current scholarship has it, could not have been more different. England has thus commonly been described as the purest form of bureaucratic kingship, based on the undeniably impressive and highly sophisticated administrative apparatus at the king's disposal.[4] Germany, by contrast, has been portrayed as a loose assemblage of territories, ruled over by archaic forms of governance, drawing largely on ritual or other forms of symbolic communication.[5] There was no imperial administration to speak of, and imperial means of rule were thus infinitely more numinous if not ephemeral. This book will not challenge the facts underpinning this picture (there *was* no imperial administrative apparatus to speak of, and the English king *did* have a more elaborate bureaucracy at his disposal), but it will challenge the inferences historians have drawn from them. It will not, however, engage in simple revisionism – this, to use Nicholas Vincent's phrase, is not a case of turning the Plantagenets into Ottonians with Pipe Rolls.[6] Rather, this study will argue for a more complex image, based on the ideals and mechanisms as they emerge from a close and comparative reading of the evidence. While German chroniclers, for instance, gave short shrift to Frederick II's invocations of royal honour, and while they normally ignored acts of ritual self-representation, English chroniclers criticised Henry III because he failed to show sufficient concern for his honour, and they spent considerable time dealing with form of public, symbolic and ritual communication. Why was this so? What does this tell us about the relationship between the structural framework of politics on the one hand, and the ideals and means of political action on the other?

We will also encounter examples of seeming parallels disappearing at closer investigation. German and English chroniclers might thus invoke similar values, but what they meant by referring, for instance, to justice or appropriate counsel could be very different, and yet highlights deeper shared structures and beliefs. The same goes for the tools and mechanisms of politics. This book will focus on the public nature of politics – we will find evidence of debates, of conflicting discourses of legitimate political power and so on, and if we want to appreciate politics properly, we will need to understand how such debates could be conducted, who engaged in them and how they functioned. We will focus on the elites engaged in political exchanges, and make no apologies for that, but these elites, too, consisted of a variety of different groups with different concerns and with different means of engagement at their disposal. More importantly, we are also dealing with a period of transition; new actors begun to emerge (and they are given due weight), while, especially in England, new and more formalised structures for conducting processes of political communication among these elites began to be formed.

By using political entities as unlike each other as England and Germany, it is thus possible to establish paradigms and trace developments applicable across much of the medieval West. If differences dissolve once looked at more closely, if we are able to trace common values and basic organisational mechanisms which could nonetheless be interpreted according to and modified to fit very different structural frameworks, this has implications beyond the immediate focus of this book. Moreover, it may provide a model for somewhat different approaches to studying medieval political history – a subject that has largely developed along modern national lines,[7] and comparative studies are few and far between. There is very little exchange between those working on English and German (or, for that matter, French, Iberian, Italian or Scandinavian) history, and while there have been collaborative volumes published in recent years, they normally consist of neatly compartmentalised contributions which focus on a particular region, without necessarily engaging with more than one of the component parts of the Latin West.[8] Alternatively, scholars have taken a broad trans-European sweep, in an attempt to highlight common forms of organisation.[9] While the former thus exaggerated differences, the latter cannot always do justice to the subtle variations, the fine distinctions and the more complex background to specific cases. By focusing on two realms, this book will avoid either of these pitfalls, and will thus enable us to gain a more subtle, detailed and nuanced understanding of what politics meant in a medieval context.

This book makes no claims of being comprehensive in its coverage. Even so, it fills a number of gaps in our understanding of medieval politics, and does so in terms of perspective, approach and methodology. There is, for instance, as yet no comparative study of political culture in the Central Middle Ages.[10] Similarly, there are a number of volumes seeking to place England within a broader European context,[11] but these are often histories of exchange, rather than detailed and focused comparisons. Once attempts are made at offering broader comparisons, they are in danger of reducing the European context to France – and one of the reasons Germany was chosen was that it falls outside the comparative paradigm within which those few studies of England's place in Europe normally move.[12] If we really want to compare the realm established by William the Conqueror and his heirs, then we should compare it with regions and polities that fall outside the wider Frankish world of which England still formed part. Otherwise we reduce medieval Europe to just one of its component parts.

Equally, there is an often unspoken assumption among historians of medieval England that there was a kind of English exceptionalism that clearly and from as early as the eleventh century set England apart from some shadowy yet homogeneous norm that existed across the Channel.[13] Much of this centred on the more elaborate administrative apparatus at the disposal of English kings, rivalled only by that of the crown of Aragon from the thirteenth century, or that of some Italian communes. It would be unjust, however, to lambaste historians of England alone for a narrow focus: on the German side, the situation is not much better, with most studies either covering relations between Germany and its immediate neighbours[14] or reducing Europe to Northern France.[15] Similarly, while English historians stress English exceptionalism, German historians stress a *Sonderweg*, or separate route, that, in the Middle Ages, separated Germany from a common European norm, normally meant to be that evident in France, of centralised governance and administration, foreshadowing the rise of the modern nation state. Instead, Germany remained a highly regionalised society, where means of symbolic communication, of ritual and ceremonial, compensated for a lack of the kind of centralising apparatus familiar from England.[16] Quite apart from the fact that this sets aside the regional divisions plaguing France, for instance, it does not reflect the reality of Italy, much of the British Isles, Scandinavia or Eastern Europe, where political entities often shared features with medieval Germany rather than France or England. Undoubtedly, there was no administrative system comparable to the English one, and politics were more regionalised, but the reality of politics, we will see here, was infinitely more complex than such neat historiographical models would suggest.

This study also forms part of a debate about the nature of medieval politics and political organisation. In part perhaps helped by the degree to which legal and administrative history in German academia is pursued within departments of law rather than history,[17] also reflecting the sheer excitement that new approaches in anthropology and literature offered to the study of medieval narrative sources, much current scholarship on medieval Germany focuses on questions of ritual, symbolic action, the image and representation of secular power.[18] Much of this work has been associated with Gerd Althoff, and his is a name we will encounter frequently. Althoff has argued fervently for the importance of gesture and ritual in medieval politics, primarily as a means of communication, also as a means of governance and government: it was through the power, status and influence that controlling and applying the public expression of that status (through ritual and symbolic acts) conveyed, that power relations were conducted and established.[19] Similarly important has been the role of honour in Staufen politics, recently highlighted by Knut Görich: honour was the visible expression of power and status, and thus became a principle of ordering and defining politics in late Staufen Germany, partly at least in compensation for other means of exercising, representing and expressing lordship. Conversely, many of the challenges facing Frederick, especially in Italy, emerged out of a legally and administratively more refined way of thinking that rejected such elusive and numinous concepts.[20] We will return to several of these points as this book progresses, but it is worth stating from the outset that, while agreeing with the broad principles of this approach, we will also seek to modify it, and point out some of its inherent weaknesses. We will see, for instance, that while Frederick II and his son engaged in a discourse of honour, this was largely ignored by their subjects, who instead highlighted different means of exercising power, and stressed due process and legal mechanisms instead. Much of this was born out of the specific circumstances of the 1230s (and we will deal with those), but it also points to some of the inherent tensions within the German kingdom, and is thus of wider significance, beyond current academic debates about the uses and significance of ritual.

We are partly able to do so, and able to argue against some of the grain of current scholarship on medieval Germany, because many of the mechanisms Althoff and Görich have pointed to are more clearly evident in the English materials than the German ones. Again, this reflects the specific types of evidence we have to work with, but it is similarly something that goes against established trends in scholarship on twelfth- and thirteenth-century England. Here, the administrative, fiscal and juridical mechanisms of royal lordship have traditionally been emphasised, and relatively little work has been done on ritual aspects of power.[21] There are numerous reasons for this, but perhaps one of the most important is the overwhelming wealth of administrative sources at our disposal, which did not make it necessary to engage with the narrative materials to the same degree German medievalists, for instance, had been forced to.[22] In fact, most of the important narrative sources for the thirteenth century have still not been properly edited, and historical writing in this period has not yet been explored in any way comparable to the detail German historians or those of twelfth-century England have lavished on their narrative sources. It is in these materials, though, that we will find evidence for the kind of phenomena Gerd Althoff and Knut Görich, have written about. While not ignoring the administrative materials, what follows will pay greater attention to the narrative sources and will thus be able to show the degree to which an emphasis on honour, for instance, the importance of gesture, ritual and ceremonial, was by no means a particularly German phenomenon, nor was it something that necessarily denoted administrative weaknesses.

I do not intend to offer a book that merely inverts roles, with Englishmen fretting over royal honour and Germans getting unduly excited about the more arcane points of tenurial law. Rather, I would like to show that the reality of medieval politics, from what we can judge, was infinitely more complex than modern historiographical traditions would suggest. Yes, ritual mattered more in England than historians have been wont to recognise, but this did not override, nor did it ignore, the administrative reality of English kingship. What we have to do instead is explore how these different means were used and perceived by contemporaries, how they reflected, but also how they modified, more familiar means of governance. Equally, in the German case, we should not set aside the more fragmented and regionalised nature of imperial politics (and we will encounter ample evidence for the ways and means by which this formed both the norms and the practice of politics). Neither should we ignore the subtle variations, the debates and conflicts between different norms and expectations, and between different means and mechanisms of royal and princely lordship. Furthermore, only by setting the English and the German experience alongside one another will we be able to see what was specific to either, and what they had in common, and what this ultimately can tell us about the culture of politics not just in England and Germany, but thirteenth-century Europe as a whole.

This book falls into three parts. The first offers an outline of events and will use these to highlight some of the structures underpinning politics. The first two chapters will also offer an introduction to German and English politics in the period – based on the assumption that historians of England may not be familiar with the former, or those of Germany with the latter, and in the hope that this book may attract readers which so far have been familiar with neither. The third chapter will offer a broader contextualisation: what do we mean by rebellion, where do these rebellions fit within the political history of the respective realm, how typical or atypical were they in each case, what do they have in common, where do they differ?

The second part will highlight the ideas and norms of political behaviour. How did contemporaries or near-contemporaries view these events? What do their accounts tell us about norms of legitimate political action? How did the actors themselves seek to legitimise their activities? We will see that the two do not necessarily coincide and will find traces of political debates for which otherwise very little evidence survives. We will also be able to sketch the relationship between the framework of politics and its ideologies. What was the impact of English administrative kingship on the values and norms of politics? How did the more fragmented and decentralised nature of German politics influence the representation of political values?

The third and final section will focus on the tools and mechanisms of politics. More specifically, it will deal with the public framework of politics. Chapter 7 will offer an outline of how that public was created and how it functioned as a political tool. Chapter 8 deals with means of communication: how was that public addressed? Particular attention will be paid to the respective uses of and the relationship between symbolic (ritual, ceremonial) and administrative forms of communication. This brings us to the heart of perceived differences between England and Germany, and also enables us to look at a broader framework of politics. Chapter 9, in turn, will look at the groups constituting that public, their role within the political process and the means they had at their disposal of influencing it. While the first two parts will thus have dealt with political culture from a broadly intellectual–ideological angle, the third will deal with the social reality of politics: how did these processes and exchanges work in practice? How did ideals influence the exercise of power (and vice versa)?

Part I

Kingdoms in Turmoil – The Structures and Framework of Revolt

1

To Be King in Name as well as Deed: the Revolt of Henry (VII) in Germany (1234–5)

I

In the autumn of 1234, worrying news reached Emperor Frederick II: his son and heir, Henry (VII), the king of the Romans and emperor-elect, had allied himself with the Lombard League, the towns and communes of Northern Italy which, under the leadership of Milan, had repeatedly resisted Frederick's attempts at establishing full authority in the north of the peninsula.[1] This threatened to undermine the precarious hegemony which Frederick had been able to establish in Lombardy, and it also endangered a project which during these years had become central to his relationship with Pope Gregory IX: when Frederick, in the summer of 1234, announced that he was to visit Germany the following year, he had done so with the clear intention of using the visit to prepare for a new crusade.[2] This was not merely a formality, or, as has frequently been suggested, an attempt by the emperor to exploit his contemporaries' religious sensibilities.[3] Rather, it was a way by which pope and emperor had been able to find a modus vivendi which allowed them to put aside, at least temporarily, the differences which only a few years earlier, in 1227, had led to Frederick's excommunication, and which, in 1239, were to result in a second excommunication and, in 1245, even his deposition.[4]

Henry's rebellion went to the very core of Frederick's ability to exercise and expand his authority. At the same time, it occurred when Frederick was at the height of his power. In 1227, he had set aside his excommunication, set sail for Jerusalem and negotiated a temporary return of that city to Christian control.[5] On returning to Europe, he overpowered an army sent by Pope Gregory: by 1231, he had been fully reconciled to the pope. Over the next few years, he greatly expanded the range of his

3

authority into all the constituent parts of his domains – the kingdoms of Sicily and Jerusalem, and the Italian and Burgundian parts of the Holy Roman Empire,[6] much of this with papal backing.[7] Henry could not have chosen a less suitable moment to rise up in arms against his father: Frederick's enemies had been overcome, or had at least been rendered impotent, while the sole figure that might have sought to restrain Frederick's power – Gregory IX – had thrown his lot in with the emperor. Yet Henry's uprising reveals the precarious nature of the emperor's hegemony. If Frederick's own son took up arms, a dangerous precedent would be set for those in Lombardy, the Holy Land, Sicily and Burgundy who, so far, had been muted in their resistance.[8] We should thus not allow us to be deceived by the increasing rhetorical bombast of the imperial chancery,[9] or by the apparent ease with which Frederick had been able to overcome resistance. As the way he dealt with Henry's rebellion shows, much of Frederick's power rested on the fact that he was not forced to use it.

All these point to some salient features of imperial lordship in general. The emperor's domains stretched across several lands and kingdoms. As emperor, Frederick ruled over Germany, Northern Italy and the kingdom of Burgundy; he had inherited from his mother the kingdom of Sicily, including Sicily and Sardinia, and much of southern Italy; by right of his second wife, and as regent for their son Conrad IV, he was king of Jerusalem. In each of these regions, different rules of political engagement applied; different legal, political and cultural traditions prevailed. This study will focus on the culture of politics in Germany, largely because this was the heartland of the Holy Roman Empire, and it was on the affairs of Germany that the ability to exercise the imperial office ultimately rested. Yet German affairs cannot be viewed in isolation. The emperor's role as king-regent of Jerusalem mattered, as it both required that he continue to assist crusading efforts in the Holy Land, while also offering him a repertoire of ideas and values which allowed him to press his claims more firmly; but so did his governance of Sicily, which coloured papal perception of his attitudes towards the Church, but which also provided him with financial resources far exceeding those of Germany, and those of Lombardy (which could not be settled without the manpower he hoped to muster in Germany, and which ultimately were to force him into a fatal showdown with the papal court). Henry (VII)'s revolt mattered because it brought to the fore these concerns and because it crystallised the complex web of structures, beliefs, values, ambitions and traditions which constituted the wider framework of imperial politics in the thirteenth century.

II

Henry's elevation to the German throne in 1220 had been a compromise. It was the price Pope Honorius III demanded for Frederick's coronation as Holy Roman emperor. Uneasy about the prospect of one and the same person ruling over Apulia and Calabria to the south, and Lombardy to the north of Rome, Honorius had urged a separation of Sicily from the empire, but in the end settled for the coronation of Henry as king of the Romans.[10] Although it was not unusual for emperors to secure the election of their eldest son as king during their lifetime,[11] Henry's elevation was an altogether different matter. Henry's enthronement did not occur after his father had fully secured his grip on the realm, but at the very outset of his reign, and it had been agreed upon with the express purpose of limiting Frederick's hold on the Holy Roman Empire. There was no precedent which could have defined how exactly the relationship between father and son was to work once Henry came of age in 1227.[12] This lack of clarity had already caused difficulties during Henry's minority, when the regency council frequently sought to counteract the emperor's decisions,[13] and the situation did not improve once Henry himself assumed the reins of government. Frederick insisted, for instance, that, in the person of Duke Louis of Bavaria, Henry (VII) accept the authority of a procurator even after he came of age.[14] A clash between father and son was avoided between 1227, when the emperor's failure to set out on crusade led to his excommunication by Pope Gregory IX and a series of attempts to impose an anti-king in Germany,[15] and 1230, when emperor and pope were reconciled in the Treaty of San Germano. All this only delayed a showdown between father and son.

In 1231, Frederick called on his son to attend an assembly – a *diet* – at Ravenna, aimed to prepare for a campaign against the Lombard League,[16] which Henry refused to attend. They eventually met in spring 1232, when Henry (VII) was forced to accept a series of humiliating terms. Were he to violate these, the German princes were called upon to revoke their fealty and to appeal directly to the emperor for support against his son. To make Henry's humiliation complete, this agreement was confirmed not by the king himself, but by the nobles and prelates in attendance.[17] The meeting thus amounted to a public degradation of the young king, whose status was reduced to that of an imperial official, with authority that could be revoked at will. That Frederick had called upon the German princes to oversee his son's administration amounted to a vote of no confidence in Henry's ability, as if without princely oversight he would not only act unwisely, but was also unlikely to keep his word. This was not the only level, however, on which Henry suffered humiliation: in April 1233, Henry (VII) approached Pope Gregory IX and requested that should he in future disregard his father's orders, the pope would excommunicate him.[18] We may assume that the driving force behind this letter was not Henry, but his father.

Henry's frustration finally erupted in the autumn of 1234. In September, he and a group of allies, mostly bishops from southern Germany and a number of *ministeriales* – unfree imperial knights – met at Frankfurt, and the rebellion began.[19] Henry soon tried to find allies outside Germany, and opened negotiations for a marriage alliance with Louis IX of France,[20] while in November he sent his Marshal to Lombardy to meet with representatives of the Lombard League,[21] with an agreement concluded in December 1234.[22] Henry's Lombard alliance may have been an act of desperation (reflecting his lack of support in Germany), but it was also the single most effective means he had of forcing Frederick to respond to his concerns, and of putting up a credible military and political challenge. It was also a fatal mistake: Henry had drastically reduced his father's room for manoeuvre, and now only a complete quelling of the revolt would do.

The exact course of Henry's revolt is difficult to ascertain, partly because it was to be overcome with such relative ease. Henry's support seems to have centred largely on the Alsace and parts of Swabia, that is, traditional Staufen heartlands, and perhaps Franconia: when, in the summer of 1235, Gregory IX ordered those clergy to come to Rome who had sided with the king, he only listed the bishops of Augsburg and Würzburg, and the abbot of Fulda, as well as two canons of Würzburg cathedral.[23] The bishop of Worms sided with Henry, but there is little sign of support from among the German princes, and the secular backing he seems to have received was largely limited to *ministeriales* and knights.[24] That this is not the whole story and that support may have been more widespread is indicated by the fact that when the emperor later in 1235–6 began to wage war on his namesake, Duke Frederick of Austria, one of the crimes the duke was accused of was his support for Henry (VII).[25] Similarly, Matthew Paris, an English monk and historian, reported that when Henry III's sister Isabella, soon to become Frederick II's new wife, arrived at Antwerp in spring 1235, she had been given a strong bodyguard as rumours abounded about plots to thwart the marriage.[26] Finally, Frederick imposed heavy fines on some imperial officials in Alsace after his arrival in Germany and subsequent to Henry's defeat and imprisonment.[27] Although it is difficult to link these men directly to Henry's revolt, their official function and the fact that they had been active in those areas close to the king's centre of power seem to suggest that they may in part have been punished either for their failure to thwart the revolt, or for their role in it. All this may indicate that Henry had received stronger backing than his ultimate failure would at first suggest.[28]

The backing Henry managed to assemble proved insufficient. More importantly, he even encountered resistance from those whom, in the past, he had gone out of his way to support. The citizens of Worms, for instance, one would have suspected of showing sympathy for the king, as during the early 1230s, Henry had frequently supported them against their episcopal lord.[29] In 1235 they were, however, among those most strenuously resisting him. Henry was soon forced to take desperate measures to shore up his support, demanding hostages and oaths of loyalty from them.[30] The reasons for their change of attitude are complex, linked, as they were, to the internal affairs of Worms. For much of the thirteenth century, the commune and the bishop had been locked in conflict over how the governance of the town was to be divided between them.[31] By 1234, a new bishop, Landulf, had been chosen, who took a more uncompromising stance, and who soon clashed with the commune. More importantly, he was closely associated with Henry (VII), and the citizens' refusal to come to Henry's assistance was thus linked above all to their fraught relationship with the bishop. The citizens had not resisted Henry because they objected to the principles he evoked to justify his rebellion, but because he was aided and abetted by their bishop.

III

Initially, Frederick II treated his son's uprising with flagrant disregard. There is little indication that he had mustered troops beyond those already in his entourage: in fact, when leaving the Sicilian *regno* not long after Easter, Frederick sent many of his Sicilian officials back before proceeding towards the Alps,[32] which he did not reach until April,[33] several months after news of the rebellion must have reached him.[34] His subsequent progress could best be described as leisurely, and he did not enter Swabia, the heartland of Henry's rebellion, until late June.[35] Instead, he spent some time at Regensburg in Bavaria, where he met various, mostly south German princes,[36] before entering the old Staufen lands of Franconia. By the time he reached Kornburg, just outside Nuremberg, in June, his entourage had been swelled by princes from across Germany, including the dukes of Lorraine and Saxony.[37]

Frederick's progress was, however, as remarkable for its leisurely pace as for its peacefulness. There were no armed battles, no skirmishes or sieges. Frederick relied largely on a display of wealth and power to overcome Henry's already meagre support, and this approach seemed successful. The emperor's subjects, as one chronicler put it, flocked to him wherever he appeared, while those who had sided with his son took refuge in their castles and fortified places, leaving the king deserted and alone.[38] Henry's partisans, in the words of another, were immobilised with fear when they beheld the emperor's might and glory.[39]

Henry soon realised that he would stand little chance of resisting his father, and already by June, his emissaries were said to have offered Frederick submission.[40] The exact chronology of Henry's final weeks in power remains unclear.[41] He eventually approached his father in person at Wimpfen in Swabia but was not allowed into the emperor's presence.[42] Instead, he was ordered to submit to the emperor at Worms in early July 1235, where he was put in chains, given into the duke of Bavaria's custody at Heidelberg, before being dispatched to Apulia, where he died in 1242.[43] Frederick's triumph was complete. He spent the remainder of his time in Germany pushing through one of the most radical reforms of the governance of Germany attempted by an emperor until the fourteenth century, before he left for Lombardy again in 1236. He returned in 1237 to oversee the campaign against Duke Frederick of Austria, and it was while Frederick was at Vienna that the chapter of Henry VII's kingship was finally closed, and the German princes elected in Conrad IV, another of Frederick's sons, a new king of the Romans.[44]

The imperial response did not, however, end with overcoming the young king's rebellion. Frederick used the remaining months of his German sojourn to propose and propagate not only an increasingly hostile view of his son's uprising, but also a more elaborate and far-reaching interpretation of imperial power.[45] The great *diets* of Worms in July, which coincided with Frederick's wedding, and at Mainz in August 1235, focused on the heinous nature of the crimes Henry and his allies had committed, but also on the lessons to be drawn from them. At Mainz in particular, the issue of the *Reichslandfrieden*, one of the fundamental laws of the Empire until its dissolution in 1806,[46] was employed to propagate this new reading.[47] This was not merely a matter of the charter's content, but above all the emphasis which Frederick put on the degree to which princely (and, in the case of his son, royal) authority derived through the emperor from God, and how it had to be used to assist in performing the duties of ruling the empire.[48] A violation of these principles was not only an insult to the emperor's majesty but also to God. Henry, in turn, had been punished not only because he rebelled against his father but also because he had failed to perform his duties.

In the weeks after Mainz, this line of argument was soon extended to others, most notably to Duke Frederick II of Austria. The exact circumstances of the duke's falling out with the emperor are difficult to ascertain, but were at least in part connected to Duke Frederick's unwillingness to meet the emperor outside Austria.[49] While this may, at first sight, seem a slight offence, it amounted, in fact, to a rejection of imperial power, and an act of barely veiled rebellion (and one to which we will return in Chapter 7). To this were later added accusations that the duke had sided with the Lombards against the emperor, and that he had supported Henry's rebellion. Above all, though, the duke was attacked because of the numerous crimes he had committed against his own subjects.[50] By violating their duties, Henry and Duke Frederick prevented the emperor from performing his own: both had oppressed their noble subjects (and thereby forced the emperor to intervene), and both had failed in their duty to do justice and maintain the peace (by attacking their neighbours and princes instead). By 1236, the emperor led an army against the duke, and in 1237 took full control of the duke's lands: in the words of one contemporary chronicler, due to the duke's incompetence and tyranny the duchies of Austria and Styria had returned to the empire.[51] The princes' participation in the governance of the empire was no privilege, but a most solemn duty. Similar ideas had been espoused before, but it was to some extent the ease with which Henry (VII) had been overcome that enabled Frederick not only to propose so wide-ranging a reading but also to enforce it against others who, like Henry, continued to defy his authority.

This, then, was the course of Henry (VII)'s revolt, and it has already revealed a number of defining features. There was, for instance, the decentralised nature of imperial lordship, the role of the princes and the somewhat haphazard nature of imperial administration. These three, in turn, were intrinsically linked to the international nature of the empire which, though not unusual, still went far beyond what we can see, for instance, in England. Frederick ruled lands he held by too many different claims, and that were geographically too far apart for centralised imperial government to develop. What imperial administration there needed to be done (such as administering the imperial domain, organising the movements of the court or overseeing its production of documents) relied on clerics (often seconded from bishoprics or abbeys), merchants,[52] or the citizens of imperial towns (like the family of the mayor of Aachen, which also provided the imperial chamberlain).[53] In addition, Frederick had recourse to a particularly German institution: *ministeriales*, that is, unfree knights. Anselm of Justingen, for instance, Henry (VII)'s marshal and the one sent to Lombardy to negotiate his alliance with the League, was a member of such a family, and they also ranked among Henry's foremost supporters during his rebellion.[54]

Many of the functions which in England had been exercised by the king or his officials, such as the raising of revenue and taxation, the keeping of the peace, and the control of weights and measures, in Germany fell to local lords and the princes. There was, for instance, no system of general taxation. The exercise of royal justice was, equally, delegated to princes, and even such important economic prerogatives as the right to mint coins or to levy tolls was shared with secular and ecclesiastical lords. German princes thus exercised a more wide-ranging role than their English counterparts. While Richard Marshal, for instance, who led resistance to Henry III in England in 1233–4, and who, as earl of Pembroke, was one of the most powerful magnates in the realm, had possession of continuous stretches of land only in the border regions of the English kingdom (in south Wales) or in Ireland, the remainder of his estates was distributed across most of the realm.[55] In Germany, by contrast, one of the defining features of thirteenth-century politics was the degree to which the power of princes was increasingly concentrated in certain areas. Sometimes these were small stretches of lands, and men like the duke of Limburg, for instance, rarely managed to escape the control of mightier and more powerful neighbours (in his case, the archbishop of Cologne). Others, like the landgrave of Thuringia, the duke of Bavaria or the duke of Austria, controlled most of the lands of which they were nominally in charge. They still faced rivals – other princes, the emperor, towns, monastic houses or cathedral chapters – but the degree of control they exercised far exceeded that of an English earl.[56] This did not necessarily bring with it a weakening of imperial authority – quite to the contrary, as we will see – but it raises questions about the relationship between the wider framework of politics and the norms and means of political behaviour. These will become even more pronounced once we set the German alongside the English experience of revolt and politics in the 1230s.

2
The Marshal Rebellion in England (1233–4)

We do not know how Henry III responded to news of Frederick's German troubles. We can be certain, though, that he knew about them: after all, Henry (VII)'s final submission coincided with the wedding of Frederick II and Henry III's own sister, Isabella.[1] Henry III may, however, have been struck by the marked differences between Frederick's experience and his own. For by the summer of 1235 Henry III was recovering from the most serious challenge to his authority since his accession: the revolt of Richard Marshal (1233–4). Superficially, both the context and the outcome of the Marshal revolt had been quite different from its German counterpart. While Frederick had overcome his son's revolt with relative ease, and while the emperor had been able to turn his son's revolt into a means for strengthening and expanding imperial lordship, Henry had been forced to concede to the rebels' demands, and only the Marshal's death had spared him even worse humiliation. Once we look (over the following chapters) at some of the arguments used, however, and the mechanisms employed by the rebels, some quite remarkable parallels will emerge. First, though, let us turn to the context of the Marshal rebellion, and its course.

I

The revolt originated in the internal politics of Henry's court, and the vexed history of his accession to the throne.[2] The young king's succession had been far from smooth. When, in late 1215, his father, King John, had sought to renege on Magna Carta, a number of English barons had called upon Prince Louis, the oldest son of the king of France, to claim the English throne. Those who had remained loyal to the monarch, most notably, among the barons, Earl Ranulph of

Chester and the aged William Marshal, earl of Pembroke, and, among the prelates, Stephen Langton, archbishop of Canterbury and Peter des Roches, bishop of Winchester, must have been relieved when John died in October 1216. Yet they were now faced with the challenge of securing the throne for a nine-year-old boy.[3] Even Henry's coronation had been a highly improvised affair, and one contemporary chronicler commented on the haphazard nature of his regalia, the hastily produced coronation garments and the air of insecurity surrounding the proceedings.[4] So unusual were these circumstances, that, in 1220, Pope Honorius III demanded that Henry be crowned again.[5] The regency council, under the leadership of William Marshal, and soon supported by legates dispatched by Pope Innocent III, set out to win back the rebellious barons. In this context, the confirmation and reissue of Magna Carta began to play a major role. Almost as soon as Henry had been crowned and knighted, his regents reissued the Great Charter, omitting some of the more radical clauses, but in essence conceding to the demands of the more moderate rebels. It was this reissue of Magna Carta which laid the foundation for the role which the Charter continued to play in English politics for much of the thirteenth century. That, in turn, centred not so much the document itself, as the principles which it enshrined.[6]

It was, however, only one in a series of steps undertaken to state publicly that Henry III would not hold as unlimited power as his father had done. Equally significant was his re-crowning in 1220, which was combined with the translation of the most famous victim of royal tyranny in England: Thomas Becket.[7] Similarly, worries over the king's willingness to abide by the principles his government had espoused continued to dog the regency. The 1216 reissue of Magna Carta, and all the grants and promises made by the king's regents were valid only until he came of age. Once that date had been reached, they would be null and void unless reissued and confirmed by the king. Worries over Henry's willingness to abide by the spirit of Magna Carta thus led to a series of moves to postpone his official coming of age. In 1223, when Henry turned 16, a compromise had thus to be found which limited the king's ability to exercise power in full, and he did not assume full power until 1227. Furthermore, in 1225 his regents reissued and confirmed anew Magna Carta, with a separate reissue of the clauses relating to the royal forest, and also with demands for the continuing role of Hubert de Burgh, the justiciar in the young king's government.[8] In short, then, by the early 1230s, Henry had become king in name, but not necessarily in deed. Like Henry (VII), Henry had not been trusted with running his own affairs, and remained under the tutelage of his regents longer than was customary. Last but not least, he exercised royal authority under the threatening shadow of baronial revolt – unrest had broken out repeatedly during the 1220s, most importantly in 1223–4, and in 1227. By 1232, when our narrative proper of the Marshal revolt sets in, Henry must have been eager to assert his authority as king, both in relation to his barons, and those who continued to exercise authority on his behalf.

Before turning to the revolt itself, we must consider the relationship between two of the chief players at Henry's court: Hubert de Burgh and Peter des Roches, for the rivalry between them triggered the crisis of 1233–4, and only after their removal from court did Henry's personal rule begin.[9] Both de Burgh and des Roches had come to prominence under King John, but whereas des Roches had been one of the most despised and hated of the king's ministers,[10] de Burgh had gained the respect both of royalists and rebels. He soon played a prominent role among the regents of Henry III, and in 1223 had landed a major coup against des Roches by accusing the latter of treason and by having des Roches' allies removed from the king's administration.[11] Peter des Roches, as bishop of Winchester, had been able to avoid the harsher punishment meted out to some of his supporters, but ultimately deemed it more prudent to leave England. He took the Cross, joined Frederick II's crusade of 1227, and did not return to England until 1231. The bishop soon set out to settle scores.

By the summer of 1232, des Roches had regained Henry III's confidence, and sought to draw political gains from the king's recent setbacks in Wales, and from the court's worsening financial malaise. By July 1232, his triumph was complete: de Burgh was deposed as justiciar, and Stephen of Seagrave appointed in his place, with many of des Roches' allies once again occupying those positions they had lost in 1223. When, in the summer of that year, riots erupted against foreign (mostly Italian) holders of ecclesiastical benefices in England,[12] Peter was given a means to assure himself of papal support. Des Roches accused de Burgh of having masterminded the attacks. Furthermore, he ordered his predecessor to give full account of his income and expenditure during his time as justiciar – and did so in violation of previous royal grants which had exempted de Burgh from exactly this type of investigation.[13] Hubert was aware that this move had been driven not by a desire to reform the king's finances, but to destroy whatever political clout had remained on de Burgh's part. Consequently, he renewed his crusading vow, and took refuge in the chapel of Merton priory.[14] Peter des Roches was, however, unwilling to settle for his success thus far, and in November forced Hubert to stand trial at Westminster.[15] Hubert pleaded guilty, was, deprived of his royal fiefs, and imprisoned at Devizes castle for the remainder of his life. Even his ancestral lands, although they were to pass to his heirs, were held during his lifetime in the custody of the earls of Cornwall, Warenne, Pembroke (i.e. the earl Marshal) and Lincoln.[16]

II

This, in short, was the immediate background to the Marshal's revolt. This is not to say that the earl had played a prominent part either in des Roches rise or de Burgh's demise. Like most of the secular and ecclesiastical barons of England, he remained absent from the royal court during the critical summer months of 1232. This was partly due to the fact that, while certainly not a supporter of the bishop of Winchester, Richard was by no means a follower of Hubert de Burgh either. Nor should we believe the picture painted by contemporary chroniclers, of a man who steadfastly defended abstract principles of justice against a tyrannous des Roches. For, in November 1232, Richard had been quite willing to condone the king's revocation of his own earlier safe conducts and the imprisonment of de Burgh. After all, not only was he, as earl of Pembroke, appointed as guardian of part of de Burgh's inheritance, but Richard was also one of those responsible for keeping de Burgh confined at Devizes. In fact, Nicholas Vincent has recently suggested that the Marshal began to distance himself from court exactly because the rewards for his role in de Burgh's fall were nowhere as generous as he might have expected.[17] Rather, the earl's increasing disenchantment with the king and the king's court was related to old grievances over the inheritance of his brother William Marshal II, who had died in 1231. According to the most recent estimate, the earl was in danger of loosing nearly a third of his English revenues, with further losses looming in Ireland and Wales.[18] Even so, Richard stayed on in Henry III's entourage, and in January 1233, he was at least condoning (though not openly supporting) a renewed attack on Hubert's former colleagues: while at Chepstow, one of the Marshal's most formidable castles, Walter Mauclerk, the treasurer, was forced to render account of his handling of the king's finances.[19] This was ironic, as, according to at least one contemporary observer, it was along other crimes of the regime, Mauclerk's dismissal that drove the marshal to rebel.[20]

The earl's disillusionment with his prospects of promotion culminated in early 1233 and was related to a dispute over the manor of Upavon

(Wiltshire) between the Marshal's close kinsman, Gilbert Basset, and Peter de Maulay, an old partisan of Peter des Roches.[21] The case was, furthermore, tied up in the rivalry between des Roches and de Burgh: a close dependant of the bishop of Winchester, Peter de Maulay had found himself dispossessed in 1228, with the manor granted to Gilbert Basset by the king. In 1233, Henry decided to reopen the case, and granted the estate to Peter de Maulay.[22] This made clear to the Marshal that his continuing presence had brought few rewards. That he was unable to protect even his own kinsmen must also have made evident his loss of standing and influence over the king. In early 1233, he thus joined the increasing number of magnates and prelates who had withdrawn from court.[23] Not only had he been unable to utilise his continuing loyalty to the king, but he had also been isolated from and humiliated before his peers. Ultimately, it was his time in Ireland which laid the foundations for the Marshal's final confrontation with the king's court. Before we turn to that, though, we should take the opportunity to highlight some key features about the nature of English politics and kingship in the early years of the thirteenth century.

The Marshal rebellion was a very different kind of uprising from that of Henry (VII): it was not a dynastic dispute pitching father against son, but one between a monarch and a powerful subject. At stake was not the division of power between a ruler and his chosen successor, but the role and influence of the leadings secular elites of the realm. This also points to one of the distinguishing characteristics of English politics from the late twelfth century onwards: unlike in Germany, the composition of the king's administrative apparatus mattered. When, in 1235, Frederick II appointed a justiciar to treat legal cases on his behalf, the name of that individual survives in the legal documents recording his judgements, but not the narrative sources.[24] Building on the administrative procedures of the late Anglo-Saxon kingdom, the Norman and Angevin kings had developed a range of procedures and mechanisms unparalleled for most of the Middle Ages.[25] The rivalry between des Roches and de Burgh, for instance, manifested itself in a struggle over access to the king and to the means of governance. The ability to raise and maximise the king's revenues was both the tool by which predominance at court could be established, and an instrument with which rivals could be fought. De Burgh was toppled not by brute force, but by the gradual withdrawal of grants and privileges, by being forced to render account for his financial administration, and the full exploitation of the bureaucratic and legal apparatus at des Roches' disposal. Similarly,

Richard Marshal's fall from favour expressed itself in his inability to receive the legal and fiscal rewards he had hoped for, a loss manifested in his failure to protect Gilbert Basset in the legal proceedings initiated by de Maulay.

III

As in the case of Germany, English politics cannot be viewed in isolation. The king of England had manifold interests beyond the borders of his kingdom. There were, for instance, his British neighbours, with the Marshal drawing on allies in Wales, and some circumstantial evidence suggesting links with Alexander II of Scotland.[26] Equally, the conflict between des Roches and the Marshal had, to some extent, emerged from the loss of Normandy in 1204 and that of Poitou in 1224: Henry III had to find new means of rewarding those who, out of loyal service to the king and his father, had lost their ancestral lands. This meant an increasing demand for royal patronage, and one which increasingly pitched newcomers like des Roches against the established ranks of the Anglo-Norman aristocracy. This international dimension equally applied to Henry's subjects. Richard Marshal had been brought up mostly in France, and it was to Capetian concepts of royal authority that he was indebted,[27] while one of the newcomers of the 1230s, Simon de Montfort, had not previously ever been to England.[28] These links could lead to astonishing cross connections: Peter des Roches, for instance, on returning from crusade, had spent some time at the court of Emperor Frederick II, and some later observers in England were in fact to portray him as a fifth columnist, who secretly sought to bring England under the emperor's dominion.[29]

On the surface, Henry III, like his imperial counterpart, thus presided over a conglomerate of lands which he held (or claimed to hold) by a variety of rights, and where his authority was exercised in a number of ways: by inheritance (England and Gascony), in fief (Normandy and Poitou), by right of conquest (Wales and Ireland), as overlord (Scotland and parts of Wales). His hegemony rested on direct military force (in relation to most of his British neighbours), but also on the resources with which his English kingdom provided him. England, furthermore, played a more important role within the domains ruled over by Henry III, than Germany did in those of Frederick II. To the emperor, his heartlands mattered politically and symbolically, as an area in which he had to exercise control if he wanted to maintain his imperial status, but his political preoccupations lay elsewhere (notably Lombardy), and his financial resources ultimately derived not from the empire, but the kingdom of Sicily. Whatever tools of governance Henry III had at his disposal, by contrast, overwhelmingly depended on his control of English affairs. It was from his English lands and subjects that he received the financial means with which to pursue the recovery of his paternal inheritance, and by which to maintain and extend his dominion over the Scottish, Welsh and Irish; his wars depended on the military backing of his English subjects, and it was on his relationship with the barons and clergy of England that his position on the wider European stage rested. A challenge in England thus had to be answered quickly and decisively.

When Richard returned to England in the summer of 1233, he could not have done so at a moment more inconvenient for Henry III. The financial demands of his system of alliances against Louis IX had forced him to find ever more unpopular means of raising funds,[30] while, the debate over the election of a new archbishop of Canterbury, which had dragged on indecisively since 1231, was coming to a head.[31] Both the king's and des Roches' situation had become more tenuous. Several members of the aristocracy had begun to withdraw from court,[32] while unrest loomed in the Welsh marches. As the king's army approached Gloucester, news reached it that the Marshal was planning to hold a tournament at Worcester,[33] dangerously close to Wales. This was taken as an act of open defiance, and Henry initiated a procedure of distraint against the Marshal.[34] This was shortly thereafter extended to others who were to play a prominent part in the Marshal rebellion, among them Gilbert Basset,[35] and William Ferrers.[36] Richard and his allies failed to attend a parliament called to Oxford for late June, where it also became clear that Henry would not be able to count on the full backing of the assembled prelates and barons.[37] Nonetheless, it was only after Richard Marshal and Gilbert Basset had held a meeting with their armed followers near London, that Henry decided on the use of force.[38] The rebellion had begun.

By late August 1233, the king's army laid siege to the Marshal's castle of Usk, while many of his partisans had been brought to heel and had sought to regain royal favour.[39] At this stage, it also seemed as if Marshal and Basset were hampered by an inability to recruit support beyond their own immediate households.[40] However, while Richard Marshal might have recognised this, many of his followers, among them Gilbert Basset and Richard Siward, did not. The latter, in particular, was to play a major part in the renewed outbreak of hostilities in the autumn of

1233. In an act of bravado, Siward, a man famed for his martial exploits, but of limited means and previously doubtful loyalty, and his band had attacked the bishop of Winchester's manors, and had made off, among others, with the bishop's harness.[41] This was soon followed by a raid on Devizes (where Hubert de Burgh was held prisoner) and the freeing of the justiciar. This undermined the king's moral, political and military authority. To many contemporary observers de Burgh's imprisonment and rescue encapsulated the tyranny of des Roches regime and the justice of the Marshal's case. Siward's rescue of de Burgh became an iconic moment of resistance, of pinning justice against tyranny, valour against treachery. Moreover, this had not been Hubert's first escape: he had initially sought refuge in the parish church at Merton, and at Devizes had sought sanctuary once more when he heard that des Roches was to be appointed as his keeper, and that the bishop was planning his murder. To make matters worse, the king ordered Hubert to be taken from the Church and returned to the castle, thereby violating ecclesiastical sanctuary.[42] Although the raid achieved little in military terms – most of de Burgh's former proteges had shown no inclination to come to his support before, and they certainly did not flock to his defence now – it was a major blow against the king's reputation.[43] Henry and his court appeared not only as riding roughshod over basic principles of political behaviour, as cruel, unjust and tyrannical, but also as incompetent and easily defeated. They were not just villains, but inept ones to boot.

The violation of sanctuary at Devizes (which had resulted in the bishop of Salisbury excommunicating the garrison and voicing his protest before the king) was not the only issue to sour relations between king and prelates. Henry's remained unable to settle the succession to the archbishopric of Canterbury, while the treatment meted out by the king's officials to Walter Mauclerk – who had been assaulted by the garrison at Dover as he sought to depart for exile in Flanders – did little to improve matters.[44] It thus comes as no surprise that the clergy, too, began to urge the king to seek a settlement with Marshal. Matters came to a head during a meeting of the royal council at Westminster in October 1233,[45] when des Roches was said to have made his infamous statement that there were no peers in England as there were in France, and that the king had the right to exercise freely his judicial authority, mediated by his officials.[46] To contemporaries, this may have sounded not a little like a full-scale dismissal of Magna Carta itself (which, after all, had aimed at defining the limits of royal jurisdiction in relation to the free men of his realm), and thus also explains why the rift which had begun to open between the king's government and the Church at large continued to widen. It was then, too, that the precarious truce which had been established with the Marshal collapsed, culminating in the confiscation of the earl's estates.[47]

IV

With the campaign against des Roches unlikely to move beyond the current stalemate, Henry withdrew to London.[48] By February 1234, he faced renewed pressure from the Church, led by Edmund Rich, the new archbishop of Canterbury. In fact, events at the royal council meeting in February were to provide another high point in the description of des Roches' tyranny. Our main sources for these events are Roger of Wendover and his reviser and continuator, Matthew Paris, both monks of the Benedictine house of St Albans,[49] who constructed events as a final showdown between those eager to aid the king in reforming the governance of the realm, and the pernicious force that was Peter des Roches.[50] In reality, Henry III had already begun to distance himself from the bishop, had forged closer ties with Archbishop Edmund Rich, issued a safe conduct to Richard Siward's wife, and allowed Hubert de Burgh's wife to reclaim some of her possessions.[51] This, in combination with an unexpected breakthrough for royalist forces in Wales and the Marshal's departure for Ireland in March, brought about the desired result: during a council at Northampton a temporary truce was declared, with a full settlement to be reached during a meeting scheduled to convene in London in early April.[52]

Des Roches' days in power were numbered.[53] Although the bishop still attended the consecration of Edmund Rich on 2 April, by June his disgrace was complete: while away on diplomatic business at the court of Louis IX of France, his letters of credit were revoked, he was fined £100, and Gilbert Marshal and the citizens of Winchester were allowed to open court proceedings against him.[54] Des Roches' fall was followed by that of some of his close associates, and by a formal reconciliation with Gilbert Marshal and many of the chief rebels. This was the end of Peter's role in English politics,[55] and this end was formally sealed by the initiatives undertaken by the new regime under Edmund of Canterbury, which issued a series of missives reforming the governance of royal justice with specific reference to Magna Carta, and who combined this with a programme of ecclesiastical and moral reform, at least in part aimed at distancing itself from the real or alleged practices of des Roches' regime.[56] In many ways, the rebels had won: Gilbert Marshal and even Richard Siward were reconciled to the king, Hubert de Burgh was allowed to enjoy at least some of his properties, while des Roches and his key allies had been disgraced. It was, however, a bitter-sweet victory, overshadowed by news of the Marshal's death in Ireland.

The exact circumstances of the Marshal's death remain unclear. Roger of Wendover and other chroniclers painted a picture of betrayal and treachery, centring on the king's court, juxtaposed with the noble resistance of Richard Marshal, who died in the defence of liberty and justice. There survives, however, little evidence which could have confirmed that portrayal, and its value lies primarily in the image it allows us to paint of the ideas and values by which Wendover and his peers judged political actions. To some extent, the Marshal's revolt had been doomed to fail from the moment he left Wales for Ireland.[57] Shortly thereafter, Llewellyn concluded a truce with the royal government, while the Anglo-Irish barons remained at best neutral, and at worst viewed this as an opportunity to settle their own scores with the Marshals. Although there is little indication of sympathy with des Roches, Maurice FitzGerald, the royal justiciar, managed to assemble as sizeable army to lead into the field against the rebels. Their armies met on 1 April, initially to negotiate a truce. Seeing that this failed, Richard led his troops into battle against a far larger force, and was eventually felled.[58] Mortally wounded, he was brought to a nearby castle, where he died two weeks later.[59]

V

The impact of the Marshal rebellion is difficult to ascertain. Henry certainly lost one of his most trusted advisors, and he was forced to concede control of his government (albeit temporarily). Events of 1233–4 are also eerily reminiscent of the second major crisis of his reign in 1258–65, when, in another struggle over access to royal patronage and the desire to control the appointment of royal ministers, Henry was even placed under the tutelage and wardship of his barons.[60] There were important differences between the two (with the latter, for instance, able to attract a far wider range of popular support),[61] and some of the complaints made by contemporary observers about the king's governance during the 1230s continued to resurface, but we should be wary of ignoring the quarter century that had elapsed in between. The post vacated by Hubert de Burgh, for instance, was never refilled, and for the next twenty-four years, Henry exercised a remarkable degree of independence over his choice of ministers and the running of the royal government. Des Roches' demise marked thus a resurrection of royal authority, and heralded a degree of independence on the king's part that makes it not implausible to describe the resignation of des Roches as the end of Henry's minority.[62] Matters are, of course, complicated by the fact that in Matthew Paris we have a prolific hostile comment-ator on the king's actions. While, as we will see, Matthew constructed events as a continuous critique of the king's person, rather than his government, most of those who had lived through the events of 1233–4 took a more forgiving view of the king. In this respect, the Marshal's rebellion had only a limited impact. It set the tone for the way in which future rebellions or acts of resistance could be reported, and became the model on which resistance was based, and against which it was judged, and the same can be said about the mechanisms that were honed and developed in dealing with the Marshal's uprising. It did not, however, immediately curtail or limit Henry's ability to reign with a considerable degree of independence from his barons and magnates. It has shown, first, the degree to which a pattern of political communication, of ideals and values was established that was to dominate English politics for most of the thirteenth century, and, second the importance of the ques-tions at the heart of this book: what does all this tell us about the ideology and what about the means and mechanisms of politics? How do divergent frameworks and mechanisms influence the ideology and the mechanisms of politics?

3
Rebellion in Context

The differences between the Marshal's revolt and Henry (VII)'s were manifold, and perhaps most evident in how they were portrayed by contemporary and later observers. Richard Marshal, in death, achieved victory; Henry lived, but remained a prisoner for the remainder of his life. For some time, Richard Marshal remained the paragon of the wronged vassal who valiantly stood up to the repressive actions of a king's corrupt ministers. It was not until the 1260s and after, with the death of Simon de Montfort at the battle of Evesham in 1265,[1] that Richard was displaced as the beacon of noble resistance. Even so, in the fourteenth century, for instance, Robert of Gloucester still glorified the Marshal's stance, praised him for the resistance towards des Roches, and extolled the valour of his deeds in Ireland,[2] while in the turmoils of the Edward II's reign, Marshal's rebellion was still remembered as an example of resistance, honourable and just though futile, to the king's mistreatment of his barons.[3] Richard's reputation was tied to the image which contemporary chroniclers had constructed of him as a defender of the proper norms of royal governance.

Henry (VII)'s reputation also began to change, but the shift centred on the manner of his fall, not the conflict that had triggered it. If Marshal was a heroic victim of royal tyranny, Henry was a tragic one, evoking pity, not admiration. Most contemporaries had condemned his revolt, and it was the manner of his death and the cruelty of his punishment that continued to be remembered. His deposition and captivity encapsulated – as it did to the anonymous author of the *Vita* of the emperor's most fervent opponent, Pope Gregory IX – the ruthlessness and ingratitude of Frederick II.[4] There was thus a reason why Frederick lamented the passing of his son so publicly, and to correspondents as far afield as the king of England.[5] At the same time, this change in attitude was by no means limited to those already hostile to the emperor. In the early fourteenth century, for instance, the author of the *Österreichische Reimchronik* (Austrian Verse Chronicle) cited Henry's fate as a warning example to all rulers: had Frederick II tempered his wrath with mercy, his son would not have died in prison.[6] To later generations, Henry became an unfortunate prince, punished well beyond what was due, and a token of his father's depravity. That, though, was all for which he was remembered.[7]

Despite these differences, Henry's and Richard's uprisings also had much in common. How much will become fully apparent once we turn (in chapters 4–9) to the ideals and the mechanisms of political exchange. Already they tell us something about the wider framework of politics, the role of violence in medieval politics and the underlying structures of governmental organisation in England and Germany. By placing Henry and Richard in their historical context, we can more easily grasp the importance and significance of their actions. What follows will not offer a comprehensive overview of their revolts (which would require a book length study of their own).[8] Rather, it aims to sketch out some key questions and seeks to place the violence of Richard's and Henry's rebellion within its broader contemporary context. Neither was the first or the only challenge to Henry III's or Frederick II's authority, and one of the questions we thus need to ask is to what extent the political actors of 1233–5 may have been influenced by established models of behaviour. This framework of rebellion, after all, also determined how Henry III and Frederick II responded to those challenges, and how their subjects perceived and interpreted them.

I

Let us begin with Richard Marshal. The precedent invoked by at least some of the Marshal's contemporaries was the events leading up to and following Magna Carta. A continuation of the *Margam Chronicle* from South Wales, for instance, likened the events of 1233–4 directly to those twenty years before: the conflict had sprung from des Roches' attempt to bring aliens to England with whom to oppress the clergy and people, 'just as had been done under King John'.[9] At the same time, this is the only explicit reference to Magna Carta and the turmoil of King John's reign. Our main source for the events of 1233–4, for instance, Roger of Wendover, constructed his account in very different terms. While under John, conflict had arisen over the king's exactions and undue financial demands, and while it had clearly pitched the king against his people, in the 1230s, this was a conflict between the nobles of England and those that prevented them from gaining access to the king. The conflict was not about abstract liberties (although these were, of course referred to), but about who should advise and counsel the king; and it did not pitch Henry against his barons, but Henry's barons against those who usurped the royal council. At the same time, striking echoes remained which should not be ignored. At one point, for instance, Richard Marshal threatened that he and other barons would withdraw from the royal council unless justice was done.[10] In 1215, this had been the first step leading to the elevation of Prince Louis as rival claimant to the English throne,[11] while Peter des Roches' alleged response to the Marshal's demand that he be judged by the peers of England – that in England, unlike France, there were no peers[12] – may have contained echoes of a key clause in the 1215 version of Magna Carta: clause 39 that 'no free man shall be taken or imprisoned or disseised or outlawed or exiled or in any way ruined except by the lawful judgement of his peers or the law of the land.'

Certainly, the king's need to take counsel was intrinsically linked to the clauses of the Great Charter, and the 1215 document had also set a precedent by stipulating a clear and well defined right to withdraw one's allegiance should the king continue to violate the freedoms of his people, the laws and customs of his realm. This was not a peculiarly English principle (we will encounter some striking parallels from Germany), but the role it assigned to the magnates as overseers, evaluators and judges of the king's government (ultimately, the reason Wendover and others saw as driving the dispute), and the ease with which a royal dereliction of duty could justify formal resistance, were new, and became more pronounced in the course of the thirteenth century. The legal treatise ascribed to Bracton, and probably composed in the household of William de Raleigh during the 1230s, *De Legibus et consuetudinibus Angliae*, On the Laws and Customs of England, listed a number of instances in which the barons of the realm were duty-bound to restrain and correct the king, and to do so by force if necessary: first and foremost among them whenever and wherever he failed to act in a fair and just manner.[13] When, probably around 1240, Matthew Paris revised Wendover's account of King John's succession, he similarly included a section which reflected the thinking of the 1230s, rather than of the years around 1200. Like Saul and David, John was told, he had been chosen, not because he was closely related to his predecessor, but because he was the most suitable candidate: it followed that should he prove incapable of fulfilling his duties, he could just as quickly be deposed again.[14] No such statement had been recorded by Wendover, who in fact simply reported the king's coronation and gave an outline of John's coronation oath.[15] While we should avoid over-interpreting this insertion by a chronicler notoriously hostile towards royal authority, that it chimed with other accounts of events in 1233–4 suggests that there was more to this than one especially querulous monk giving vent to his frustrations. Armed and forceful resistance to royal actions became more common in thirteenth-century England, and more easily legitimised, than in other parts of the medieval West.[16] Marshal was thus linked to Magna Carta and the 1215 uprising not by the king's tyranny, but by the principles he invoked, and the ease with which these principles could be called upon to legitimise what, after all, had first and foremost been a squabble over access to the royal person, and the flow of royal largesse.

All this may furthermore explain the mixture of panic and intransigence in the court's response. We will deal with both the ideas and the actions brought into play by Henry's chancery over the next few chapters, but it is worth remembering that while, on the one hand, violence was used sparingly and gradually, on the other the rejection of the Marshal's claims was most forceful. While Richard was thus portrayed as a traitor and a brigand, some evidence suggests that the public display of condemnation hid a less visible and rather anxious desire to appease him. Marshal was simultaneously fashioned as someone prepared to sell his king and kingdom to Welsh savages, and was in secret offered full restitution of his status if only he submitted, and if he did so publicly. In fact, the force with which the king insisted on a public display of submission (and hence acknowledgement of guilt) adds to the impression of something close to desperation. Events were probably too reminiscent of Henry's early years (the prolonged civil war and slow recovery of royal power after 1216; the activities of Faukes de Breaute, which, in 1224, had tied up resources which otherwise could have been used for the defence of Poitou), and any display of violence against the king's authority was eyed as in danger of pushing the realm to the brink of civil war. It was this fear that drove the king's administration.

II

In Germany, the last time an emperor had faced a challenge from his son had been in 1105, when Henry V deposed his father, Henry IV. Circumstances then had been unusual: the challenge occurred at the height of the investiture controversy, and may have to be viewed as an attempt by Henry V to extricate himself from the more and more dangerous situation into which he had been manoeuvred by his father.[17] Nothing comparable had happened in the 130 years since, partly, too, because only twice during this period did a son directly succeed his father – in 1190 and 1196 – and only once was a son old enough to exercise authority during his father's reign (Henry VI, who had been knighted in 1184).[18] German royal sons thus had fewer opportunities to rebel against their fathers.

At the same time, German politics were a more violent affair. There may have been fewer revolts than in England, but the use of political violence was both more widespread, and more easily accepted. Henry III's subjects, too, faced their fair share of unrest: in 1232, for instance, Robert Tweng, a Yorkshire knight, had led a series of violent attacks on Italian clergy.[19] In 1235, a cleric who had insulted the memory of Richard Marshal died under mysterious circumstances,[20] and Matthew Paris gives a detailed description of how a scuffle between the entourage of Cardinal Otto of St Nicholas, the papal legate, and the citizens of Oxford in 1238 deteriorated into a lethal brawl: some of the good men of Oxford had come to pay their respects at the legate's quarters, but were turned away by a particularly haughty janitor. The resulting argument escalated when a cook of the legate's poured a pot of boiling water over a clamouring cleric. In turn, an especially bellicose Welshman, 'like a second Nebuchadnezzar' killed the cook with a shot from his bow. From thence, there was no holding back, the legate had to seek refuge in a tower, and the king send knights to pacify the situation.[21] In 1269, a dispute between the citizens of London and Winchester (over who was to provide the butler for the king's table) similarly escalated so far, that the king had to cancel the banquet and crown-wearing that had been planned for the occasion.[22] These were conflicts quite different from the ones we might encounter, for instance, in records of judicial eyres or court proceedings, which dealt with the violent antics of drunken Englishmen.[23] This difference, in turn, rests largely with the political subtext of the examples just given. Robert Tweng led riots because he felt his rights of patronage infringed upon, and the Oxford disturbance of 1238 may have given vent to still lingering misgivings about Peter des Roches and his dependants.[24] We should, however, also notice the personnel involved: these were conflicts started not by the leading men of the realm, but by those of low rank and social status. This was only in part intended to show popular support for those critical of the king:[25] one of the distinctions drawn by English chroniclers in their description of the Marshal revolt was that between the rebels, who never or only reluctantly engaged in low level violence, and that of their Poitevin opponents, who held no such scruples. That is, brawls, attacks, killings and similar acts were a sign of behaviour unbecoming of a truly noble agent. This was the kind of activity Poitevins engaged in, but not those worthy of being the king's councillors.

In Germany, such killings were equally frowned upon, but they still occurred with some regularity, and were not as socially determined. One of the surviving documents in the *Urbar* (list of conveyances) of the counts of Falkenstein from the 1160s, for instance, was a letter in which the count seems to condone (or even order) the assassination of a rival.[26] This extended to the highest ranks of society: in 1208, for instance, Frederick's uncle, Phillip of Swabia, had been murdered over a property dispute (by the count Palatine of the Rhineland, that is, a leading member of the imperial aristocracy),[27] as was, in 1225, the first leader of Henry (VII)'s regency council, Archbishop Engelbert of Cologne,[28] and, in September 1231, Duke Louis of Bavaria, Engelbert's successor as regent.[29] Similarly, one of the most spectacular killings of the 1230s was the murder of Conrad of Marburg, who had overseen the persecution of heretics in Germany.[30] The way this killing was reported in contemporary narrative sources is worth noting. The Chronicle written at Worms showed little compassion: Conrad had endangered many of the Rhineland nobility by his persecution of the family of the count of Sayn – even after the count, supported by numerous clergy, had cleared himself of accusations of heresy, Conrad persisted. While the count appealed to the pope, some unnamed knights, whose relatives had unjustly been pursued by Conrad, murdered him and one of his companions, instigating what can best be described a serial killing of friars across Germany. Far from being outraged, Pope Gregory IX was described as joking about the matter, and merely ordered the Germans to desist from killing friars in future.[31] The Erfurt annals, written by a Dominican, unsurprisingly took a slightly different stance. Even so, the anonymous annalist recorded the hostility felt by many towards the inquisitor: one unnamed noble was said to have suggested exhuming and burning Conrad's remains (a treatment reserved for heretics).[32]

This is not to say that such killers normally got away lightly: both those of Phillip of Swabia and Archbishop Engelbert were eventually executed. We should, equally, notice that these killings were so widely reported at least in part because they were such spectacular events. One later biographer of Engelbert even sought to mould him in the style of Thomas Becket, as a martyr for ecclesiastical liberties.[33] Equally, that this cult did not take off, that such killings happened with some frequency, and that they were perpetrated by knights and nobles (in the case of Conrad, the counts of Sayn and Solms were the key suspects),[34] should alert us to the degree to which violent settlements of disputes were a more familiar phenomenon in German than in English politics, and be it just to remind ourselves of the (often fluid) distinction between revolt (which we are concerned with here) and violence (which we are not).[35]

Without doubt, English magnates, too, used force against one another, but they also had other means by which to conduct power struggles, and ones that were less risky and perhaps more effective. In England, since the reign of Henry II at least, a myth had developed, mostly in the writings of contemporary historians and chroniclers, that feuds (in the sense of armed encounters between political actors below the level of king as a regular means of pursuing conflicts) occurred only in times of royal weakness (as during Stephen's reign or in the immediate aftermath of Magna Carta in 1215).[36] The reality was a little more complex, as Paul Hyams has demonstrated,[37] and as is also suggested, for instance, by the emphasis on magnates arriving at parliaments with a suitably armed entourage, or the ease with which men like Richard Siward, the earl Marshal, but also, in 1238, the earl of Cornwall, could assemble and mobilise armed bands.[38] Most importantly, we must be aware of regional variations: in the Welsh marches, for instance, in the palatinate of Durham, or in Ireland, royal authority was felt less strongly or directly, and there is some indication that violent conflicts between nobles were by no means a daily occurrence, but that they happened more frequently than in other parts of the realm. Furthermore, we need to keep in mind that there was a distinct difference between contemporary realities and contemporary ideals of political behaviour: most chroniclers did not record noble feud, unless they, their institutions or their patrons were directly involved.[39] Finally, in those parts of England where royal authority was strongly felt, different means were available to deal with one's opponents – the royal courts, and the mechanisms of patronage and influence. Dependent on the degree to which a party was able to call in favours, to activate links of relationship or friendship, this provided a less dangerous but no less effective means of getting back at one's foes.[40] It was this ability and need to influence the composition of the king's court and household, in turn, which had made the figure of Peter des Roches such an important one: the bishop of Winchester had monopolised access to the king's person, and thereby excluded his rivals to such a degree that, ultimately, armed force was the only means at their disposal to gain the hearing they had been denied.

III

In Germany, Henry (VII)'s case was unusual not only because it was the first time in over a century that a son rebelled against his father, but also because it was the first time since the 1180s, when Frederick Barbarossa clashed with Henry the Lion, that an imperial prince openly defied his emperor. This is not to say that German princes were normally meekly accepting of imperial authority: to the contrary, they were highly adept at getting emperors to change their minds, and they had a variety of means at their disposal. They could ignore them (although that was a risky strategy), plead with them, seek to have the same issue discussed repeatedly at a succession of *diets*, get others to side with them and so on. This partly reflected the fact that emperors, in order to rule effectively, needed the support of their princes. There was no elaborate machinery of government, and the raising of troops or revenue, the keeping of the peace and so on could only be accomplished with the backing of a ruler's princes and prelates. Under these circumstances, armed resistance was neither necessary nor desirable.

The exception to this rule was kings who faced a rival for the throne, and, to some extent, twelfth- and thirteenth-century Germany seems peopled by anti-kings: between 1125 and 1308 only two rulers did not face a rival candidate for the throne – Frederick Barbarossa and his son, Henry VI. At the same time, matters were not as straightforward as they may appear. In fact, between 1138 (with the first Staufen king) and 1245 royal successions ran relatively smoothly. In 1198, the problem had been a more familiar one of a powerful relative ignoring the claims of an under age prince, when Phillip of Swabia decided to make a bid for the throne, allegedly in order to protect the needs of his nephew, Frederick.[41] Only the involvement of Pope Innocent III, and of Richard I of England, had turned the 1198 election (which had pitched Otto of Brunswick and Phillip of Swabia) into such a protracted struggle.[42] After 1245, matters were again complicated by the involvement of the papal court: in 1245, at the council of Lyon, Innocent IV had Frederick deposed as emperor and king, and the need to find a suitable rival dominated imperial politics until the emperor's death in 1250. Furthermore, 1198 was an election routed in a much older tradition of rivalries and conflicts, pitching Frederick Barbarossa's son against one of Henry the Lion's. Although not too much should be made of the old myth of a rivalry between the Staufen and Welf families,[43] this was first and foremost a conflict between rival clans, rather than an accepted means of voicing discontent towards the emperor or king.

The situation was thus remarkably different from that in England. The closest parallel to the uprising of Henry (VII) was that by Henry the Young King, Henry II's eldest son, against his father in 1174. They also invoked strikingly different principles of legitimisation, and reflected fundamentally different political cultures. The English king quite explicitly portrayed himself as a more capable ruler, and sought to justify his uprising with reference to the many crimes committed by his father. In fact, he styled himself as the true heir to Thomas Becket, and as the one who could restore the liberty of the Church, and bring justice and peace to England.[44] His German namesake, by contrast, sought to emphasise his loyalty to Frederick, and portrayed himself not as a better ruler who could replace his father as emperor, but as an aggrieved vassal seeking redress from his lord.[45] Henry the Young King was also representative of an established tradition of twelfth- and thirteenth-century English kingship. It helped, of course, to have a rival claimant who could with some legitimacy be chosen as king – there was a reason, for instance, why Henry I had kept his brother Robert Curthose in prison for over a quarter of a century,[46] and one of the factors which extended the war over Henry I's succession after 1135 was that neither his nephew Stephen of Blois nor his daughter Mathilda had an indisputable claim to the English throne. Equally, rumours about John's involvement in the murder of his nephew Arthur of Brittany seemed credible not only because of John's personality and character but also because of the very real focal point Arthur could have provided to the king's opponents.[47] No similar threats were made during the Marshal revolt, partly because of a lack of suitable candidates (the king's brother, Earl Richard of Cornwall, did in the end side with his brother). This continued well into the latter half of Henry's reign: one of the problems that faced Simon de Montfort and the rebels in 1264–5, for instance, was that all the likely candidates they could call upon to act in Henry's stead firmly sided with the king: his brother Richard, his sons Edward and Edmund, and his brother-in-law, King Louis IX of France.[48] When Simon thus had to act as the king's regent, he brought upon himself the very situation which had faced English kings in the past: those affronted by his demeanour, or disillusioned with his displays of undue favouritism, expressed their opposition by transferring their allegiance to someone with a better claim to act as king – Henry III.

Electing an anti-king was thus not a particularly German phenomenon, but there were fundamental differences in the way the great men of the realm used and responded to the question of anti-kings. German princes, too, had their gripes which could lead them to support one candidate over another (as perhaps best exemplified by the resurrection of Frederick II's claims after 1211, which had originated in disillusionment with the governance of Emperor Otto IV).[49] Until 1298 (with the possible exception of Ottokar of Bohemia's complaints about Rudolf of Habsburg in 1273–4),[50] they did not, however, employ the threat of electing a rival king as a means of voicing opposition towards a monarch's regime or his running of the realm.[51] Neither Henry (VII) nor those like Frederick of Austria who fell foul of the emperor in 1235 considered inviting a rival claimant to the throne. Henry had no need to do so, but even so he avoided seeming desirous of the imperial crown: he did not aim to dethrone his father, but to receive the degree of respect and authority that was his by right. The princes were certainly alert to the possibilities which a split election or a rival claim to the throne could offer them, but they would not have thought of making statements or of taking steps like the ones taken by the English barons. They happily exploited rivalries, but did not normally set out to create them. To some extent, and this will be a recurrent theme, this may have reflected the rather different degree to which an emperor could directly interfere in the affairs of his noble subjects. What mattered was not so much the identity of a king, but the ability to build up a network of supporters, of allies, friends and relatives who would aid a prince against his rival, and who would allow him to bargain more forcefully with his imperial overlord. As we will see, this did not amount to a rejection of imperial lordship, but rather to a paradoxical situation in which even the princes granted the emperor larger powers in theory, in the expectations they had of him and what they wanted him to accomplish, than they might have been willing to countenance in practice.

While Henry's revolt was thus unusual, it nonetheless reveals structures and mechanisms which are representative of thirteenth-century German political culture. It was, for instance, embedded in a whole series of conflicts: between Henry and Duke Otto of Bavaria; Bishop Landulf of Worms and his citizens; Henry and the citizens of Worms; the archbishop and commune of Mainz; the count of Sayn and the early friar inquisitors; or the duke of Austria, and his neighbours in Bavaria, Bohemia and Hungary. We will return to several of these, partly because this local context frequently conditioned the way in which events like Henry's rebellion were recorded and interpreted, but also because these conflicts shared with the king's rebellion a number of important characteristics. The use of violence was to some extent an admission of defeat, of an inability to overcome one's opponents by other means, but it was also normally applied in the hope that it would bring about the involvement of others who would then exert pressure on one's opponent to seek a settlement.[52] Henry (VII), for instance, used violence as a means of soliciting support from the German bishops in dealing with his father. That acts of political violence occurred more frequently in Germany than in England reflected the absence of the effective judicial machinery through which Englishmen conducted their feuds.[53]

Furthermore, violence was normally directed not against the king or emperor, but against one's immediate neighbour or lord. This was not a sign of anarchy, but of the political realities of thirteenth-century German society: often the local prelate or prince was the one most likely to threaten or able to grant the liberties of a town, for instance, not the king of the Romans or the emperor. King and emperor still performed a legitimising function, but it was first and foremost the immediate lord who exercised the authority which it was necessary to resist or invoke. This was thus one of the key differences between the English and the German experience of political violence, but it also helps to contextualise Henry (VII)'s uprising and explain its relevance for the kind of comparison we are seeking to undertake here. The king's rebellion was not unusual because of the ideals it invoked, or because of the mechanisms it employed, but because it was directed against the emperor. At the same time, it was directed against Frederick II because Frederick performed in relation to his son the kind of function Bishop Landulf, for instance, performed in relation to the citizens of Worms: his was the immediate authority against which Henry had to define his own. This raised Henry's uprising above the normal level of strictly localised violence, but it also meant that it differed from the other outbreaks of revolt in the level on which it was played out, not in the means employed in conducting it, or the ideals invoked in justifying it.

What have we learned from all this? Certainly, to appreciate the degree to which Henry's and the Marshal's revolt reflected the different concerns, but also the fundamentally different mechanisms of lordship that distinguished England and Germany. The framework within which Henry (VII) rebelled was a very different one from that within which the Marshal conducted his campaign; Richard, after all, placed himself within (and to some extent helped to create) a distinct tradition of political violence. In the eyes of his partisans, this was a struggle not merely over access to the king, but over the hallowed principles according to which the kingdom should be run, the limitations imposed upon royal authority, and the provenance and status of the monarch's councillors. They went to war over principles which most German observers would have assumed to be either self-evident (for instance, that a ruler had to take the advice and counsel of his leading subjects, and that they shared in the governance of the realm), or which, to them, dealt with problems that simply did not arise (because no emperor could command a comparable administrative and bureaucratic machinery to impose his will upon them). That they still invoked similar principles, and that they and their rulers employed similar mechanisms of rule is therefore all the more remarkable, and is thus one reason why these two rebellions have been chosen. The other is that, in very different ways, they highlight essential features of their respective political communities. They offer a snapshot, a rare glimpse into the complex reality of political ideals, norms, concerns, means, tools and mechanisms inhabited by Europe's political elites. Let us now turn to these ideas and values, the norms and mechanisms.

Part II

The Ideals and Norms of Politics

Historians of medieval Britain have often been reluctant to discuss ideals and concepts or to see magnates and kings motivated by lofty principles and norms of ritual behaviour.[1] This may reflect the nature of the evidence. In a sketch of British and French approaches to the medieval past, Nicholas Vincent has pointed out that, to nineteenth-century historians, the abundant administrative sources surviving from medieval England provided a more fruitful area of research than the opinionated ramblings and pious imaginings of monastic chronicles. Consequently, research has focused on questions that draw on the record of royal or baronial administration, while French historians, having to rely on narrative sources and a considerable number of charters, have been guided by the concerns of their sources, and focused on issues such as ideology and sacrality.[2]

Something similar applies to the German case.[3] The amount of administrative materials surviving for Frederick II clearly pales when compared to the English sources: during his nearly fifty-year reign, Frederick issued about 3,200 charters and mandates,[4] while a conservative guess would put the *annual* output of Henry III's chancery at about 5,000 items. There was thus a reason why German historians have increasingly shunned administrative history, and the quantity and type of surviving evidence has forced them to ask different questions. More recently, ways have parted even further: while many German historians have embraced the emphasis on ritual and representation pioneered by Gerd Althoff and Hagen Keller,[5] their British counterparts have stuck to more familiar questions about the organisation and workings of royal governance. Historiographical traditions have thus exacerbated existing differences and have raised these to a degree of distinctiveness that is not always warranted by the evidence. There were, of course, real differences in the political structures of England and Germany. At the same time, once we begin to put the kind of questions to the English sources that German and French historians have asked of theirs, some remarkable parallels emerge. This is, to some extent, a one-way exchange (as no comparable wealth of administrative materials exists for Germany). It will not, however, lead to an image of English as a mere reflection of German politics, a mirror image with no peculiarities of its own.[6] Rather, we will encounter some familiar differences, but also unexpected parallels, and even more unexpected inversions of established concepts.

What follows is an analysis of the political culture of thirteenth-century England and Germany and will rely mostly on chronicles and other narrative sources. Chroniclers were, of course, frequently ill-informed, dependent on hearsay, rumour and highly partisan accounts.[7] We will be concerned not with the accuracy of their reporting, but with the values they espoused. The more imaginative and fantastic an account, the more useful it is for our purposes. Chroniclers, after all, had to make sense of these accounts, reconcile and interpret them. In doing so, they were frequently guided by the values and expectations of their institution, intended audience and patrons, and also by those of the wider political community within which they lived and wrote. Their interpretation of events, their remodelling and imagining thus provide a fruitful source for those ideals and values. Moreover, historical writing had a distinctly pragmatic function. It provided a record of events, of the rights, privileges and properties of a monastic house, for instance, and chronicles were increasingly utilised as such: when, later in the thirteenth century, Edward I prepared to claim overlordship of Scotland, a mandate went out to English abbeys to search their historical records for evidence that could justify this claim.[8] When, in 1257, Henry III met Matthew Paris, he recited a list of English kings venerated as saints, and asked the chronicler to incorporate them in his writing.[9] Similarly, in 1235, Frederick II ordered the events of the Mainz *diet* and the crimes of his son to be incorporated into annals and chronicles.[10] We will return to this particular function when exploring the public nature of thirteenth-century politics, but it is important even at this stage to keep in mind the role of monastic chronicles as part of communal memory. Consequently, historical writing also had a distinctly didactic purpose, with an expectation that chroniclers would judge and evaluate as well as report events. They were meant to illustrate the consequences of evil deeds, praise good men, and show how good men were meant to act. They may have misrepresented events, but when they let their imagination run free, they still sought to record what, ideally, should have happened, and aimed to fit their narratives of events within an established framework of rules and norms.

Historical writings give us only the view of one section of society: that of educated clerics. Writings by laymen are few, and they are virtually non-existent for the Marshal rebellion. This will pose a problem, and one for which no obvious solution exists: even in Plantagenet England, there are limits to the evidence we can use. It is here, however, that the German sources can be used to highlight the English situation (and vice versa). Most importantly, they will allow us to tackle questions for which insufficient evidence survives in England, and will do so because, although the quantity of the surviving sources is more limited, they survive in a wider range of genres. While, with the exception of one mandate, no evidence survives which would allow us to tackle the self-representation of Henry III, and nothing to gauge the reasons of Richard Marshal (where we have to depend on the chronicles alone), in Germany the various letters sent by both Henry (VII) and his father have been preserved. We will thus be able to highlight not only the norms and values by which the actors themselves wished to be judged but also those by which their contemporaries did choose to judge them. The two, as we will see, do not always coincide. Last, but by no means least, in Germany, we also have access to a corpus of vernacular writings, composed according to quite different rules and to meet different concerns from the Latin texts, and thus enabling us to trace yet another perspective on the events of 1234–5. In England, by contrast, we will have fewer narratives at our disposal, but those we have will compensate with a far richer coverage. Roger of Wendover's *Flores Historiarum* (*Flowers of History*) and Matthew Paris' *Chronica Majora* (*Major Chronicle*) in particular, which amount to 2,500 and 3,000 pages respectively in their modern printed editions, far exceed anything German chroniclers produced. We thus have available a narrative of unparalleled richness and colour, which, in turn, allows us to ask questions which the sparseness and brevity of the German materials would make impossible to pose. While we will not superimpose the English onto the German evidence (or the other way round), comparing the two will nonetheless allow us to make more informed guesses about the gaps in our evidence. This is not necessarily and not just a case of seeking to fill these gaps, but also of exploring how they came about. The kind of event chroniclers reported, and how they reported it, may tell us more about the intellectual framework within which they wrote, and its relationship with wider political structures, than the actual report itself. With these preliminaries out of the way, what were the values espoused by those writing about the revolts of 1233–5?

4
Loyalty, Justice and Honour: Henry (VII) and Frederick II

I

Henry (VII)'s reasons for rebellion survive in their most detailed form in a letter he sent, probably in the autumn of 1234, to the bishop of Hildesheim.[1] The king used three overlapping lines of argument: he had been appointed as king, and should thus have the power of one; he had acted solely with the interests of the empire at heart; and his father had not only been unjust towards him, but had also frequently spurned his advice, and sought to undermine his authority as consecrated ruler of Germany. There seems to have been an awareness that Henry's past activities might be held against him. In fact, the specific actions he referred to – his wars against the dukes of Bavaria, the destruction of noble castles and the hostages he had demanded of the margrave of Baden – were the ones his father was to cite as evidence for the young king's tyranny. One of the first points made in his letter was thus that his actions were legitimate and just: while holding an unusually well attended *diet* at Frankfurt, called 'to restore the peace and tranquillity of the fatherland at the advice of the princes and magnates',[2] he had received complaints about illicit castles, and was asked to destroy them by the common judgement of the assembled princes; he had taken the duke of Bavaria's son as hostage to ensure himself of the duke's loyalty, while the margrave of Baden had surrendered his son voluntarily. Henry, therefore, had acted not in order to satisfy his own ambitions and desires, but solely at the behest of his princely subjects, and with their support.

We should note the role Henry assigned to the princes. He argued within an already established framework of defining the governance of the empire, which had always been perceived as a joint undertaking of emperor and princes. This was, of course, not a peculiarly German tradition,[3] but the collaborative nature of imperial lordship was more pronounced than elsewhere, and applied to all levels of imperial politics, as illustrated by a mandate of 1231, originally issued by Henry (VII), but later confirmed by his father. This document decreed that lords could not pass new laws in their domains, 'unless they had first secured the agreement of the better and greater men of the land'.[4] That is, just as king and emperor were bound by the judgement of their leading subjects, so these men, too, had to abide by that of their own knights and nobles. The emphasis on collective governance should not be misread as a sign of imperial weakness,[5] but rather as aimed at tying the German princes into the joint maintenance of peace and justice. Princes who refused to share in this task deserved to be punished, while those who refused to take the advice and counsel of their subjects were no better than tyrants. Far from challenging Frederick's reliance on the princes, Henry thus placed himself in an established tradition of collective rule.[6] It is thus worth noting that his letter ended with an appeal to the prelate, in which Henry once again emphasised the role of the princes: 'the empire largely rests on you' (*imperium maxime consistat in vobis*), and it was only with the prelate's backing and that of the other princes that peace and concord could be restored. Frederick II violated the very principles on which the governance of the empire was to be based, and it was up to Henry as much as the princes to restore the right order of politics.

The king's letter proceeds from his campaign against the duke of Bavaria to listing examples of Frederick's harmful interventions: having returned triumphantly from his campaign against the duke, Henry called a *diet*, where, at the behest of the princes and with heir advice, he sought to reform the realm. Although Henry had thus acted in unison with his noble subjects, and although the duke of Bavaria had been asked for hostages only after two previous warnings had been left unheeded, and despite the margrave of Baden offering his son voluntarily, without pressure, and as token of his good will, Frederick overruled Henry. More importantly, he continued to treat his son in an unheard of manner, contrary to all custom and precedent: he refused to receive the king's envoys or letters, and instead secured a papal mandate that Henry was to be excommunicated should he be accused or denunciated by any of the princes. This, Henry declared, was contrary to all law, both ecclesiastical and secular, as he would be punished without a public hearing or previous warning. These complaints refer to the oath which, in 1232, Henry had been forced to offer, authorising the German princes to renounce their fealty should he resist or oppose his father.[7] It also seems to echo letters issued by Frederick II and Gregory IX in 1234, asking the archbishop of Trier to remind Henry of his promises, and to warn him of the consequences should he fail to do so.[8] Henry faced a combined front of pope and emperor, and many of his subsequent actions (such as his alliance with the Lombards) may have been an attempt to break up that particular alliance. That his letter was addressed to the bishop of Hildesheim and that he emphasised the ecclesiastical status of his emissaries to Frederick II – the archbishop of Mainz and the bishop of Bamberg – may point in a similar direction. It is as much an indication of the need to win over (or at least to secure the intercession of) Gregory IX, as of the support Henry lacked among the secular princes.

In Henry (VII)'s eyes, Frederick's actions were simply tokens of the continuing and unjustified disdain in which Henry was held by the emperor. The contrast with Henry's way of doing things was under-lined repeatedly: the king only acted after taking the advice and counsel of his princes; he responded to an immediate necessity, and acted on behalf of his subjects and at their behest, in order to maintain and safeguard peace and public order; due process was carefully observed (even the duke of Bavaria had been given several warnings). In every respect, Henry (VII) thus acted like a model ruler, strictly abiding by the norms and conventions of imperial politics. All of this was lacking in the emperor's dealings with his son: Henry could be condemned by rumour and denunciation, without the right to argue his case; without warning; and without reason. Henry's letter painted a clear contrast between the rightful exercise of kingship – royal rule in consultation with the nobles, in loyalty to the emperor, and with due respect for the law and its processes – and the arbitrary injustice he had suffered at his father's hands.

All this was linked to yet another complaint: the emperor's violation of Henry's honour. Henry's letter ended with a request to the bishop of Hildesheim to plead with Frederick not to diminish or change 'our honour, which we deem to hold by his grace and that of God'.[9] This was by no means a central complaint – Henry was more concerned with Frederick's violation of established custom and precedent – but neither can it be ignored. The emperor's implied tyranny and his violation of Henry's status and standing were merely two ways of describing the same phenomenon. *Honor* could mean property and legal rights (in this case, to exercise the authority of king), but also more generally and diffusely status and standing, and the latter was all too often the public and symbolic manifestation of the former.[10] A lord or ruler exemplified his authority and standing, the extent of his wealth and influence, by means of public display and demonstration. Both meanings mattered in the case of Henry (VII). The king's repeated humiliation at the hands of Frederick II undermined his standing and authority: in 1232, before the assembled princes, he had been forced into an act of humiliation and submission; in 1234, his envoys were publicly refused access to the emperor. That is, he was demonstratively and publicly denied the authority to rule, and Frederick thus effectively deprived the king of his royal status. This forms the context within which the reference to Henry's honour should be read: Henry had acted to the best of his abilities, and like a good ruler should act, but it seemed as if his father had already decided to strip him of his royal dignity.

The effectiveness of Henry's self-justification rested on his loyalty towards Frederick: he never denied that his authority and power were ultimately rooted in that of the emperor, and his letter thus started out by listing his acts of faithful service. When Gregory IX had sent Cardinal Otto to Germany after Frederick's 1227 excommunication, Henry had prevented him from entering the empire; and when Duke Louis of Bavaria sided with the enemies of the empire, Henry had waged war on and subdued the duke. He exercised authority on the emperor's behalf and through the emperor's grace, and it was the emperor's and the empire's welfare that had guided his actions. All this made his treatment at Frederick's hands all the more cruel and unjust. Naturally, this also contained a suitable note of realism (reflecting his lack of support among the princes). There is thus no indication that Henry aimed at overthrowing his father, and he did not ask the bishop to become his ally, but to intercede with the emperor, to counsel on how the tranquillity and stability of the empire might be maintained, and to ensure that the honour due to all subjects of the empire were granted to their king, too. This was not a plea to replace Frederick II, but to remind him of his duties and obligations, and to grant Henry the access, the authority and the dignity which he had so far been denied. The empire rested on the joint governance of princes and ruler, and it was now up to the princes and prelates to restore the equilibrium which Frederick had so wrongfully disturbed.

In all this, we must note the contradiction at the heart of Henry's letter: while, on the one hand, he presented his case as that of an aggrieved vassal seeking redress from an unjust lord (violence was a last resort, the only means still at his disposal by which he might yet be able to gain a fair hearing), his grievance rested in part on the fact that he was more than a simple prince. He was, after all, the crowned and consecrated king of the Romans, and it was the denial of the rights and privileges that came with his status that had forced him into an act of open resistance. Somewhat paradoxically, Henry sought to claim greater authority by outlining how frequently that authority had been denied; he sought to be treated as king by lamenting how frequently he had been treated as worse than a common criminal. This argument was born out of a clear understanding of the unequal balance of power between father and son, but it also points to the fundamental dilemma at the heart of Henry's relationship with his father. He was king, but only in his father's name, and what exactly that entailed for Henry's ability to govern had never been clarified. As we will see, Henry was not alone in this attitude – similar concerns emerge from the way in which contemporary and near-contemporary observers portrayed the events of 1234–5 – but it was not a concern he or his subjects shared with Frederick II.

II

In January 1235, Frederick wrote to the archbishop of Trier, outlining his complaints against Henry.[11] The emperor's grievances centred on two closely related points: the king's disobedience, and his hostility towards the princes. When Frederick had called Henry to the helm of the empire, his expectation had been that Henry would never offend the *ministeriales*, nobles, citizens and other faithful of the empire. Frederick was thus saddened to hear that Henry had turned against these men – the eyes and lights of the *imperium* – and had taken hostages from them. When Frederick reprimanded his son, he received a most solemn promise that henceforth Henry would abide by his father's mandates. Importantly, Frederick points out that this undertaking had been given 'at the advice of the princes who attended, and in their presence'.[12] Moreover, Henry had sworn not only to abide by his father's wishes but 'above all that he would show and treat our princes with particular respect (*honor*), and that he would generally do justice to all our faithful'.[13] Frederick was, however, to be disappointed a second time. For Henry set aside the fear of God (*timor Dei*) and the reverence he owed his father, and began to plot against the emperor's honour (*in honorem nostri machinari*), took hostages from the emperor's faithful, seized castles and sought to force Frederick's supporters to break their oaths of fealty. Therefore, the emperor requested that the archbishop aid him in setting right the wrongs committed by his son.

While the examples Frederick gave of his son's tyranny were those actions which Henry had been most eager to defend, the emperor otherwise ignored his son's grievances. There was, in fact, little in Frederick's responses that made any direct reference to Henry's complaints, and Frederick instead resorted to general accusations about his son's ingratitude and tyranny. Nor does he refer to Henry's overtures towards the Lombards and Capetians, or – with one notable exception – the outbreak of violence. If we had Frederick's letter alone, we would never know that a rebellion had taken place.[14] This was symptomatic of the emperor's response: he sought to overcome Henry's revolt by denying its existence. Even once Frederick entered Germany in the spring of 1235, he consciously reduced his entourage,[15] and decided on a slow and ceremonial progress, periodically interrupted by a very public exercise of those rulerly duties which he had accused his son of violating.[16] Although he also assembled a formidable entourage, and despite the splendour of his progress (involving, one chronicler claimed, a lavish display of exotic animals and treasures),[17] a military confrontation was to be avoided: the preposterous nature of Henry's rebellion was to be revealed by the ease with which it was overcome. There was thus little acknowledgement of Henry's military threat, either in the emperor's letters or his actions, until it had been overcome.[18]

In June 1235, for instance, Frederick wrote to his allies in Lombardy, emphasising the willingness with which the German nobles had flocked to his court, the splendour of his reception, and his willingness to return to Lombardy soon: his enemies should not believe that Henry's revolt had in any way impeded his ability to attack them, too.[19] Henry's submission was mentioned more in passing: far greater room was given to the emperor's imminent wedding, and to his plans for a *diet*, to be held at Mainz in August. The account of the king's surrender is sandwiched between these two topics, and the marginality of Henry's revolt is made clear in the language of the emperor's letter. Having outlined the splendour of Frederick's and Isabella's reception, the next sentence opens with a *preterea* (furthermore, incidentally) – because our son, the king, had realised that all those whom he had reluctantly dragged to his side deserted him after our arrival,[20] he offered his submission, first at Trifels, before sending envoys to Nuremberg, where he surrendered unconditionally. This is the first time that Frederick acknowledged to those not immediately concerned by Henry's rebellion that something like unrest had taken place (after all, the king had some, though unwilling, followers).

This established a pattern: resistance was acknowledged only once it had been overcome. In August 1235, the *Reichslandfrieden* of Mainz, for instance, dealt not only with the reform of the realm but also with what actions were to be taken against sons who rebelled against their fathers,[21] while one contemporary chronicler reported that the Mainz *diet* was used to make public the many crimes committed by Henry (VII).[22] Furthermore, at some point between 1236 and 1239 someone, as Herbert Beumann has suggested,[23] either at the imperial court or close to it, produced a life of St Elisabeth of Thuringia, the so-called Zwettl *vita*. The text ends with an account of the translation of the saint's relics in May 1236, and the emperor's participation in it. This, in turn, is preceded by a short outline of the event's historical context: Frederick had appointed Henry as king in Germany, so that the presence of the son might compensate for the absence of the father. However, Henry had become jealous of his half-brother, Conrad IV, and rose against his father. The emperor, accompanied by Conrad, came to Germany to quell the revolt and respond to the needs of the empire. Having subdued the rebels, he visited Marburg to give thanks to God.[24] The further in the past Henry's revolt, the clearer its condemnation by the emperor, and the more explicit the references to its military nature. The reason given for Henry's initial appointment as king is worth noting: he was to act as his father's representative, the extended arm of Frederick's governance, thus also highlighting themes that permeate Frederick's letters. They espoused a concept of governance that viewed power as emanating from and being legitimised by the emperor. The legitimacy of Henry's revolt, in turn, was rejected by denying its existence; painting the king as faithless and incompetent, rather than as a dangerous inciter to violence; highlighting the preposterous nature of his rebellion; and claiming a lack of support for him (to a degree that reduced Henry's already far from impressive following to the forced backing of a few unfortunates). As far as Frederick was concerned, there was no uprising, only a useless ruler and ungrateful son who had to be chastised and corrected.

Both in terms of the specific events he referred to, and the principles he invoked, Frederick covered much the same ground as his son. What to Henry (VII) had been an effective keeping of the peace – the hostages demanded of Duke Louis of Bavaria and the destruction of illicit castles – to Frederick was a token of his son's tyranny, and what Henry had claimed as a typical of his father's injustice – the submission of 1232 – to the latter was little more than an undertaking of future loyalty. Henry had been entrusted with running the empire on Frederick's behalf, and to protect and honour the princes. Instead, he persecuted them, demanded hostages and dispossessed them.[25] Not only did the king thus oppress the very pillars of the *imperium*, but he also violated his oath, given at the advice and behest of the princes, to abide by his father's commands. That Henry took hostages from his subjects mattered. It was an issue of concern not only of the emperor but also his people (who recorded this as the chief token of Henry's rebellious cruelty). Demanding hostages denoted tyranny,[26] and was excusable only if those who offered them did so voluntarily, or if they had a proven record of breaking their promises.[27] This also explains why Henry (VII) had emphasised that the margrave of Baden had offered his son voluntarily, and why he stressed that Duke Louis of Bavaria had repeatedly betrayed the emperor: hostages were the only means he had of ensuring that Louis would not break his word again. By stressing this point, and by using it as the chief example of Henry's despotism, Frederick placed his son in a far from venerable tradition, and one which his audience, we may assume, would easily have recognised.

Frederick's response indicates the principles on which he thought the exercise of royal and imperial power should be built: like his son, he recognised that the empire could not be governed, unless this was done jointly by emperor and the princes. Just like the king, Frederick emphasised that, at every stage, he had acted in unison with his princely subjects – it was at their behest that Henry (VII) had sworn his oath of loyalty, and it was their backing that was now needed to end the king's rebellion. This was very much in line with Frederick's general policy towards the princes, who were increasingly called upon to exercise functions on behalf of the emperor. In July 1234, for instance, when first announcing his plans to come to Germany, Frederick had called upon the archbishop of Trier to be vigilant in ensuring that the empire would not be disturbed, thereby increasing not only his own honour but also earning himself imperial rewards.[28] Similarly, in the arenga to the *Constitutio in favorem principum* (*Constitution in favour of the princes*) of 1232, for instance, Frederick explained that the just peace of the empire depended on concord between emperor and princes, a relationship, which he likened to that of head and members,[29] with similar language used in the arenga (preface) to the 1235 imperial land peace (*Reichslandfrieden*) of Mainz.[30] The princes shared in the governance of the empire, but this was as much a privilege as it was a most solemn duty.

Furthermore, just as a king or emperor was bound to take the advice and counsel of his subjects, so the princes had to take that of their own men. These obligations towards their own subjects, in turn, echoed their role within the empire: they had been elevated above others so as to share in the governance of the realm, and to join in performing the most prominent task facing those who held secular power: maintaining peace and justice. This theme permeated Frederick's dealings with the princes. When, in August 1235, for instance, Frederick enfeoffed Otto of Brunswick with the duchy of Brunswick, he emphasised his own elevated status (Frederick had been called to the helm of the realm through the grace of God, and was thus raised above all other princes), but also stressed, in more general terms, the obligations which so high a status entailed: most importantly, to maintain peace and public order. This function, in turn, was at least in part performed by turning strenuous and loyal nobles like Otto into princes, and by confirming them in possession of their inheritance and title.[31] By implication, the newly created duke had earned his elevation by his strenuous maintaining of the peace, but was now called upon to perform these duties even more rigorously. More importantly, his obligations were threefold: towards God, the emperor and his subjects. God had created the power which Otto exercised, and he also had endowed Frederick with the power with which he now entrusted the new duke. Finally, they had been granted their elevated status as a means of protecting those who could not protect themselves. A failure to perform these functions thus dishonoured not only empire and emperor but also God.

Similar thinking guided the actions taken against Duke Frederick of Austria. These matter as, to some extent, proceedings against the duke fed on the principles initially invoked against Henry,[32] and because they thus allow us to see concepts formulated more clearly which could be seen only incipiently in Frederick's response to his son. When, in early 1236, Frederick explained to the king of Bohemia why he had formally declared the duke deposed,[33] his complaints centred on the shame and dishonour which his namesake had brought upon both empire and emperor: he acted 'against our honour and the dignity of the empire', by refusing to meet Frederick when the emperor had first entered Germany in 1235;[34] 'against our honour and that of the empire' by seeking to forge an alliance with the Milanese;[35] and action had to be taken because 'the offences he had committed against us and the empire';[36] and because the duke 'ought to fear God and show due reverence in all matters, to Frederick and the empire.[37] In addition, he sought to have the mythical Old Man of the Mountain, leader of the Assassins, kill Frederick, but the duke's evil deeds extended further still. He failed to protect widows and orphans, oppressed the poor and dishonoured his nobles. He persecuted *ministeriales*, entrusted to him by the empire, raped virgins and encouraged his entourage to rape them, dishonoured matrons, arranged forced marriages, took hostages from his knights; he had dispossessed and expelled his mother and had attacked the princes of the empire. That is, the duke's crimes consisted both of his failure to perform his duties and his attacks on the emperor in person. Frederick had no choice but to end the duke's tyranny, and to end it, as he had put it in a letter to the nobles of Austria, through the power of justice.[38] Not all of the duke's crimes should be taken at face value – Frederick presented a rhetorically heightened list of the crimes committed by archetypal bad lords.[39] Some of the specific items echoed the alleged failings of King Henry – the oppression of nobles, the taking of hostages, his lacking the fear of God. Even more importantly, though, this letter points to an underlying principle also evident in Frederick's response to Henry's revolt, and his enfeoffment of Otto of Brunswick: princes received their authority from the emperor, who in turn received it from God; if they violated their duties, if they failed to do justice, it was the emperor's obligation to punish them for their dereliction of duty.

Loyalty and fealty were the twin pillars of imperial politics: those who had shown that they would not betray either empire or emperor would be richly rewarded, both with lands and privileges, and also with honour, prestige and standing. This theme had been elaborated in Otto's elevation to the duchy of Brunswick,[40] and it was a theme called upon repeatedly. When Frederick, in November 1234, confirmed the *Constitutio in favorem principum* to Archbishop Siegfried of Mainz, for instance, he emphasised that this was a reward for the prelate's past loyalty.[41] Similarly, when, probably in the spring of 1235, he exhorted the citizens of Worms to hold out in their resistance against Henry and Landulf, he praised them for their loyalty, and the due reverence in which they held both his honour and that of the empire.[42] This emphasis was by no means limited to the revolt itself: in July 1234, when announcing to the archbishop of Trier his planned visit to Germany, Frederick praised the prelate for his loyalty,[43] the citizens of Erfurt, who in July 1234 had their privileges confirmed by the emperor, partly due to their humility and loyalty,[44] and when granting Wenzel the kingdom of Bohemia in July 1231, this was again linked to the fealty of the new king and his late father.[45] To some extent, this may reflect common practice, and the language of royal charters in the thirteenth century.[46] Nonetheless, the frequency with which Frederick stressed the loyalty and faithfulness of those whom he rewarded is worth noting, and contrasts clearly with its use by Henry (VII). Loyalty and faithfulness were the chief duties of those who received power from the emperor, and the means by which they could earn the right to exercise that power. Those, like Duke Frederick of Austria or Henry (VII), by contrast, who betrayed emperor or empire, had forfeited the special status to which they had been raised. Frederick thus shifted the discourse of loyalty and a track record of loyalty, also evident in his son's epistle, onto altogether different ground, and combined it with complaints about Henry's tyranny and incompetence.

These various lines of argument came together in a letter which Frederick sent to the citizens of Worms in early 1235. Several versions of this missive survive (suggesting a wider circulation), and it is probably the earliest admission by the emperor that some sort of armed conflict was in fact taking place (a fact which even he would have been hard pressed to deny when addressing the men of Worms). Frederick emphasised familiar themes: he thanked the citizens for their steadfastness and loyalty, their spirited defence of 'our honour and that of the empire',[47] and 'the imperial name and honour',[48] and promised that their loyalty would be amply rewarded. In the meantime, they should hold out, as his arrival was imminent. The reason this letter matters is, however, because it introduces yet another theme: Henry's youth. Unlike in England, where age was as a means of limiting the king's responsibility, in Germany it was a means of heaping further opprobrium upon him. By doing so, Frederick also departed from German norms, and even from the way he himself otherwise used a discourse of age and maturity. In the duke of Austria's case, for instance, the emperor had declared that, initially, he had been willing to excuse the duke's lack of respect and obedience by his namesake's youthful inexperience: he was but a *juvenis*, young man, and one who might yet be led to the path of righteousness.[49] Henry was granted no such mitigating circumstances and was instead likened to Absalom, King's David's rebellious progeny.[50] These were not the actions of an inexperienced young man, but the archetypal betrayal of paternal trust by an ungrateful son. Frederick then continued to elaborate on the many favours his son had received, how he had been raised to the pinnacle of power by being entrusted with the kingship of Germany, and how he had repaid his father's kindness with sedition and unrest. It was this line, too, which was to dominate Frederick's response to Henry once he had been overcome. Henry was denied the opportunity to atone for his mistakes, and he was denied this opportunity because of the unprecedented graveness of his crimes, his lack of gratitude and his ineptitude. Just as Henry's attempts at proving his effectiveness had been turned into tokens of tyranny, so the one factor which, in other cases, allowed for a display of forgiveness and grace was used to heighten and exacerbate the severity of the young king's faults. In this context, we should note what Frederick did not accuse his son of: Henry (VII) did not take bad counsel. This is important, as this was to be at the heart of English representations of the Marshal's revolt (which shifted blame away from the king and onto his councillors), and because it was one of those points where the narrative sources departed from the matrix with which Frederick had provided them: while chroniclers blamed the revolt on Henry's unwillingness to take prudent counsel, the emperor blamed his son alone. There were to be no mitigating circumstances. Frederick's condemnation of Henry's actions was relentless and complete.

The young king suffered for being Frederick's son: with the exception of the duke of Austria, the emperor rarely had the means of transforming this rhetoric of imperial power into political reality. The duke, in turn, could only be attacked because he had already alienated in his subjects, peers and neighbours the very people who could have aided him against his lord. He was, in some ways, easy prey. The reality of German politics was such that Frederick would have been unable to enforce his concept of the relationship between empire and princes. Even many of those who, in 1235, had fallen out of favour, were therefore back at court once they were needed against more formidable enemies: Bishop Landulf of Worms, for instance, having been driven out of his city in 1235, won the emperor's backing against the citizens in November 1238,[51] while the duke of Austria was back in imperial favour after Frederick's excommunication in 1239, and was even considered as a possible father-in-law for Conrad IV.[52] Henry (VII), by contrast, had no independent power base, and his authority was dependent solely on his status as the emperor's son. Frederick, no doubt aided by Henry's inability to win the backing of the princes, was thus able to implement a reading of his relationship with the prince, which he would not have been able to implement in dealings with the duke of Bavaria or the king of Bohemia. Henry felt the full force of his father's ever more heightened reading of imperial power because, unlike his princely subjects, he did indeed hold power solely at the emperor's grace.

III

What, then, were the principles of political organisation propagated by Henry and his father? Both stressed loyalty, the role of the princes and the honour of the empire and its rulers. The king portrayed himself as an aggrieved vassal who sought redress from his lord. Violence was a final resort and was aimed not at replacing or dethroning the emperor, but at forcing him to concede what so far he had been unwilling to grant: justice, and recognition of Henry's merits and deserts. Implicit in this was, however, a warning: just as Frederick would violate the bonds of justice and paternal piety in dealing with his son, so he might also overrule the rights and privileges of the German princes. Henry had done nothing wrong, but had acted in line with basic principles of political organisation, at the behest and on behalf of the princes, with the interests of the empire foremost on his mind, and of indubitable loyalty towards his lord and father. If he was treated as he was, what would stop Frederick from treating the princes in a like manner?

Two concerns emerge as foremost on Frederick's mind: honour and the role of the princes. Henry (VII) had been called upon to treat all his subjects, especially the princes, with due respect; he violated these by demanding hostages and forced oaths of fealty. It was not, however, only the princes' standing he violated, but that of his father, too. Although the theme of honour was also evident in Henry's letter, it was used more frequently and widely by Frederick. Imperial *honor* could not be separated from the means by which it was violated: most importantly, Henry's refusal to treat the princes with proper respect or to take their advice and counsel, and also his disloyalty and betrayal of the emperor by failing to do justice and keeping the peace. A king or emperor could not proceed without the backing of his subjects. To some extent, this reflected the political reality of thirteenth-century Germany, but it was more than mere expediency. Giving advice and counsel, sharing in the governance of the empire, was a most solemn duty, and the princes would be called to account if they refused to share in that responsibility. Henry (VII) had proven himself unworthy of exercising imperial power: he caused dishonour to those who shared in his power; he refused to take the advice and counsel of the great men of the realm; and, in disobeying his father, had revolted not just against the emperor, but against God.

The differences between Frederick's and Henry's conception of a ruler's office were differences of emphasis, but they also point to inherent contradictions within this concept. Henry would probably not have disputed most of the elements in Frederick's understanding of the royal office: he, too, emphasised the importance of the princes, and the fact that, ultimately, his authority was grounded in the emperor's, and he repeatedly stressed his loyalty and fealty. Where Frederick and Henry differed, however, was what these principles meant in practice. While the king claimed for himself the rights he was willing to grant even the most recalcitrant of his subjects, Frederick seems to have used Henry's resistance as a means of stating a warning example. Partly because Henry was even more dependent on Frederick than the princes, he owed an even greater degree of obedience and subservience. More importantly, because of his proximity to the emperor, in terms of political status as much as family relationship, any sign of ingratitude or resistance weighed more heavily and had to be punished more rigorously. Henry may have emphasised that he was the crowned and consecrated king of the Romans, and that he received his authority from both his father and from God, but to Frederick, it was his relationship with God that ultimately defined his son's. This was a principle relevant beyond relations between Frederick and Henry. What we have yet to consider is how far it was shared, recorded or even rejected by their subjects.

5
Justice, Loyalty and the Absence of Honour: Frederick II and Henry (VII) as Seen by Their Contemporaries

This chapter addresses some overlapping questions: what does the way contemporaries report on King Henry's revolt tell us about the ideals and norms applied in judging the actions of rulers? Where do these norms overlap with, and where do they differ from those the king and his father had sought to project? What does this, in turn, tell us about the structural underpinnings of imperial politics in the thirteenth century? We will seek to answer these questions by grouping our sources into three categories. The first will deal with those texts typical of the fragmentary, often laconic and heavily regionalised perspective adopted by German chronicles, and will give us a flavour of how the majority of narratives described the events of 1234–5. The second will focus on three more detailed sources, which provide perspectives and allow us to ask questions to which the overwhelming mass of chronicle entries would yield no answers. We will finally turn to vernacular texts, both poetry and historical narratives, in which we will find dissonances in an otherwise shared, almost uniform, outlook on events.

While none of our materials compare in length to the English ones – Wendover's account of the Marshal rebellion, for instance, runs to nearly 90 pages in the nineteenth-century edition, while even the most detailed German account rarely stretches to more than a paragraph – they compensate for their brevity by enabling us to view Henry's revolt from a greater range of perspectives, and thus draw firmer conclusions about how widely shared a concept was, how typical of the political climate of Staufen Germany. Furthermore, although composed independently of each other, these texts also refer to a common source (mostly Frederick's version of events). How they made use of this material, how they reworked it, what they left out and what they added, allows us rare insights into conflicting discourses of imperial power and political values, and the process of communication between rulers and ruled.

I

German chroniclers did not take kindly to Henry (VII), and overwhelmingly condemned his actions. Most, furthermore, had little to say about Henry's fall. The entry in the *Chronica St Petri Erfordensis Moderna*, written at Erfurt in Thuringia, gives us a taste of the kind of entry we are typically dealing with.[1] The text proceeds annalistically, and Henry's fall is mentioned under the year 1235, immediately following a short report that Pope Gregory IX had called for support against the citizens of Rome. Little detail is given: that same year (*eodem anno*), the emperor Frederick had imprisoned his son Henry at Heidelberg before transferring him to Swabia. Fearing, however, that the king's partisans might cause unrest, he had him escorted to Apulia, first by the prelates of Salzburg and Bamberg, and then the patriarch of Aquileia.[2] There was little in terms of background narrative, not even the rebellion is mentioned, and the narrative sets in with Henry's defeat and imprisonment. If we stretch this a little, the *Chronica* contains an indication that Henry's overthrow may have been less secure, and his support more widespread than Frederick's representation of events would suggest: there was, after all, the fear that some of Henry's partisans might cause unrest.

But rarely was this image explored further, and then only to express more clearly a chronicler's hostility towards the young king. The *Annales Erphordenses fratrum Praedicatorum*, for instance, another text produced at Erfurt, and connected to the local Dominicans, adds that the dispute arose because Henry refused to follow his father's advice and instead prepared to resist him. In fact, the king had already tied some princes to his cause by paying them money.[3] The emphasis on Henry's disobedience is worth noting (as it reflects a theme at the heart of Frederick's response), as are illicit means he used to muster support. Although money payments were by no means unusual, they do not seem to have been common knowledge, and were in fact frowned upon once proffered openly or publicly.[4] Henry thus had to rely on bribery and the illicit use of funds to secure the support he enjoyed. That this backing, in turn, was fickle could come as no surprise. Henry had forfeited the right to be king by the means he chose to exercise his office, and he lost it because of the allies he had gained. This proved a popular image. The *Chronica Regia Coloniensis*, for example, composed in the wider environs of Cologne cathedral, reports the dubious means which Henry, acting at the instigation of evil councillors, had used to gain supporters (threats, petitions and gifts).[5] That Henry followed bad advice, rather than acted out of his own will, should not be read as exculpating the king: a good king would instantly recognise and reject morally perverse counsel, while the means by which Henry gained his backing merely underlined the illegitimacy of his actions: he gained supporters not because what he was doing was right, but because he threatened or bribed them into aiding him.

Similar themes were elaborated by the *Annales Scheftlarienses Maiores*: already in 1233, Henry and some of the princes had considered rebelling against the emperor, so as to bring about a division of the realm. When the duke of Bavaria refused to consent, he incurred the king's wrath and a campaign was planned against him. Without waiting for the return of two prelates (the archbishop of Mainz and the bishop of Bamberg) sent to the emperor to consult him about the campaign, Henry laid waste to Otto's lands, just to find out that Frederick had refused permission for the campaign to go ahead. Consequently, he became suspicious of the two prelates, who hurriedly returned to the imperial court, and brought with them letters from the princes, asking the emperor to come to Germany.[6] The *Annales'* account is also worth noting for its strongly regional focus – the dealings between father and son were viewed largely through the prism of Bavarian and more generally South German affairs (and is almost immediately followed by one of the most detailed accounts of the campaign against Duke Frederick of Austria). Throughout, Henry is portrayed in unremittingly bleak terms – he was supported by only a few princes, and aimed at destroying the unity of the empire. He was overly suspicious – blaming, it is implied, the bishop of Bamberg and the archbishop of Mainz for Frederick's refusal to condone war against the duke of Bavaria – and persecuted those like Otto, who remained steadfast in their fealty towards the emperor. To this list of Henry's shortcomings can be added sexual lust and envy: according to the *Annales Wormatienses* (*Annals of Worms*), he wanted to divorce his wife,[7] while the Zwettl *vita* of St Elisabeth claims that Henry was motivated by envy of his half-brother, Conrad IV.[8]

Intriguingly, almost identical points were made about Frederick of Austria: the duke refused to attend imperial *diets* and ignored the mandates of the emperor;[9] he delighted in rape and robbery, was unjust and persecuted religious houses;[10] he was attacked for his many crimes, and after many accusations had been levelled against him by the bishops and princes.[11] The terror of his lordship was such that he was feared in equal measure by his subjects and his neighbours.[12] Just as in the case of Henry (VII), accounts of the duke's tyranny centred on his sexual misdeeds; the oppression and dishonourable treatment of his noble subjects; and an unwillingness to do justice and maintain the peace. There were, of course, differences: the duke's tyranny did not, for instance, express itself in a refusal to take advice and counsel, and there is (unsurprisingly) no mention of ingratitude. Equally, Henry was never accused of indulging in rape or the molestation of noblewomen. Even so, the imagery used to depict bad lordship in both the king's and the duke's case remained remarkably similar and thus points to a common repertoire of norms and expectations of how those in power should act and behave.

We will return to the overall image painted of Henry's revolt in more detail a little later, but already some common features have emerged. Most importantly, the surviving accounts seem indebted to Frederick II's representation of the revolt, and thus stress the king's ingratitude as a driving motive behind his actions, the tyranny he had exercised over the duke of Bavaria, his taking of hostages and his general lack of suitability for the royal office. Some of these themes are elaborated further, in particular the dubious means by which Henry sought to gain the backing of his subjects (by bribing or terrorising them into submission), and his moral failings (especially greed, envy and sexual lust). In addition, though, themes are introduced that were not present in Frederick's letters: in particular, the unsuitable advisors on whom Henry relied, his disdain for wise and prudent men, and the notoriety of those with whom he did consort. Finally, some elements of Frederick's propaganda, in particular the honour of the empire, were ignored or at least given considerably less space than in the emperor's response. We will return to several of these, but first let us look at how these themes were played out in some of the more detailed narratives.

II

Among the narrative sources for Henry's revolt, three stand out: the *Annales Marbacenses* (*Annals of Marbach*), written in the Staufens' Alsatian heartland; the anonymous continuation of Godfrey of Viterbo, composed probably in the 1240s at Ebersbach in Swabia, another centre of Staufen power; and the historical writings emerging from Worms in the decades after 1240. They stand out because of the relative detail with which they describe events, but also, because their proximity to the events or, it seems, the actors themselves, allowed them to offer information not available elsewhere. Probably the best example for how these various factors combine is that of the *Annals of Marbach* which, for instance, give an indication of motive: Henry, who had been given the empire by his father, broke the bonds of filial duty and, driven by fear, rebelled against his father. Why Henry might have been afraid of Frederick is not elaborated, but the means Henry used to find himself some backing are: moving up the Rhine from Basle, he took hostages from the towns of Alsace. In addition, he sent the marshal, Anselm of Justingen, to Lombardy to open negotiations with the Milanese.[13] Furthermore, the king dispatched the bishop of Würzburg to the king of France, with the intention of arranging a marriage between their children. This was probably an attempt to counteract the papal–imperial alliance,[14] and it was a forceful demonstration of sovereignty (nobody but Henry decided on his or his children's marriage). That the author of the *Annales* viewed matters differently is suggested by the sentence immediately following Henry's quest for allies: 'and all that, because he feared his father' (*Et hoc omnia propter timorem patris*). Unsurprisingly, therefore, when Frederick entered Germany, many towns and princes sent envoys to greet and welcome him most joyfully. In the meantime, Henry, who had continued seeking to find allies through gifts, was swayed by the counsel of Herman of Salza to approach his father, submitted, was imprisoned and, by the judgement of God, punished.[15]

The contrast between the figure of Henry, desperate to win allies, and desperate in the means he chose to win them, and the triumphant appearance of Frederick II, whose presence was greeted enthusiastically by his oppressed subjects, is worth noting, as is the juxtaposition of Frederick's easy victory with the sad – but just – fate awaiting his son. As such, the Marbach account hardly departs from a line common to most German observers of the events of 1235. Unusually, though, it elaborated the moral message of to be drawn from these events: in times of prosperity, Henry had set aside the fear of God, and, in the manner of tyrants, had despised the counsel of virtuous and honourable men; he had broken the bonds linking him to his father, who had granted him the kingdom of Germany. The king, not content with the riches he possessed already, had destroyed it all, and did so by attacking the religious and by forcefully oppressing monasteries. Consequently, there was no peace for pilgrims and travellers. The king's trajectory was a familiar one: driven by sinful desires, he set aside the counsel of wise and prudent men, resulting in the oppression of those it should have been his most noble duty to protect. His futile attempts at winning his father's forgiveness, and his shameful captivity, were the price he had to pay for his past sins, and were almost mockingly contrasted with Henry's former wealth and glory.[16] The detail with which the *Annals* report events may be due to their proximity to events (Henry (VII) had issued various grants at nearby Hagenau in the spring of 1235,[17] while Frederick held one of the *diets* preparing for the war against Duke Frederick of Austria in the town, and wintered in Hagenau with his wife in 1235–6),[18] which also allowed them to portray these as: a clash between shameful tyranny and righteous kingship.

Let us now turn to the anonymous continuator of Godfrey of Viterbo writing at Ebersbach probably during the early 1240s.[19] Unlike the Marbach annalist, the Ebersbach account makes no direct link between the emperor's return and the deeds of his son. In fact, the emperor's visit to Germany had been mooted on rather more peaceful grounds: as the archbishop of Cologne was escorting Frederick's new wife to Germany, Frederick suggested that the wedding, too, be celebrated there. Henry (VII), however, on hearing of his father's imminent arrival, was mightily perturbed (*turbatus est vehementer*), and, together with his closest allies, began to plot revolt. He thus visited the towns of the empire, and went from prince to prince, labouring with all available means, using both threats and gifts (*minis et muneribus*), to win supporters. Many of the prelates and princes sought to dissuade him from so foolish an undertaking, but Henry, setting aside their prudent counsel, gathered a group of counts and noblemen – all of them of ill repute – and demanded hostages from the towns and cities. He, furthermore, sent troops against the citizens of Worms because they had refused to betray the emperor. It was only after Henry had opened hostilities that Frederick took action: on hearing of the oppression and misery his son had wreaked upon the poor, Frederick hastened towards the Rhine. En route, at Regensburg, he was joyfully met by several princes, and then progressed in great glory – the author described on the Saracens and Ethiopians in his entourage, the exotic animals (elephants and dromedaries) and great treasures which accompanied him – towards Wimpfen. Beholding the glory of imperial might, Henry's henchmen were paralysed with fear, and deserted the king. Betrayed by his own men, Henry submitted and was imprisoned by his father – despite the fact that many had begun to plead on the young man's behalf.[20]

As in most accounts of the young king's rebellion, not much time is spent on motives: we are told that Henry was perturbed because his father planned to come to Germany, but not why this should have been the case. Unlike the Marbach annalist, the anonymous continuator did not claim that Henry feared punishment for past misdeeds. Otherwise, the Ebersbach account largely follows an established pattern – Henry spurned the advice of wise and prudent men, surrounded himself with those of low standing and little loyalty, and used both threat and bribery to gain supporters. That this was the only way his allies could be won, in turn, was a clear sign of his moral weakness, and that of the men on whose support he relied. His opponents by contrast, as exemplified by the citizens of Worms, were true paragons of steadfast loyalty. The contrast between Henry's desperate attempts to gather a following, and the willingness and joy with which the princes greeted the emperor points in a similar direction, and this impression is further strengthened by the continuator's choice of Biblical references: perhaps in an echo of the emperor's letter to the citizens of Worms, he likens Henry to Absalom and Frederick to David. Henry's tyranny sprang from this rejection of counsel, rather than being exemplified by it, but otherwise this conforms to a familiar pattern.

Whether the Marbach annalist or the Ebersbach continuator actually witnessed any of the events they describe is difficult to ascertain. They certainly reveal information – Henry's proposed alliance with St Louis of France, or the exotic entourage of Frederick II, the pleas on Henry's behalf by members of the imperial court and so on – which, if correct, may suggest links with the imperial court or at least with those who had witnessed events. On the other hand, their account of Henry's tyranny is curiously formulaic, and seems to have drawn to a considerable degree on Frederick II's various letters (and perhaps his representation of events at the 1235 Mainz *diet*), but rarely goes into detail. As with the shorter texts we have discussed before, they depart from the imperial version of events largely by stressing the bad counsel Henry had taken – unlike Frederick, they did not portray Henry as acting on his own – but otherwise their image of bad kingship is curiously generic. Whether that is a fair assessment will be easier to determine once we consider a group of texts written from among the midst of the 1234–5 uprising: those from Worms.

The Worms materials are particularly rich, not least because, despite a number of overlaps and despite the fact that they may have drawn on a common, now lost third source, they also reflect the views of different sections of the thirteenth-century town. One, labelled the *Chronicon Wormatiense* by its nineteenth-century editor, appears to reflect the views of the cathedral chapter, the other, the *Annales Wormatienses*, that of the townsmen. At the same time, the textual relationship of these two sources is not the only problem they pose: the date of composition is also unclear. The *Annales*, for instance, somewhat mistakenly put the beginning of Henry's uprising in the year 1233, while the entry immediately following the king's siege of Worms relates to events in 1241.[21] The chronicles may, of course, have been composed and written in intervals, but all we can say for certain is that they were written at various stages from the middle decades of the thirteenth century onwards.

Let us begin by summarising the narrative: the *Annales*, that is, the version associated with the urban commune, place the beginning of Henry's revolt in the year 1233: he caused his father great offence by planning to divorce his wife Margaret, daughter of the late Duke Leopold of Austria, and to marry the sister of the king of Bohemia instead. Realising how much this would aggravate the emperor, the king feared his father might come to Germany, and thus decided to prevent him from doing so. Taking the advice of his council, he demanded hostages from the towns, and to this effect, sent emissaries to Worms. What follows paints the citizens as paragons of loyalty, and contrasts their steadfastness not only with the king's fickleness but also that of their commercial rivals. While the men of Worms risked the king's anger by rejecting his demands unanimously, the citizens of Speyer, swayed by their bishop, succumbed. Realising that the citizens resisted his demands, the king sent several noble messengers, including Landulf, their bishop, to sway them. Once this failed, Henry began to devastate the lands surrounding Worms, so that its inhabitants did not dare venture beyond the town walls. Not only did they see their properties and livelihoods destroyed but also – perhaps indicating the author's mercantile background – incurred many expenses because they had to equip knights and bowmen. The king continued to step up the pressure, and even attacked Worms itself: in late April, Henry sent an army of allegedly over 5,000 knights against the town, and that army did indeed burn about 30 houses in one of the suburbs before it was thrown back.[22] Shortly thereafter the emperor arrived.

So far, so familiar: we learn very little about Henry's motives or intentions, apart from the ease with which he succumbed to sexual desire. This may be indicative of more profound shortcomings, but these are not elaborated – no mention is made of unsuitable advisors, for instance, and although the driving force in the revolt was the king's fear of his father, these anxieties are not linked to specific misdeeds. Here was a picture of tyranny that focused on actions (the taking of hostages, for instance), but these actions followed rather than preceded the uprising itself. What matters in the present context, though, is how the Worms annalist used this as a means of legitimising the actions of his fellow townsmen, and of the values which this allowed the citizens to proclaim and uphold. Almost every step of the conflict enabled the men of Worms to prove their steadfastness by demonstrating their loyalty to the emperor, and to do so in ever more fervent ways. This established a favourable contrast not only with the fickleness of their political foes but also that of their commercial rivals. Unlike the citizens of nearby Speyer, for instance, those of Worms resisted the pleadings of their own bishop, and they maintained their stance even when Henry himself appeared outside Worms – by thirteenth-century standards a degree of political pressure which few of those on whom it was exerted would have been able to withstand. This steadfastness compared favourably not only with the king's treachery but also his motivations: the good men of Worms acted out of their love for justice and due to the bonds which linked them to their lord, the emperor. Henry, by contrast, set aside both the obedience he owed his father and the protection he was to grant his subjects, and did so for the most dishonourable of reasons: sexual lust.

Equally worth noting is the juxtaposition between the citizens' actions and those of Bishop Landulf. Although the *Annales* stop short of accusing Landulf of greed or simony, they imply a link between Landulf's pleading on the kings' behalf, and his election. This firmly situates the events at Worms within the continuing struggle between commune and bishop, and should thus alert us to the fact that the townsmen's loyalty was loyalty at a price. It seems, too, as if this strategy worked: while, in November 1234, Henry had ordered the citizens to return all rights and privileges to Landulf which had been granted by the bishop's predecessor,[23] and which the king himself had initiated or at least confirmed,[24] in May 1236, the citizens had these privileges reissued by Frederick II, as a belated and temporary reward for their loyalty.[25] The conflict between father and son was viewed from a strictly local perspective, and more strikingly so than by other sources. This may furthermore explain some of the oddities in the annalists' way of reporting the young King's rebellion: despite having been so close to events, the annalist appears to have had little information about the motivation behind Henry (VII)'s rebellion. What mattered was the impact regnal politics had on his immediate environment, and where the information was unavailable which might have allowed him to paint a more detailed picture, he either avoided too detailed a coverage or constructed one which fitted Henry's actions within a more established pattern of bad lordship. Despite its local focus, the Annals thus elaborate a set of values of universal significance.

This becomes even more apparent once the *Annales* are set along-side the *Chronicon Wormatiense*, probably written by or for members of the cathedral chapter. The *Chronicon*, too, emphasises the citizens' loyalty, but contrasts this implicitly with their previous treatment at the young king's hands: when describing the earlier conflict between the townsmen and Bishop Henry, for instance, it is stressed that they would not agree to anything without the agreement of the king, 'because he favoured them in everything.'[26] Nonetheless, once the king rose against his father, nothing could sway the townsmen into betraying Frederick. Bishop Landulf, on the other hand, was on friendly terms with the king. Even so, he was much liked by the citizens, and, with their permission, set out to Henry's court to see what he might be able to accomplish. During his absence, however, some members of the cathedral chapter began to conspire against him, and secretly sent envoys to Frederick, accusing the prelate of betrayal.[27] When Frederick eventually made it to Worms, he banned Landulf from his presence, and, despite the inter-cession of the citizens, Landulf was forced to seek refuge with one of his chaplains.[28] In all this, Henry makes only a passing appearance, and his rebellion merely serves as a means of locating events in time: Landulf was elected roughly at the time when Henry rose against the emperor, and those conspiring against the prelate wrote to Frederick because they knew he was coming to deal with Henry. Beyond this little detail is given, except for an entry from a now lost chronicle, which described in some detail the burning of some of the suburbs of Worms, and Henry's ultimate submission and exile.[29] No reasons are given for the king's rebellion, and there is little background about its build-up and course.

The *Chronicon* thus shares with the *Annales* a local focus that views imperial or regnal matters primarily in relation to the affairs of the town and chapter of Worms. The differences in describing Landulf's actions are, however, worth noting, as they reveal shared values: the bishop had acted as intermediary, at the citizens' behest and with their permission, and because of his good relationship with the king. There was no indication of evil doing on his part, and his subsequent treatment at Frederick's hands was the unjust result of intrigues spun by members of the cathedral chapter.[30] Equally important is the role ascribed to the citizens: they welcomed the bishop's attempt to intercede with Henry; pleaded for Landulf when Frederick sought to expel him; and greeted him joyfully when he returned.[31] We have already seen that in reality the relationship between Landulf and the citizens was rather more antagonistic – in fact, his reconciliation with the emperor also resulted in the revocation of the privileges the townsmen had been granted in 1236. Nonetheless, this image served to deflect criticism from the prelate, who had acted not in opposition to the citizens or the emperor, but in close association with the former, and to spare them greater evil. This only underlined the moral and political strength of his position, and the moral depravity of those who had conspired against him.

The conflicting accounts of Landulf's role and motivation also throw light on the principles according to which the Worms chroniclers judged legitimacy: most importantly, loyalty and the pursuit of justice. This was, after all, what distinguished them from Henry (VII) and his partisans: the townsmen did not reject Henry's authority, but viewed it as subordinate to that of the emperor. In fact, the annalist stressed, they were willing to grant Henry all that was rightfully his, short of backing him against his father. The king, by contrast, showed no such compunction, and betrayed the trust and authority with which he had been invested by Frederick. Similarly, Bishop Landulf, in the *Annales'* version of events, had forfeited any loyalty he might have been owed by the townsmen the moment he joined those resisting the emperor's rightful claims. Faithfulness was the moral indicator against which political actions had to be measured. Henry's decision to rebel against his father was thus reason enough to condemn him, and required no further explanation.

Loyalty was, however, also the driving motivation behind Landulf's actions. In fact, although bound to Henry by ties of patronage and friendship, there was little doubt that, in the end, he, too, was loyal to the emperor. It was, in fact, this fealty, which made his treatment at Frederick's hands all the more cruel and unjust. At the same time, the *Chronicon*, although written under the impression of Frederick's second excommunication in 1239, went to some length to soften its criticism of the emperor. His treatment of Landulf was unfair, and this injustice was underlined not only by the fact of the bishop's faithfulness but also by the resistance Frederick encountered from the citizens: in 1235, the townsmen had pleaded on their prelate's behalf; in 1237, when an imperial official visited Worms to deprive Landulf of his bishopric, they co-operated only reluctantly and under protest.[32] Even those who had stood so valiantly by Frederick, who had endured the burnings and sieges unleashed upon them by the king, recoiled at the harshness of the emperor's response. Furthermore, Frederick II listened to bad advice: when, in 1235, a group of anonymous canons had accused the bishop of siding with Henry, Frederick, rather than allowing the bishop to clear his name, forced him into exile.[33] Unlike his son, however, Frederick was allowed to redeem himself, and did so by taking Landulf back into his favour. Frederick may have acted wrongly, but he was willing to make amends, to correct wrongs committed in his name or at his behest, and to show due favour to those who had suffered on his behalf.

Loyalty was not, of course, given unconditionally, but on the assumption that, in exchange, a ruler would abide by common norms of political behaviour, most importantly a love of justice, and that he would reward those who had stood by him. If a ruler – as Henry (VII) had done – violated these principles, then his subjects could transfer their loyalty elsewhere, although they had to do so reluctantly, and there were narrowly circumscribed bounds within which loyalties could be changed. For, and this is the second key point to emerge from the Worms accounts, several overlapping levels of loyalty and obedience were at play. In this particular case, loyalty to the emperor overruled that owed to king or bishop. This also meant that one set of loyalties could be played against another: as had happened in the conflict between commune and Bishop Henry in 1233–4, and as the men of Worms were themselves to experience once Landulf had been reconciled to the emperor. That actions did not always follow the principles espoused in the historical record is unsurprising, but the ways in which actions were written up so that they could conform to these norms, throws important light on the cultural and ideological context of politics.

The Worms chronicles are representative of the way Henry's revolt was reported by most contemporary or near contemporary observers. None allow the king redemptive features, all described Henry as the driving force behind the unrest, and the rebellion as indicative of his tyranny, his political or moral incompetence. This may reflect the swiftness and totality of Henry's overthrow: he did not put up enough of a struggle to warrant much sympathy. It may also reflect the fervour of Frederick's response, and possibly that Frederick, at least from July/August 1235 onwards, represented his son's rebellion as something more dangerous than it may otherwise have been. That is, although armed conflict certainly did take place, it was perhaps the fact that Frederick treated his sons' actions as an armed rebellion that made contemporary chroniclers turn it into one. This certainly would be another reason to explain the somewhat schematic nature of the chroniclers' response, their unwillingness to tell us much about the background to events beyond a catalogue of familiar archetypes of filial ingratitude and royal tyranny.[34] Simultaneously, however, that somewhat clichéd language of royal injustice also revealed some of the abiding norms according to which politics were meant to be conducted.

III

The Latin narratives discussed so far offered a record of events as they unfolded. Abstract principles informed their judgement and perhaps even the selection of what they reported, but these norms were not something that had to be elaborated on, explained or justified in detail. Most of the vernacular materials at our disposal, by contrast, are political poems, seeking to espouse principles valid beyond the immediate political context of their composition. They thus provide a valuable perspective on events, but they also pose problems. Most importantly, thirteenth-century political poetry is difficult to date. It works by allusion to events that may have been well known to a contemporary audience, but which, several centuries later, are hard to identify and which have thus led to sometimes widely different datings. What follows should thus be approached with some caution. Although I have sought to stick to those texts which can be loosely identified either as dealing with the events of 1235, or as having been written around that time, there is no guarantee that they actually were. All we can assume with some certainty is that they were composed in the thirteenth century. At the same time, their concern for abstract ideals also means that there is no reason to be overly concerned about linking a poem to a specific event or time: if read with due caution, it still tells us something about the values, norms and ideals espoused by those writing it.

Let us now start by considering a panegyric for Frederick II, written by Reimar von Zweter:[35] the text is structured as an allegorical description of Frederick's person – he had a tongue of justice, a hand of peace and so on – centring on Frederick's love of peace and justice, his steadfastness and constancy.[36] Reimar, similarly, praised Frederick for his ability to hear everything that was said,[37] not in an allusion to his ability to listen, but as a token of his power and might;[38] but he also warned the enemies of the empire that those who conspired against it would face swift and inevitable punishment. Several of Zweter's poems of praise seem to echo the language Frederick himself had employed – in his letters to the archbishop of Trier or the citizens of Worms, the preface to the Mainz land peace, the Zwettl *Vita* of St Elisabeth, or his letters against the duke of Austria. Some of Reimar's verses in fact read almost like translations of Frederick's statements, and thus go far beyond the Latin narratives, which largely echo the themes of imperial propaganda, without adopting them wholesale, while at the same time incorporating them within a specifically local frame of reference. According to Reimar, Frederick did not want to consume the bread of the empire without deserving it, and was thus driven by a desire to do justice, and to punish the wicked, and liberate the oppressed.[39] Reimar continued that Frederick only responded to the needs of the empire and was sent by God to end the sufferings of his subjects: before Frederick's arrival, 'the empire was wasting away, its voice hoarse and darkened by its lamentations, ...'[40] This, in turn, reflected some of the narrative accounts we have already been dealing with, but it also echoes, for instance, the Zwettl *Vita*: Frederick returned to Germany to heal the wounds of his subjects.[41] The image of imperial power that emerges from Reimar's writing is one with which the imperial chancery should have been familiar and comfortable. Imperial power was interpreted as the absence of war, as the pacification of the realm and the swift and immediate punishment of evildoers. There was, however, also an important difference: while both Frederick and his son had stressed the importance of the princes, and the need to act only in close consultation with their noble subjects, this element was absent from Reimar's poetry: doing justice and maintaining the peace was the emperor's prerogative. This reflected a common attitude among Middle High German poets, as our next example will show.

Brother Werner, probably writing in the 1230s and 1240s, also eschews references to specific political events. Instead, he produced a series of poems outlining in more general terms the respective virtues and vices of popes and emperors.[42] Foremost among the latter's duties, and a favourite theme of Werner's, was that he did justice strictly and without hatred.[43] In another poem, probably written c. 1235, just before or after the Mainz land peace,[44] Werner called upon the emperor to do in Germany what he had already accomplished in Sicily, and see to it that justice be done. Frederick, who was likened to Christ (through whom he had received his power), was exhorted to heed the cries of the poor, act on their laments, and rectify the miserable state of his realm.[45] The evidence is too fragmentary to allow for overly elaborate interpretations, but the kind of virtues Werner praised (or desired) in the emperor and the princes nonetheless differ: while the former was to act as a strict but impartial judge, an enforcer of peace and justice, a poem in praise of Duke Frederick of Austria lists a somewhat different catalogue of virtues. Most notably, the duke had been generous and gentle to his subjects, irrespective of their status (counts, freemen, *ministeriales* and servants, knights and squires all became rich under him), strenuous in war and protective of the honour of his lands.[46]

While stressing different values, the distinctiveness of imperial and princely virtues is equally maintained in a praise poem on the late Duke Louis of Bavaria: with Louis someone had passed away who was without equal in his faithfulness to the emperor, and who had so skilfully protected the empire when emperor and pope had been at war. Without him, king and emperor were deprived of wise and prudent counsel.[47] The importance of princely counsel, and the danger of listening to wrong counsel, is also alluded to in yet another poem (*Swelh vürste nach dem keiser gat*), which again poses difficulties of timing and attribution. The text can be read either as urging drastic action against Duke Frederick, or as warning him against his enemies and their plots. An unnamed prince is described as stalking the emperor like a wolf, seeking to poison him with bad counsel, and waiting for him to fall. The emperor, in turn, is exhorted to face these enemies early, and to guard against them as one guards against a fire that is beginning to spread.[48] While good princely lordship thus manifested itself in loyalty towards the emperor, the princes could not relieve the emperor of his responsibility for the welfare of his people. They could share in this task, but it was by no means central to their function. At best, being a loyal and prudent counsellor was the attribute of a great prince; at worst, the emperor was advised to heed the princely wolves circling his court. The princes were also expected to display distinctive virtues: they certainly ought to be loyal and have the interest of the empire at heart, but above all, they had to be fervent defenders of their own domains, and – maybe not the most disinterested demand coming from a minstrel – be generous to their dependants.

Zweter and Werner had thus stressed the emperor's duty to do justice and indicated some of the distinctions between princely and imperial power. Similar themes were elaborated by a poet, writing c. 1235–40, known only as Brother Walter, but he also indicates a more varied attitude towards Henry's uprising. This becomes most evident in a poem which, written as a prolonged allegory, dealt directly with Henry's rebellion, and compared the king to Adam, and his rebellion to the expulsion from paradise. Like the first man, so the unnamed *iuge kúnig* (young king), too, had been given possession of paradise (Germany) on condition that he abide by his lord's commandments. Like Adam, Henry remained unable to resist temptation, and following the whisperings of one of his advisors, rose in revolt (he took a bite out of the apple).[49] Responsibility for Henry's rebellion did not rest solely on the king's shoulders: he did listen to bad advisers, and the text thus echoes a theme also evident in many of the Latin texts we have considered. Brother Walter presents, however, a more subtle reading of Henry's uprising: the king brought suffering upon himself and his subjects, but at the same time, he merely re-enacted a motif typical of human history.[50] Henry was at fault, but his fault was that of inevitable human weakness, rather than of a particularly pernicious of unfaithful disposition. By implication, his treatment at Frederick's hands could be read as unduly harsh, thus adding to the young king's tragedy.

This was certainly the stance taken by our final example: the Bavarian continuation of the *Regensburger Kaiserchronik* (*Regensburg Chronicle of Emperors*), written probably in the early 1250s. Henry was described as acting successfully and justly in his father's name. His rule was virtuous and distinguished: peace prevailed for peasants and on royal roads.[51] This was, in fact, a point to which the anonymous author returned several times in the course of the fairly short section (150 lines in total) on Henry's reign (ll. 616–18, 621–2, 755–65). It was the peacefulness of Henry's reign – for fourteen years, there had been neither unrest nor violence – that made Frederick's actions so unjust.[52] Moreover, Henry was generous, and his table always laden with food and crowded by visitors. In terms of specific events, the campaign against the duke of Bavaria was recorded approvingly, and was justified with the duke's many crimes against the empire.[53] Intriguingly, though, very little is said about the reasons for the eventual falling out between father and son: having subdued the duke, the king worried almost daily that Frederick would come to Germany and diminish his honour and standing. Eventually, he saw no other way but to ally himself with the Lombards.[54] On the one hand, the continuation thus conforms to a pattern also encountered in Latin sources: incomprehension as to why father and son had fallen out, and, like most of the former, the anonymous author stuck to simply recording the event rather than seeking to explain it. He did, though, voice a somewhat different stance: he did not condemn the king. Even the war against the duke of Bavaria was singled out as a positive achievement, and the continuation thus comes closest among our sources to echoing Henry's letter to the bishop of Hildesheim. This text, furthermore, endows Henry with good qualities that combine the traditional values of good royal lordship (maintaining the peace, punishing evil-doers and protecting the weak) with those normally the preserve of princes (generosity and hospitality). As such, the Bavarian continuation points to more far-reaching structural problems, and the time has now come to move from specific texts to the broader picture.

IV

Our sources reveal the complex and multi-layered relationship between imperial and royal politics, and the generally more localised concerns of contemporary observers. On a most elementary level, Henry was unable to get his side of the story across. Criticism of the emperor's actions was, with the exception of one text, muted and indirect, and was, moreover, limited almost exclusively to vernacular sources. Much of this does, of course, reflect the ease of Frederick's victory and the extent of Henry's humiliation. The king's imprisonment and exile, the – to German observers – unaccustomed ferocity of the punishment meted out to him and his supporters, left little room for debate: there was no conceivable avenue of celebrating Henry's achievements without criticising an emperor who, during his German sojourn of 1235–6 had so frequently and amply illustrated the range of his power, and the brutality with which he would respond to criticism and resistance. There was, however, more to this than merely that old and clichéd adage of history being written by the victors. For German chroniclers did not simply and slavishly copy Frederick's pronouncements. To some extent, Frederick was successful because his ideas and values echoed those of his subjects. Similarly, had Henry been reconciled to his father, or had he been able to put up more of a resistance, we would perhaps find more widespread references to the fact the he upheld similar principles of royal power.

Imperial lordship was based on collective rule, on monarch and princes acting in unison, and only after close and careful consultation. This had been at the heart of both Frederick's and Henry's pronouncements, and it was an ideal frequently invoked by their subjects – either directly, by stressing the advice and counsel taken by the emperor, by praising individual lords, like Duke Louis of Bavaria, for the prudent advice they had given, or indirectly, by lambasting Henry for his tendency either not to heed advice, to refuse taking it, or take it from men of ill repute and little standing. Of equal importance was the maintenance of peace and justice. Both Frederick and Henry stressed this as their chief duty. Their subjects shared this perception of the imperial and royal office: bad kingship expressed itself by unwarranted violence, the oppressive use of force and the denial of justice, while good lord-ship manifested itself in the punishment of evildoers and the main-tenance of peace. More importantly, seeing to it that justice was done remained first and foremost the duty of king and emperor. This may have reflected the more exalted thinking at Frederick's court after 1235, as evident, for instance, in the decrees of the Mainz *diet*.[55] Similarly, both the campaign against Henry and that against Duke Frederick had been legitimised with this imperial duty of acting as the fount of justice: because Henry and Frederick had refused to perform their function, because they had oppressed rather than that they protected widows and orphans, the emperor had to intervene and deprive them of their office.

Equally important, though, is what chroniclers did not report, and foremost among those issues ranks the question of imperial honour. While Frederick repeatedly stressed the shame which the king's actions had brought upon him, the empire and its princes, and although Henry, too, complained about Frederick repeatedly violating his royal honour, only one contemporary observer echoed these complaints. The honour of empire and emperor (*honor imperii et imperatoris*) remained a discourse invoked by the emperor and his son alone. This is not to say that concepts of honour did not matter: among the tokens of Henry's and Duke Frederick's tyranny, for instance, were numerous examples of the shameful treatment they had inflicted on their noble subjects: by demanding hostages, for instance, or by arranging forced marriages between noblewomen and men of lesser standing. Equally, in some of the praise poetry, noble conduct, as with the duke of Bavaria, or the honour of one's lands, as with Duke Frederick, mattered and was invoked as a token of princely virtue. Why, then, did the concept of the *honor imperii* find so limited a reception? We will probably never know for sure. One reason, though, may have been the degree to which Frederick linked that *honor* to his functions as guarantor of peace and justice: it was by maintaining those that his honour and that of the empire was maintained. That is, by highlighting Frederick's success as guarantor of peace and the rightful order of the world, chroniclers and poets high-lighted those elements of the imperial *honor* which to them mattered most.

This cannot, however, be the whole story: maybe this was at least a partial rejection of a rhetoric which to most Germans, too, may have seemed archaic, not a little overblown, and out of place. What concerned them was that Frederick did his job as emperor and that he dealt with the malaise that prevailed in Germany. This clash between imperial self-representation and the contemporary response is worth noting, as it resembles some of the problems Frederick encountered in Italy.[56] In Lombardy, Frederick's discourse of imperial honour had fallen on the deaf ears of his enemies, but in Germany, it was ignored even by those who otherwise supported his regime. This matters for a variety of reasons. It complicates the picture painted in recent scholarship about the central role of *honor* in imperial politics.[57] Honour was certainly central to imperial ideology and self-representation, but it was also something which neither to the Staufens' adversaries nor their supporters seemed worth dwelling on. Staufen imperial ideology was perhaps as outdated in a German as it was in an Italian context, and may thus indicate a more far-reaching problem than current scholarship would lead us to expect.

All this also had repercussions for how Henry (VII) was perceived by his subjects. To most of them, he was a curious hybrid between a prince, that is, a vassal and subject of the emperor, and someone who was expected to perform the functions of an emperor without being one. To some extent this, too, reflected the way the king and his father had painted their relationship: Henry, after all, had portrayed himself as an aggrieved vassal who had been wronged repeatedly and unfairly. Equally, Frederick had painted Henry as entrusted with the authority to rule, but he could rule only at the behest of his father's, and on his behalf, never in his stead. Henry's power and authority derived from Frederick, and Frederick could easily take it away again. In fact, to most contemporaries, the driving force behind Henry's insurrection had been the fear that his father would do just that. The relationship between father and son deteriorated at least in part because these contradictions were never resolved. This was a dilemma they shared with their subjects. Most had little difficulty in accepting that Henry exercised authority on his father's behalf, and this concept was accepted in equal measure by those hostile to the young king, and the few who either failed to condemn his actions outright or who sided with him. Nor, for that matter, did Henry dispute that he exercised authority through his father, and on his behalf. Once chroniclers describe specific actions performed by the king, a similarly contradictory attitude emerges, and Henry was thus portrayed either as incapable of or as excelling at keeping the peace and of ruling with justice.

However, we also find ideals of rulerly action referred to, which in other cases were associated with princes, rather than kings. The evidence in all this is rather limited, and we should thus avoid over interpreting it. Nonetheless, when Henry was praised, it was because he combined virtues more typically associated with an emperor – the keeping of the peace and the maintenance of justice – with those more commonly ascribed to princes (and princely patrons): generosity and splendour. The combination of failings laid at the young king's door by hostile sources – his sexual lust, greed and so on – points in a similar direction: they echo, after all, those, presented as typical of Duke Frederick or, in some accounts, Duke Louis of Bavaria.[58] In Germany, unlike Italy, few of these played much part in reports condemning Frederick II (after 1239), who was more commonly lambasted as a tyrant and oppressor of the Church, rather than a lecherous pursuer of young women. That is, when the emperor was criticised, he was lambasted for failing in his duties as guarantor of peace and justice, and as protector of the Church, not for personal moral failings (which remained the weakness of princes, not kings). This phenomenon cannot be reduced to the question of relative familiarity alone, that is, the fact that, unlike his father, Henry had been continuously present in Germany, and that his various misdemeanours and sinful acts were thus more widely known. The image of Henry's revolt in the narrative sources coincides with that emerging from Frederick's and Henry's own letters: there was uncertainty as to what the young kings' role should be. He was judged by criteria which mixed elements of a standard catalogue of imperial virtues with that more normally reserved for princes. That the exact relationship between father and son had never been clearly defined ultimately brought about the conflict of 1234–5, but the history of tensions between the two had left its mark on the expectations of Henry's subjects, too. To them, Henry was somehow neither prince nor king nor emperor, neither fish nor flesh nor fowl.

The one to profit from all this was Frederick II. In fact, in comparison with the English sources, the degree to which the emperor was exempted from responsibility remains striking. Problems or difficulties facing Germany were squarely blamed either on the king or on the princes. In fact, even those who lamented the state of Germany, its suffering and the anguished cries for justice emanating from its people, stayed well clear of implying a link with Frederick's fifteen-year absence. This may reflect conventions of genre and literary writing, but remains remarkable when compared, for instance, with the portrayal of Frederick II in Italian sources,[59] or that of his grandfather, Frederick Barbarossa, in Germany.[60] This is true even if we exclude the kind of panegyric we have encountered in vernacular sources. While largely exempted from responsibility for the affairs of Germany, and while only rarely criticised for his treatment of Henry, and never blamed for the outbreak of his son's rebellion, he was also faced with expectations that may well have exceeded the capabilities even of a man like Frederick II. He had portrayed himself (perhaps in response to these expectations) as harbinger and source of justice, and this was exactly what his subjects expected him to be.

Attacking Henry may thus have been a means of criticising Frederick. Not only had Henry been admonished for failing in the functions viewed as a ruler's foremost duties, but his deposition and exile had also made him a safe and convenient target. We should not, of course, exaggerate Frederick's grasp on Germany – there would have been manifold opportunities to voice criticism of Frederick without him ever becoming aware of it. Rather, what we have here is a curious combination of the expectation that Frederick would accomplish what he had accused his son of failing in, perhaps strengthened and radicalised by the emperor's fifteen-year absence; relief at the arrival of a ruler who would have the authority (and the means) to fulfil his duties; and an attempt to list, in the context of Henry's rebellion, the evils which the emperor's subjects desired him to address, and which, in part at least, may have arisen because of that prolonged absence.

It is furthermore worth noting that, unlike Henry III, the king of the Romans was granted no opportunity to redeem himself. To some extent, this may have been the case because Henry III, unlike his German name-sake, was the ultimate source of governmental authority in his realm: Henry (VII) suffered for the fact that, in his father, an authority existed which could be called upon to exercise rulerly functions in his place. No such alternative existed in England. While much of the blame for the Marshal's uprising was thus shouldered by royal officials and advisors, and while the king was granted numerous opportunities to redeem himself politically and morally, Henry (VII), and Henry (VII) alone, had to take responsibility for his actions. Some sources may have accused him of listening to evil councillors, but whereas in England blame for civil unrest rested with these advisors, in Germany Henry was blamed for appointing these men and listening to them. Moreover, his failure expressed itself primarily as personal and moral failings, from which his political shortcomings sprang. This, too, is an image very different from the one we will encounter in the English sources. That personal short-comings and political misfortunes were closely linked was, of course, one of the stables of medieval writing on kingship,[61] but the degree to which success or failure rested with the individual ruler exceeded what we know from other parts of medieval Europe and may thus reflect the swiftness of Henry's overthrow, and the impact of Frederick's propaganda, but it may also point to a more personalised concept of imperial lordship in Germany (and as such is a theme to which we will frequently return).

We should, however, avoid drawing hasty conclusions about the nature of German politics. There certainly were no administrators who could shield the ruler from criticism. Neither, though, should the personalised nature of Henry's tyranny be understood as denoting archaic forms of governance: the situation is more complex, as we will see once we turn to the means and mechanisms of politics. Equally, we should not be deceived by chroniclers failing to deal at length with processes of imperial administration (e.g., by naming imperial officials or recording decrees like the Mainz land peace). They may not have been particularly interested in the workings of royal government (and may thus have stressed the moral failings of the king and his general acts of tyranny, rather than the specifics of his rule, the breaking of legal norms or processes), but they were also quite capable of ignoring Frederick II's exuberant rhetoric of imperial honour. Furthermore, different concerns were at play on different levels of politics. As we will see, those writing history were interested in the administrative and legal mechanisms of power once these had an immediate and direct impact on their locality, institution and community. Equally, though, that imperial power was not described in these terms had more to do with specific notions of how an emperor should act in politics, than a real or perceived lack of imperial power. Administrative lordship mattered on the level of princes and prelates, but it was something beneath the dignity of a king or emperor.

Exploring the image of Henry's revolt has enabled us to trace a series of processes and highlight distinctive features of Staufen political culture. We have been able to sketch out the complex relationship between royal and imperial self-representation on the one hand, and its reception by contemporary observers on the other. Most importantly, while evoking similar values and propagating similar ideals (such as loyalty and prudent counsel), rulers and ruled also diverged on a number of points. The concept of honour, for instance, so central to Frederick II's image of imperial lordship, was given fairly short shrift by the chroniclers. Similarly, the emperor's emphasis on the princes sharing in the governance of the empire was only partly held by his subjects. This was not an act of hostility towards the princes, but a case of Frederick falling victim to the expectations he had raised among his subjects. The question we should consider next is how this compared to the English experience, and it is there, too, that we will encounter some remarkable inversions. English chroniclers espoused similar values (loyalty, the need for advice and counsel) but gave them a somewhat different practical meaning, and, above all, they were much more concerned with issues of moral behaviour, royal honour and public action. Why this may have been the case and what it tells us about English political culture, about the distinctiveness of Staufen and Plantagenet politics, will be at the heart of the next chapter.

6
Loyalties True and False: Political Values in England

In dealing with the English sources, we must be aware of the degree to which most narrative accounts of the revolt drew on one another, with often only subtle variations. Roger of Wendover's *Flores Historiarum* and Matthew Paris' *Chronica Majora* dominated thirteenth-century historical writing. Even the *Margam Chronicle* continuation, for instance, was closely modelled on Paris' revision of Wendover,[1] while the St Albans *Flores Historiarum* started out as a reworking of Paris' *Chronica Majora*.[2] In the German case, no single source dominates the historical record to the same extent. Even so, when chronicles copied Wendover and Matthew Paris, they did so because they deemed them reliable, and because they agreed with the fundamental thrust of their narrative and interpretation. We thus have to treat our sources with caution, and will have to compare them repeatedly to each other, and to those few pieces of writing not directly related to the tradition established by Wendover and Paris. In exchange, the richness of detail, subtlety and colour of narrative in these sources far exceeds that of the German materials, and allow us to ask questions that the evidence in the latter case would not even let us pose.

There is, however, a second problem: although the English evidence is more detailed, it is also more limited in range. There are, for instance, no vernacular sources. The closest we have is a short entry in Robert of Gloucester's chronicle, written at the turn to the fourteenth century, and drawing much from Roger of Wendover. Changes are few, and, following his source, Robert emphasises the cruelty of Peter des Roches, the unfair treatment meted out to Hubert de Burgh, and the king's ultimate show of contrition.[3] Similarly, no letters survive like the ones sent by Frederick II and Henry (VII). The closest we have to a statement by the king is a mandate, to which we will turn shortly, but nothing like the detailed justifications dispatched by the emperor and his son. As far as the earl is concerned, at best his family's close links with St Albans – Roger of Wendover's mother house – and with the Cistercian abbey of Margam in the Welsh marches, endowed by Richard and his family, where he had staid during the conflict with the king, and from where one of the most detailed accounts of the Marshal's uprising survives, may give us an indication of how he perceived himself. Circumstantial evidence also suggests that the Marshal family was adept at using historical writing for its benefit. Most famously, perhaps, this had been the case with the *Histoire de Guillaume le Mareshal*, written within a few years of William the Marshal's death.[4] Equally, though, the *Song of Dermot and the Earl*, describing the Anglo-Norman conquest of Ireland, has been associated with the Marshal family.[5] This both complicates the picture and allows us some insights into the kind of arguments used in the 1230s. It complicates matters because we cannot *prove* that the Marshal and his partisans influenced the way Roger of Wendover or the *Margam Annals* reported the events of 1232–4. Considering, however, some of the detail Roger of Wendover was able to record, especially that relating to the earl, it is plausible to assume that at least some of this information had been passed on by those siding with the Marshal. Even if we cannot with certainty declare these to be the Marshal's views, they nonetheless reveal the attitude of one of the most widely copied and trusted observers of the contemporary political scene. If Wendover's and Paris' contemporaries believed them to offer an accurate rendition of the values at play, this enables us to offer a plausible interpretation of ideals and norms that were widely accepted, regardless of whether the Marshal had voiced them or not.

I

In August 1233, Henry III issued a mandate ordering the confiscation of the Marshal's lands. This mandate, our most detailed evidence for Henry III's view of events, was made out to the sheriff of Worcester, with copies sent to those of Berkshire, Sussex, Warwickshire, Oxfordshire, Buckinghamshire and Wiltshire, and recounted the most recent instalment in the prolonged struggle between the Marshal and the king. Richard, Henry claimed, had approached him at Wycombe, surrounded by an armed retinue. At the behest of several magnates, the king had granted the earl a respite and safe conduct: Richard was to return to his estates, together with those of the king's men who had accompanied the earl, armed against the king, and who the earl had maintained in his retinue contrary to the king's commands. These men were then to approach the king and submit themselves to his mercy, or to the judgement of his court, with the earl following suit later. However, the earl had not only failed to send back his retinue, nor had he submitted to the king's mercy, but had also attacked the castle of Hay – which was part of his barony and which he had received in exchange for his promise of faithful service – seized and fortified it against the king. Having done so, he sent envoys to the king at Hereford, asking for royal grace, while at the same time seizing yet another castle – much needed in protecting the Welsh marches – which had not even been part of the earl's lands, and fortifying it against the king. For these and other excesses against the king's peace, the sheriff was ordered to seize all of the Marshal's properties in his county, and return them to the king.[6]

This document tells us little about how the conflict between king and earl started. Its main purpose was, after all, to initiate and authorise a specific bureaucratic process. Even so, it fulfilled some functions similar to those of Henry (VII)'s and Frederick's letters: it was distributed widely (across several counties), and justified a particular course of action to a wider audience. It sought to anticipate criticism, and muster support for the king's actions. We will return to the role of the political public in the next chapter, but it is important to remember the significance of county courts and county communities in establishing that public.[7] They were the primary means by which decisions, events and debates could be carried from the court to the realm at large,[8] and this mandate was thus one way in which Henry could communicate his view of events to that wider audience. The detail with which Henry sought to justify the earl's dispossession is unusual for this kind of public mandate, and may thus indicate an awareness that the conflict threatened to engulf more than just the Welsh marches. What, then, were the arguments which Henry III used to deflect criticism and muster support?

Richard broke the peace, endangered the security of the realm, disregarded royal prohibitions on armed retinues, and failed to keep his word. He thus violated a series of legal, moral and political codes. That Richard met the king armed, and with an armed entourage, was already a breach of protocol, a threatening gesture which clearly indicated his rebellious nature and hostile intent.[9] The Marshal thus also violated the royal peace, and acted contrary to the most basic bonds of fidelity. He repeatedly broke his word – he had, after all, promised to make his men return to the king unarmed, and to follow suit himself; and the earl seized the castle at Hay, which he had received in exchange for his promise of loyalty and faithful service. He was not to be trusted. While the earl was supported by unknown traitors – 'our men who had come armed against us' – Henry III, by contrast, acted in unison and at the behest of his subjects. It was, after all, at their suggestion that the earl had been received, and that he had been granted a safe conduct, and it was at their behest that he was now deprived of his lands. Henry III emerges as a paragon of patient forgiveness. Only after the earl had broken his promises, had seized royal castles and armed them against the king – and only after Richard had attacked the king's faithful servants – was action taken against him.

When the Marshal was allowed to return to his estates, his men were meant to surrender themselves to the king's mercy or the judgement of his court. Both the question of what royal mercy entailed, and whether the judgement of the king's court was to be accepted, were central to the conflict. When, during the Westminster parliament in late 1233, the bishops and magnates had asked the king to abstain from further action against the earl, as he had not been found guilty by the judgement of his peers, Peter des Roches replied that there were no peers of the realm as there were in France, and that the king could pass judgement through the justiciar he had appointed.[10] This should not be understood as a rejection of Magna Carta, but as defending the principle that judgements in royal courts were passed after they had been presided over by royally appointed officers.[11] Nonetheless, once the identity of that official and the legitimacy of his appointment were in doubt, the judgement itself was unlikely to be accepted. Moreover, the treatment meted out to de Burgh would not have inspired confidence, nor would have the rumoured attempts by des Roches to have the Marshal tricked into captivity or even assassinated.[12]

The king's mercy poses similar problems. Wendover reports a conversation between a Friar Agnellus and the earl while the latter was staying at Margam.[13] This was one of the central passages in Wendover's reporting and justification of the revolt, and much of that justification turned on what seeking royal grace entailed. The friar claimed he had overheard the king say that although the earl had behaved unjustly and treacherously, he would nonetheless forgive him, take him back into his favour, guarantee him safety of life and limbs, and even grant Richard sufficient estates for him to live honourably. All the earl had to do was give himself over to the king's mercy. In fact, Agnellus continued, Stephen de Seagrave, the justiciar, had made a similar offer to two of the Marshal's friends, while many at court urged the earl to surrender, well knowing that he would be safe. There were good practical reasons, too, for the Marshal to do so: he had no other means of protecting himself.[14] What matters at this stage is that the expectation that the

Marshal throw himself at the king's mercy was not the unconditional surrender as which it might at first appear. The difference (to be elaborated further in Chapter 8) rested with the public against the private nature of the Marshal's submission.

The former denoted an unconditional surrender, and, in this case, an acknowledgement that the Marshal had been in the wrong and had treacherously attacked his sovereign. Ultimately, this was also the reason why Richard rejected Friar Agnellus' offer: he had done nothing wrong but only demanded that justice be done. The latter, by contrast, softened and mellowed this submission, and guaranteed that the earl would avoid the penalties which would normally be inflicted on those betraying their king. Similarly, when, in May 1234, Richard's remaining allies were reconciled to the king, the language used was that of surrender and seeking the king's grace: Gilbert Marshal, his brothers Walter and Anselm, Hubert de Burgh and others were granted a safe conduct 'to petition for the king's grace'. However, this safe conduct, in turn, was immediately followed by a list of pardons and grants which restored many of their possessions.[15] That this language was still used after des Roches and his allies had already been sidelined, and after the Marshal's remaining supporters had effectively won the war, may thus underline the degree to which seeking the king's mercy had become a formula which by no means carried with it implications of the full rigour of the law. Rather, it was an acknowledgement of defeat, and of accepting royal authority. What mattered to Henry was not so much to take revenge on the Marshal, but for the Marshal to acknowledge the illegitimacy of his actions, and to do so before as wide an audience as possible.[16]

The manner in which Henry and his chancery represented the conflict thus reveals important points about what they deemed to be rightful forms of political behaviour, and the principles that were meant to underpin them. At its heart were the twin pillars of consultative governance (the king acted at the advice and the behest of the magnates) and the monarch's role as the font and overseer of justice. That, in turn, was not administered by the ruler himself, but by those he had appointed to do so on his behalf. At the same time, and as the emphasis on royal mercy stresses, he had the right to soften or dismiss judgements, but not necessarily that of imposing them himself.[17] This was not a conflict between a totalitarian 'continental' and a 'libertarian' English model of royal authority, but was a clear acknowledgement of the principle that royal authority was limited and was to be guided by the advice and counsel of the king's leading subjects. Furthermore, the concept of a community of the realm (whose peace was threatened by the Marshal's actions) existed alongside a series of personal bonds, tying the great men of the realm directly to the king. These were, moreover, the bonds most clearly violated by the Marshal, who, despite his earlier oaths of loyalty, had led 'our men armed against us' and who had seized and fortified castles 'against us'. Inevitably, considering the type of document we have at our disposal, the rhetoric was less exalted, and the king's claims less detailed or far-reaching than those of Frederick II or Henry (VII), but they espoused similar principles: the Marshal's main offence had been to violate the royal peace, and undermine the stability of the realm by aiding its enemies.[18] Like the emperor, the king of England viewed safeguarding the peace and tranquillity of the realm as his foremost duty. The differences must, however, be noted, too. There was no reference to royal honour, and while Henry III had made indirect reference to the Marshal's alliance with the Welsh, Frederick did not even mention his son's ties with the Lombards. Even with these distinctions in mind, the parallels between the principles invoked by Henry III and Frederick II remain striking. Let us now see whether this also applied to how his subjects viewed the conflict.

II

One of the striking features about how English chroniclers described the Marshal's revolt was that, while fully supportive of the Marshal, they did not condemn the king outright. Wendover set the tone. He did not take kindly to des Roches, but he also exculpated the king from responsibility for the unrest: it was at the advice of Peter des Roches that he removed the *homines naturales* from his court in 1233,[19] and des Roches was responsible for the fact that the unjust administered justice, the lawless the law and the quarrelsome the peace.[20] Peter was the one who escalated the conflict by calling on the king to seize the manors of disaffected barons and to call on Poitevins and other aliens to guard royal castles,[21] while in October 1233 it was the bishop of Winchester yet again who dismissed the references to Magna Carta made by the earl Marshal.[22] The king, by contrast, played at best a supporting role and was to some extent the victim of the conflict, rather than its instigator. When, shortly after de Burgh's arrest, for instance, a number of Hubert's enemies approached the king, accusing Hubert of treason and demanding that he be punished accordingly, Henry rejected their demands: 'I would rather be known as a foolish and forgiving king, than as cruel and a tyrant'.[23] This also explains Roger's later description of the king as *rex simplex*, who, believing the lies of the Poitevins, entrusted them with the guardianship of royal castles.[24]

That this should not be read as a straightforward condemnation of the king is illustrated by *Annals* of Osney's account of the king's character, given in the 1280s. Looking back to the events of 1234, Thomas described the king as a *rex simplex* who feared God, was generous in his alms-giving, lavishly endowed monasteries and built many churches.[25] A *homo simplex* was a man of extraordinary piety. It was not a characteristic that equipped a ruler for the workings of royal government.[26] In the case of Henry III, it was this reputation for pious simplicity which made Dante place him in purgatory, in the valley of hapless kings, and which moved Salimbene to tell mocking anecdotes about him.[27] In Wendover's case, however, it also provided a means of exculpating the king from responsibility for the actions of his councillors. He was a simple and peace-loving man. It was because of this naturally benign disposition that he frequently rejected the more rigorous demands of his advisors (thus sparing Hubert de Burgh, for instance, or investing Richard Marshal with his inheritance). It was also because of this simplicity that he trusted men like des Roches or Stephen Segrave. Wendover's narrative thus centred on the need for good and prudent advisors, who would offer the guidance which a king so singularly ill equipped for royal government needed.

The degree to which Henry's simplicity was both an impediment to effective royal lordship and a means by which the king could redeem his authority is exemplified by the events leading up to des Roches' fall and disgrace. When confronted with the united opposition of the English bishops in 1234, the king acted humbly, and piously sought to accommodate their demands.[28] He, unlike des Roches, wanted to maintain the peace by any means necessary.[29] Henry's character was wholly redeemed when he heard of the Marshal's death: in the presence of bystanders he broke into tears, and hurriedly ordered his chaplains to read the office of the dead for Richard, while, the following morning, he distributed particularly generous alms among the poor.[30] This was an act of remorse, recognising the king's past mistakes, but it may also have been modelled on the reaction some chroniclers had ascribed to Henry II on hearing of the murder of Thomas Becket: for three days the king refused to eat, and for five weeks to talk to anyone.[31] Furthermore, this change of heart had not come easily, nor had it come out of the king's own volition. In fact, while the king lamented the Marshal's passing by exclaiming that he doubted a similar man would exist in England,[32] a few months earlier he had called the Marshal a traitor.[33] What had brought about the king's change of heart were the resolute measures taken by Edmund Rich, the new archbishop of Canterbury, and his episcopal colleagues, who not only excommunicated the king's closest advisors but also threatened to excommunicate the king.[34] Nor had this been the first time that the bishops protested against the king's actions: Archbishop Lucas of Dublin had done so when the king first moved against Hubert de Burgh;[35] in June 1233, a number of unnamed bishops claimed that peace would not return to England as long as Peter des Roches and his ilk were at large;[36] later that year, it was Bishop Richard of London who first intervened forcefully against the treatment inflicted on Walter of Carlisle,[37] and who later, jointly with the bishop of Salisbury, excommunicated those who had forcefully dragged Hubert de Burgh from the chapel at Devizes.[38] This list could easily be extended, but an important point has been made: this was not the first time that the prelates of the realm had intervened with the king and expressed their hostility to des Roches and his actions. Henry's resolve crumbled under the pressure of political events (the inability to subdue Marshal), ever more rigorous protest (by his clergy and barons), and the authority of St Edmund. The king was thus not free of guilt: he listened to bad advisors, and easily succumbed to their dishonest counsel. At the same time, Henry III himself was not blamed for any of the actions which drove his subjects to revolt: it was Peter des Roches who publicly dismissed Magna Carta, and Peter des Roches and Stephen Segrave were blamed for the sinister plots that led to the Marshal's murder in Ireland.[39] The king, a *rex simplex*, atoned for it by seeing his errors, by regretting the many misdeeds which had been committed in his name, and by reforming the governance of his household and his kingdom.

Wendover's view was widely shared. A continuation of the *Annals* of the Cistercian house of Margam, probably written c. 1246–7, displays an equally complex attitude towards the king. While condemning the imprisonment and shameful treatment of Hubert de Burgh, de Burgh's fall from grace is explained by the fact that his spirit had toughened into pride and arrogance, which turned the king against him.[40] The justiciar's demise was the result of his own shortcomings, and not a sign of the king's devious personality or even the machinations of des Roches alone. Similarly, on hearing that the king had disinherited de Burgh and the Marshal, and that he had done so unjustly and without the judgement of his council, the bishops appealed to the king against this decision. Their intervention had, of course, little effect, but the king was described as a *rex puer*, as a boy king, that is, as someone whose weaknesses and shortcomings were the result of his immaturity and young age, not of a devious personality.[41] Finally, once a new archbishop of Canterbury had been enthroned in Edmund, and once the king had taken the counsel of the very people on whom he was meant to rely (i.e. the native clergy and aristocracy), he dismissed des Roches.[42] In general, then, the king's conversion is treated in less detail but follows a similar pattern: Henry listened to bad advice, sometimes driven by thoroughly praiseworthy motives (a dislike of the proud and haughty), sometimes due to his inexperience and youth, but once confronted with the counsel of men like Edmund, he saw the error of his ways and acted accordingly. Equally, little doubt is left as to the depravity of des Roches and the fact that he was the driving force behind the turmoil engulfing England: the conflict between earl and king erupted because of the many aliens who Peter had brought with him to oppress the clergy and people of England.[43] At the same time, the king was not granted as many redeeming features – in the *Margam Annals*, there was no outpouring of grief over Richard's death. Similarly, though, de Burgh's fall from grace was the inevitable consequence of the justiciar's arrogance and haughtiness, and not of the king's or his minister's tyranny.

This reflected a broader trend. The mid-thirteenth century *Flores Historiarum* also attributes a greater degree of responsibility to the king. When Richard Marshal had complained about his treatment and that of other magnates, and demanded that they be restored to the king's court, the king got so angry that – truly, a token of cruel tyranny – he exiled them to Wales.[44] No mention was made of Peter des Roches forcing the king's hand.[45] The *Annals of Tewkesbury*, similarly, describe the king as the driving force in the actions against the Marshal, but also point to the willingness with which he took Edmund's advice,[46] and so do the *Annals of Winchester*,[47] Waverley[48] and Matthew Paris' *Life of St Edmund of Canterbury*.[49] The *Annals of Dunstable* add to this by describing Henry's lamentations of hearing about the Marshal's death: he grieved for the earl like David had grieved over the deaths of Saul and Jonathan.[50] This scriptural imagery matters: this was a just king grieving over those he had been close to in the past, but who had also sought to depose or kill him. More importantly, while in high medieval exegesis, David was perceived as a just king, he had also sinned against his God and his people, but then atoned for his transgressions.[51] The king of England was not a tyrant who violently oppressed his people.

All in all, this amounts to a view of the king and his actions, very much unlike that we have encountered in Germany. In the English narratives, royal advisors performed a function which, in Germany, was reserved either for Henry (VII) or a town or region's lord (such as the bishop of Worms or the duke of Austria). To some extent, as we have seen, this reflected the bureaucratic reality of English kingship: the identity of the person who presided over the running of the king's administration mattered, because he would have a real impact on the day to day affairs of the king's subjects. At the same time, as Joel Rosenthal has pointed out,[52] this also provided a means by which the institution of monarchy, and, more importantly, the person of the king, could be protected. In England this began to change during the 1240s and 1250s, when Henry III continued to be lambasted for his running of the realm, aided, no doubt, by the fact that it was not until 1258 that the administrative offices were filled that had been left vacant since 1232–4.[53] By freeing himself of the advisors and officials who might have curtailed Henry's ability to rule, he also took on a larger responsibility for the criticism, invective and resistance which previously might have been directed at these advisors. Certainly, if we compare Wendover's portrayal of the king (as a meek and pious king not quite up to the job, but ultimately a good man) with that of Matthew Paris (Henry as kind, but often foolish, profligate and weak), we get a flavour of this shift. Henry's subjects did not suddenly seek to expel the king, and much of the reform movement in 1258, for example, still looked to the king's relatives and protégés as scapegoats, rather than the king, and demands for reform were thus still couched in the language of determining the selection of those who were meant to advise and counsel the king. Only as the 1258 compromise collapsed, did criticism focus with increasing harshness on the king. Even then, much of that invective was reserved for his son Edward or his brother Richard.[54] We do, in fact, have to look to the fourteenth century and the kingship of Edward II for this tradition fully to change. Nonetheless, in 1233–4, Henry was still protected by his age, and by the fact that he had a government against which dissatisfaction could be voiced while at the same time remaining loyal to the king.

English and German chroniclers shared a view of kingship and politics which relied on the ruler's position being defined as one step removed from the actual exercise of power, while at the same time expecting him to exercise continuous and thorough oversight. Kingship depended for its effectiveness on a layer of authority and power between itself and its subjects. Equally, the king was meant to control that layer and oversee it so as to prevent the very excesses which could be blamed on his officials. It was, in fact, the mark of a true tyrant that he took decisions personally,[55] rather than relying on his officials, but it was also the mark of an ineffectual king that he did not rein in and oversee firmly the actions of his underlings.[56] This both restricted and liberated royal lordship. It offered an avenue for voicing dissent, but it also enabled the ruler to prove his suitability for office by mending his ways.

III

There still remains, of course, a stark contrast between the portrayal of the king, and that of the rebels. Roger of Wendover painted a particularly careful portrait of the Marshal as a martyr for the common good. The earl, on seeing many just men removed from court, joined them, driven by a zeal for justice (*zelo justitiae provocatus*), and courageously (*audacter*) approached the king, humbly asking that Henry correct the situation. That is, in Roger's account at least, the setbacks which Richard and his men had suffered weighed less than the Marshal's desire for the right ordering of the realm. More importantly, he gave the king due warning: he approached him humbly (*humiliter*) and requested (*rogabat*) that Henry amend his governance of the realm. At the same time, Richard warned that, should the king continue to violate his duties and obligations, he and other magnates would withdraw from Henry's council.[57] Even that did not result in an immediate outbreak of hostility, as the rebels agreed to a series of meetings where a compromise could have been reached. Only when these were thwarted by the machinations of des Roches, did they resort to the use of arms.[58] Violence, in turn, was limited, and directed at the king's ministers, rather than the king.[59] In fact, Roger claims, Richard refused to join in the battle of Grosmont, as he did not want to attack his lord.[60] Similarly, when the Marshal rejected the offer of surrendering to the king's mercy, even if his life were safe, he did so not only because he felt that he did not require a royal pardon (on the contrary, he had been the victim of Henry's officials and advisors, who, furthermore, attacked not only Richard, but the kingdom of England), but also, because, while trusting the king and the king's words, he could not extend this confidence to the king's ministers.[61] Richard rebelled against des Roches, not the king.[62]

The Marshal's death completed his apotheosis. The exact details surrounding Richard's Irish sojourn remain murky, and Roger of Wendover gave a somewhat fanciful account of events (claiming that des Roches and Segrave had forged a letter ordering the Marshal's assassination).[63] On encountering his opponents, Richard was tricked into a hopeless battle by the evil machinations of Geoffrey de Marsh – Richard was goaded into confronting a far superior force when Geoffrey accused him of being unworthy of his father's name.[64] The moment Richard took de Marsh's advice, the latter absconded and left the earl to face his enemies with just a handful of men. It was at this point that Marshal declared that 'to me it seems better to die with honour for the cause of justice, than to desert the field in flight, and thereby forever bear knightly shame'.[65] Marshal was eventually overcome, not by his noble foes, but by a mob on foot (as Wendover specifically points out), carrying lances and pitchforks. Wendover concludes with a carefully crafted deathbed scene, in which the Marshal forgave his enemies, sought the king's favour, but, above all, commended his soul to God.[66] Wendover represented the Marshal as the embodiment of secular virtues: he was pious and valiant in equal measure, took the advice and counsel of his household, and was, above all, driven by pure motives.

In this respect, too, Wendover set the tone for later commentators. The *Flores* similarly portray the Marshal as driven by the common good,[67] as do the *Annals of Waverley*: the Marshal excelled in honour and virtue (*honestas*), was distinguished by his noble pedigree, well versed in the liberal arts, strenuous in knightly exercises, and in all his deeds had God's will in mind.[68] He was driven by a desire to safeguard the peace of the realm, and initially sought to act as a wall between the king and disenchanted magnates, before being himself driven into rebellion by the king's councillors.[69] The *Annals of Oseney*, finally, put the Marshal in a long line of martyrs for just causes: some, like Roland, fictional, others, like Judas Maccabaeus, biblical.[70] Richard died a martyr for justice and the common good. He never regretted his actions, but acted as he did because they were right and because they were guided not by concern for his own person, but a desire to do what was best for the community of the realm.

IV

We must not lose sight of Hubert de Burgh. His fall was, after all, a central episode in the Marshal's revolt.[71] Relations between Hubert and Richard had not always been cordial,[72] and the earl going out of his way to plead de Burgh's case thus demonstrated the integrity of his motives. More importantly, the harsh terms of de Burgh's imprisonment had turned him into a cause celebré, while the suddenness of his fall enabled contemporary historians to highlight the injustices of des Roches' regime. Even the king recognised this: according to Wendover, Henry rejected demands that de Burgh be treated as a traitor not only because he preferred to be viewed as a lenient king rather than a tyrant, but also because of the justiciar's loyalty: 'From childhood Hubert has faithfully served, as I have heard, first my uncle King Richard, and afterwards my father King John. Although he may have behaved badly towards me, he will not die a shameful death because of me.'[73] Matthew Paris inserted a similar anecdote in his reworking of Wendover's text, which makes the same point even more forcefully: an artisan, ordered to procure a particularly strong set of chains, on hearing they were for Hubert de Burgh, erupted into a lengthy speech of surprise, wondering whether this could be the same Hubert de Burgh who had faithfully served in Gascony and Normandy, whose constancy was even praised by his enemies, and who had so successfully defended Dover against the armies of Prince Louis during the king's minority.[74] If even the men on the street knew and recognised Hubert's past deserts, the bishop's injustice became all the more obvious. Nor was this limited to the St Albans tradition. The *Annals of Waverley*, for instance, while shunning Wendover's or Paris' invective, started out by elaborating on the stature and standing of de Burgh before dealing with his fall.[75] In addition, de Burgh's treatment underlined the degree to which the bishop of Winchester and his henchmen turned against even the most loyal of the king's supporters. It was this act of ingratitude, but also the brutality of de Burgh's fall, which was to be referred to repeatedly by the Marshal and his allies.

The injustice of Hubert's treatment continued to permeate accounts of his imprisonment and flight. At first, these focused on the fact that he was kept in chains while incarcerated:[76] an especially demeaning treatment, particularly for a man of noble standing, and one that could only be justified if the prisoner was of so perfidious a nature that he could not otherwise be restrained.[77] The pernicious nature of his imprisonment was lovingly elaborated by Matthew Paris: Hubert was put on a horse, his feet tied together underneath the horse's belly – again, a most demeaning treatment.[78] The tone having thus been set, the image of an unjustly persecuted but faithful servant of his king was developed further. Hubert had initially been kept at Brentwood.[79] However, he managed to slip out and sought refuge in the castle local church, before having to surrender due to a lack of food and water.[80] This was soon followed by a second attempt at escape, triggered, Wendover claimed, by rumours that des Roches was planning to murder his old adversary.[81] The second time, though, Hubert's enemies felt unrestrained by the fact that he had sought refuge in a Church, and burst into the building to recapture him. This gave Wendover the opportunity to portray de Burgh in terms which, to his audience, may well have been reminiscent of the martyrdom of Thomas Becket: bursting into the Church, they found Hubert clutching a crucifix, and violently dragged him from the altar.[82]

Wendover's account of the Marshal's death echoes here: the earl was felled in battle not by a noble host, but by a mob carrying pitchforks, and de Burgh, similarly, was abducted not by his noble foes, but their servant rabble.

This image also carried undertones of penance: de Burgh threw himself at the mercy of God, as he would not receive it from his king. This theme was dwelled on by other chroniclers, too. The Tewkesbury annalist claimed that Hubert affixed the cross he had recently assumed to his garments on hearing of his imminent arrest,[83] while the *Margam Chronicle* even exceeds Wendover in its depiction of de Burgh's piety and the brutality of his captors: Hubert was dragged out of the church by his feet, cruelly whipped, and had his arms and legs locked in heavy irons. Hubert, though, did not give up hope, but read the Psalter which he had been able to take with him, and put his trust in the Virgin Mary.[84] He was rewarded for his faith when Siward came to rescue him. De Burgh's flight to Wales was similarly rich with religious imagery: when freeing Hubert, Siward addressed him with words echoing the Psalms: 'Come with us and fear not. There is no man in the world who has done as much evil to me as you have, but I forgive you for it. Now I repay you evil with good.'[85] Miraculously, moreover, a thick fog descended which allowed de Burgh and his liberators to slip away undetected. A little later, when reaching Gloucestershire, the party sought to set sail for Chepstow. By this stage, Hubert was once again in despair, and implored the aid of the Virgin. His pleas were answered by a voice who told him not to be afraid, as 'the lady' would free him. True enough, while sailing into the marches, de Burgh and his rescuers were attacked by a fleet from Bristol, but managed to defeat them and sail into freedom and safety.[86] Siward acted because freeing de Burgh was the right thing to do. That he did so despite the evils he had previously experienced at Hubert's hands only highlighted the morally exalted nature of his own actions, and compared most favourably with the injustice and cruelty of des Roches. The justiciar's piety, in turn, underlined the integrity of his motives, and complemented the Marshal's stance, and made all the more visible the divine favour shown to de Burgh, Marshal and their band of followers.

Hubert's erstwhile adversaries, by contrast, cut a far less impressive figure: called to account for their tenure of the king's offices, they refused to do so. In fact, Peter de Rivallis of all people sought refuge in the Church of Winchester, while Stephen Segrave turned to the Church of St Mary at Leicester, where he hurriedly remembered his clerical orders.[87] A similar strategy was adopted by des

Roches: when eventually coming before the king in July 1234, he appeared in clerical garb and tonsured scalp. Somewhat ironically, when found guilty of various misdemeanours, he pleaded privilege of clergy and was thus escorted back to Winchester.[88] De Rivallis and Segrave claimed for themselves a privilege which they had been so unwilling to grant Hubert, and the contrast between their treatment and that they had inflicted on the former justiciar only served to underline the depravity of their actions.[89] Almost every step of their submission thus echoed the initial moves against de Burgh: Hubert, too, had been asked to render account for his conduct of the king's financial affairs,[90] and Hubert, too, had initially taken flight. Moreover, both de Burgh and his adversaries initially refused to give account, for at first sight similar reasons: Hubert feared the king's wrath and had heard rumours that he would suffer a cruel death if he attended the royal court.[91] De Rivallis and Segrave, too, feared the king's wrath, but did so because they would be held to account for the crimes they had committed.[92] They thus had just cause to be afraid, but, with Edmund Rich rather than Peter des Roches leading the proceedings, they were granted what, previously, de Burgh had been denied: a safe conduct. In short, the superficially similar structure of events only served to highlight fundamental moral differences. These distinctions were further underlined by the very different public behaviour of respective actors: the pious humility of de Burgh, the Marshal's brave und upright demeanour, Edmund's unwavering rectitude, as opposed to the king's wrath, des Roches slyness and Segrave's cowardice. Piety, loyalty, forgiveness and a love of justice confronted vindictiveness, perfidy, blasphemy and most cruel injustice.

V

We have, so far, dealt mostly with the moral disposition of the chief actors (the king, Marshal and de Burgh). This disposition, in turn denotes more general political values, and it is to these that we will now turn. What, in the eyes of contemporary English observers defined tyranny? Where, in turn did this coincide with and where did it differ from the German experience?

The bishop of Winchester and his men were aliens not just by birth, but also by disposition and action: they wilfully ignored, set aside or overturned basic rules of moral and social conduct. Much was, therefore, made of their sexual behaviour. That this, in turn, was closely linked to issues of social status is illustrated by complaints about marriages to Poitevins of low breeding that, as a first consequence of des Roches' return to power, had been forced upon English noblewomen.[93] Although des Roches, unlike the duke of Austria, for instance, was not accused of condoning rape,[94] moral and social boundaries were still transgressed, and the sexual politics of Peter's regime thus played on fears of moral and social purity. It is thus also not surprising that Peter des Roches was rumoured to have broken his vows of chastity,[95] just as stories about Duke Frederick's sexual antics continued to make the rounds.[96] Sexual transgression denoted moral depravity, and denied to those engaged in it (who were all too often of low breeding, too) the right to rule others. In des Roches' case, it only served to deepen the chasm separating the Marshal and de Burgh from the bishop's depraved, violent and low-born ilk.

At stake was not only the kingdom's morality but also its political safety. According to the *Margam Chronicle*, the war between the Marshal and Henry had erupted because of the aliens Peter and Peter des Riev-aulx 'had brought to England to oppress the clergy and people'.[97] It was Wendover, however, who elaborated on this theme in most detail: having expelled all the keepers of the royal castles, des Roches and his nephew called on Bretons and Poitevins to come to England, and these aliens oppressed the *homines Angliae naturales et nobiles*, the noble and indigenous men of England.[98] In fact, when the magnates threatened to absent themselves from the royal council, the bishop advised his monarch that he could call upon more aliens to defend him against those proud and haughty men.[99] This went to the heart of the liberty of the king's domains, as the Marshal explained to Friar Agnellus. When told that the king had many more men at his disposal than the earl, Marshal replied that whoever Henry might be able to enlist would hardly come from his own lands, nor would those men really serve the king: Peter des Roches, Richard had been told, was secretly plotting to deliver England into the hands of Emperor Frederick II.[100] The Poitevins had expelled those whose task it was to defend the realm, and had put those in charge of its defences who were already in the pay of foreign enemies. They were driven by greed, and plotted to dethrone the king who so foolishly had put his trust in them. Marshal's accusations against des Roches thus bring us back to a theme at the heart of Wendover's account: the contrast between the true loyalty of those fighting Henry's government, and the treachery of those shielding him from his people.

This contrast extended to questions of royal honour, an issue of far greater interest to English chroniclers than their German counterparts. Moreover, this concern exceeded not only that of the German sources but also that of Henry III: from what we can reconstruct, the king had not invoked his honour or that of the realm in dealing with the Marshal. The chroniclers more than made up for this. Honour and shame played themselves out on a number of levels, ranging from detailed images of the ignoble treatment inflicted on de Burgh to short statements like that in the *Flores Historiarum* that the *homines naturales* were driven from court *contemptibiliter*, shamefully.[101] Nor was this specific to the revolt: in 1231, for instance, the barons were said to have objected to Henry's plans to marry a Scottish princess, as her older sister was already married to Hubert de Burgh – this was unbecoming of the king's dignity;[102] that same year Peter des Roches and his allies curried favour with the king by complaining that the frequent incursions from Wales caused grave scandal to his crown;[103] and in his entry for 1234, Roger reports a peculiar encounter between the earl and the king. Henry having laid siege to one of the Marshal's castles, ran out of supplies. He therefore sent envoys to the Marshal, asking that the earl withdraw *propter honorem ipsius regis*, for the honour of the said king, so that it did not appear that Henry besieged the castle in vain.[104] We should not ignore the obvious mockery of the king's concerns, who tried to avert the appearance of shameful defeat by admitting it to the very man whom he sought to overcome. Nonetheless, all this indicates (and other examples can easily be found)[105] that, as far as chroniclers were concerned, royal honour was an obvious means by which royal actions could be explained or triggered. It thus concerned the rebels as much as the king.

In 1233, for instance, the bishops refused to excommunicate the Marshal, as this would be *indignum*, that is, both inappropriate and shameful.[106] We have already seen that Friar Agnellus was said to have offered Richard honourable retirement to his estates, provided he publicly admitted he had been in the wrong. It may perhaps have been the shame which such unconditional surrender implied which made Marshal reject the offer, as much as the other reasons he listed. Equally, the earl's death was ultimately triggered by concern for his and his family's honour: Geoffrey de Marsh goaded the earl into battle by claiming that Richard's refusal to do so made him unworthy of being his father's heir. After all, William Marshal, who, by his wisdom and counsel, his valour and audacity had defeated all the knights of the West. By contrast, Richard's dithering was shameful, inconsistent and a disgrace to William's legacy.[107] Richard's words on finally charging his enemies played on a similar theme: it was better to die with honour for the cause of justice, than to flee the field of battle.[108] Regardless whether these were Roger's sentiments or those of the earl, they indicate that honour and status – the way political actors were perceived by their peers, dependants and neighbours – mattered, and that they were expected to be of concern to those who acted righteously and justly. Honour was thus a central aspect of this conflict, something which had to be restored, protected and defended. The language in which the *Annals of Dunstable* describe the reconciliation of Gilbert Basset and other former rebels with the king is thus worth noting: they were fully redeemed, and Henry restored them in everything, that is their reputation, as well as their lands and possessions.[109] As far as Roger of Wendover was concerned, one of the chief characteristics distinguishing the Marshal from his Poitevin foes was that Richard showed true concern for the king's honour. We have already seen how des Roches insinuated himself to the king by pointing to the shame that Henry's inability to control the Welsh, and his penury had brought upon him. That is, the bishop of Winchester expected to be able to use Henry III's anxieties about his prestige and standing as a means of overthrowing the regime of de Burgh. This, in turn, was reflected in the frequent references to royal honour which Wendover had the Marshal make. The earl was not simply out to defend his lord's honour but to defend what was truly becoming of royal honour. The Marshal's encounter with Agnellus remains a key passage in this respect: it would not be honourable to the king, the Marshal claimed, if he submitted to him,[110] while it was shameful that the king had turned his own subjects into rebels.[111] It was not the Marshal's honour that was at stake, but the king's. Similarly, the magnates' honour heightened the king's.[112]

A king acquired true honour by acting righteously, taking the advice and counsel of men naturally suited to do so, and maintaining the rule of law and justice. As far as the king's subjects were concerned, showing concern for the king's honour and giving appropriate counsel was the key to acquiring and defending one's own status and honour. Moreover, if the king or his court violated their duties, after they had been advised and counselled repeatedly and in a manner respectful of their status, then force could be used to protect the values and institutions which it was a king's foremost duty to uphold. Consequently, there was nothing noble or honourable about des Roches and the Poitevins. Whenever referring to des Roches' advice, Wendover portrayed it as primarily a matter of greed and financial gain. The move against de Burgh was thus triggered by rumours that he had left a treasure with the Templars,[113] while des Roches had gained the backing of the earl of Chester and other magnates by paying each of them 1,000 marks.[114] As in the German sources, which highlighted the illegitimacy of Henry's revolt by pointing to his use of bribery and force, so the English sources, too, revealed the illegitimacy of des Roches regime and the moral depravity of his following by the means through which he had gained it. To some extent, those means reflected the king's penury, but that, in turn, had been self-inflicted and was due to his profligate generosity: when complaining about his lack of funds, Henry was told by his ministers that this was the case because he had given away honours and custodies and alienated them from the royal fisc. That he shortly thereafter appointed Peter de Rivallis as his treasurer obviously only made the matter worse.[115] The actions of the Poitevins were tainted by money, and so were their motivations and character. The Marshal, by contrast, defined royal honour as it should be defined: as dependent on the ruler's willingness to take the advice and counsel of his subjects.[116] Other sources emphasise similar points, though in less detail.[117]

Why this concern for honour? Length and detail of narrative certainly played their part: it was easier to elaborate on righteous forms of behaviour if they formed part of a more extensive narrative. On its own this does not, however, suffice as explanation. We should thus first note what royal and baronial honour entailed, and remind ourselves that honour was also a shorthand for a series of more wide-ranging values and abstract norms (and we will turn to these in a moment). Certainly, the way narrative sources used honour reflects the broader moral contrast they sought to establish: the king, because of his youth and pious simplicity, was unaware of the evils plotted around him. Not only had he allowed himself to be deprived of the services of astute, honourable and wise men like the Marshal, and had them replaced with the bishop of Winchester, but he was also unaware of basic norms and ideals of political behaviour. Just as he was in danger of loosing his kingdom by trusting aliens, he also violated his and his kingdom's honour by not showing enough regard for it. Honourable action also mattered as it revealed moral disposition, and because it was performed before a wider audience (about which more in Chapters 7 and 8), and it was in this public side of honour that its uses for chroniclers lay: they were not normally privy to the inner workings of the court and the royal government. They had to work with those actions that were performed with the intention of conveying complex messages to a wider audience. They could, of course, rewrite, modify and interpret them, but it was because of this public communicative aspect that a display of honour mattered. The way it was used by contemporary observers was thus also different from how it had been employed by Frederick II: as a repertoire of communicative actions that made reference to a set of abstract principles, rather than as a principle in its own right. What had concerned

German chroniclers was that the most visible manifestation of imperial honour (doing justice and keeping the peace) had yet to be enacted by Frederick. English observers, on the other hand, required an assurance that the all-too visible actions of royal government were guided by the principles honour entailed.

What, then, were these values? Most importantly, perhaps, they focused on loyalty, and on the identity and moral character of those advising the king. True loyalty expressed itself in upholding transcendental values, which, however, were rarely described in detail: by his demeanour and actions, the Marshal revealed his honourable intentions and inner moral rigour, but, beyond a desire to rid the court of aliens, his intentions were not elaborated upon. The conflict was couched in terms of a clear contrast between good and evil, but this contrast manifested itself in actions not ideals. Once we delve deeper into our sources, however, a more complex picture emerges. Most importantly, royal power had to be restrained, not necessarily as wielded by the king, but as wielded by those acting on his behalf. This tied in with questions of what constituted proper advice and counsel, and who should provide it. Partly because of the king's and his government's ability to make a real impact on the lives of his subjects that power had to be controlled. It had to be controlled, however, by the giving of sound advice, rather than by more formal means. Advice and counsel should furthermore have the king's best interests at heart, but these should not be separated from those of the kingdom at large. While des Roches had thus played on Henry's penury, the means by which he sought to rectify the situation went against the interests of the realm. Des Roches, in short, sought to separate the king from his kingdom, and did this both by the advice he gave, and by the means with which he sought to implement it. Hence, too, the emphasis on aliens and the rumours that the bishop was secretly plotting to deliver England into the emperor's hands; and hence, too, the efforts to define what constituted true loyalty. These wider concerns were summarised in the principle of royal honour, defined as the maintenance of justice, and the defence of the realm against foreign invaders (be they Welsh, Poitevin or Staufen).

Somewhat ironically, perhaps, most of this would have encountered little opposition from the king. Both the earl and his ruler emphasised the need to protect the realm against foreign invaders, and both agreed that the king should be bound by the advice and counsel of his magnates. We do not have sufficient evidence to trace how far issues of royal honour and status might have mattered to Henry III during the rebellion, but over the years following the uprising, there was a remarkable increase in celebrations of the divinely ordained and hence spiritually exalted nature of Henry's kingship – most evident in the regular singing of the *Laudes Regiae*, the liturgical acclamation of the ruler, during the 1230s.[118] It was in the years following the revolt, too, that Henry began to celebrate the cult of St Edward the Confessor.[119] There may be no direct causal link between the rebellion, and this increasingly exalted notion of kingship. It is, however, reminiscent of the increasingly elaborate celebration of imperial authority which could be witnessed in Germany in the months following Henry (VII)'s demise.[120] Status that had been challenged was restored by an ever more elaborate celebration of its elevated and divinely sanctioned nature.

That a king should take and be guided by the advice of his clergy was another point which, we may assume, Henry would hardly have disputed. Where the king and his earl differed was, obviously, what these abstract values meant in practice, but then this was a situation no different from that facing any other king or rebel, as we have seen in the case of Germany. Henry and Richard shared, after all, a common frame of reference, and they sought to address (or at least reflect the views of) similar audiences. More interesting for the purpose of this book is where, as far as the values are concerned which they espoused, English and German sources converged with, and where they differed from one another.

VI

English and German observers stressed similar norms, but often gave them different meanings. This is evident, for instance, in the emphasis on loyalty (the question of true versus false loyalty in England; the king's ingratitude in the German case), but even more so in the role of counsel and advice, of the role which the great men of the realm played in its running. Frederick was desperate for the German princes to take upon themselves the role which the English rebels so eagerly desired. The emperor's emphasis on the importance of the princes, on the degree to which they shared in the governance of the realm was not mere flattery, and it certainly was no surrender before the particularism of the German princes. Rather, it was an attempt to make them share in the burdens of ruling the empire, and to take a more active role in its running.

It is thus perhaps also worth noting that some of the values which to English chroniclers were central to the king's honour – most notably defending the realm against alien invaders – hardly mattered in the

Empire. Frederick II, for instance, made little reference to his son's alliance with the Lombards, and neither did the chronicles. On the other hand, these values mattered on a princely level, as we have seen in the context of the vernacular German sources: among a prince's most noble duties was that he defend his lands, and that he maintained their honour and integrity. Conversely, doing justice was a distinctly imperial occupation (although one which, at times, might be shared with the princes). This reflected political realities: it was not until the 1240s that the Capetians aggressively expanded into the once imperial domains of Burgundy and Flanders, and that the Mongols approached the eastern borders, and there was thus little need for the emperor to excel in fending of foreign hordes. It also mirrored the political structures of the empire: the problem with Duke Frederick had thus been not only that he oppressed his own people but also that he waged war on his neighbours in Bavaria, Hungary and Bohemia, and it is thus not surprising that the duke of Bavaria, example of, was at least in part measured by his ability to fight off such hostile advances. That, viewed from this perspective, Henry III combined the duties of a German prince with those of the emperor reflected the distinctive structure of the empire, and is thus another example of the degree to which the structural framework moulded the ideas and norms of politics.

Equally, both German and English observers linked moral disposition to correct political action. German chroniclers emphasised the moral shortcomings of the king, his ingratitude, sexual lust, disobedience and so on, and English chroniclers the Marshal's moral rectitude (who kept his word, was loyal, protected those, like Hubert de Burgh or Gilbert Basset, who could not protect themselves) and Peter des Roches' pernicious nature (he was at least implied to have broken his vows of chastity, was devious, greedy, a traitor to his king, spiteful and unjust). Quite clearly, moral and political failings were inseparable. Even so, once we deal with specific expressions of tyrannical action, differences emerge. There was, for obvious reasons, little about the abuse of fiscal and bureaucratic mechanisms in the German evidence, but that German observers, unlike their English counterparts, stressed the taking of hostages as token of Henry's bad lordship is worth noting. This comes as somewhat of a surprise, as, unlike in Germany, we actually have several surviving documents that outline the promises made by hostage givers,[121] but this also seems to have been a practice by no means limited to the king. The *Annals of Tewkesbury*, for instance, report that the Marshal accepted hostages from the barons and knights of Glamorgan and the citizens of Cardiff.[122] That both parties engaged in the practice may be one of the reasons why chroniclers did not make too much of it, but it may also indicate that the taking and offering of hostages was a more commonplace phenomenon in England: it was certainly not something viewed as tyrannous. However, just as in Germany, there was a strong emphasis on hostages being offered rather than demanded: the charters of security enrolled in the Close Rolls, for instance, stressed that hostages and promises of future good service were given out of the grantors free will. In 1233–4, there were other, more worrying, expressions of tyranny in England.

Foremost among those was that Englishmen were displaced by upstart foreigners. In the empire, by contrast, the provenance of imperial and royal administrators simply did not matter.[123] Why was this so? The issue of ethnic affiliation as such rarely occurred in a German context. This was partly the case because Frederick kept his Sicilian administration separate from that of Germany, but also because of the much more pronouncedly multi-ethnic nature of the empire. Even the *regnum Theutonciorum*, the kingdom of the Germans, was, in terms of languages, cultures and peoples a more varied entity than England, and included, for instance, the kingdom of Bohemia, but also francophone Burgundy. This was yet another instance, too, where the decentralised nature of imperial administration mattered. Those active in one region were unlikely to be engaged in activities in other parts of Germany, while the imperial aristocracy increasingly amassed lands and rights in specific regions, rather than across the realm. This meant that, on a princely level, too, officials and servants normally originated in the region in which they were active. In addition, the different legal customs and practices of different parts of a ruler's or prince's domain were by the thirteenth century so firmly enshrined that a lord did not normally dare to employ, for example, officials from Styria in Carinthia. This is not to say that ethnic rivalries did not exist – from the later thirteenth century onwards, Bohemia, for instance,[124] with clashes between German incomers and the native Czech aristocracy, provides an important parallel with England – but they did not normally play themselves out on a regnal level. Rather than focusing on ethnicity, complaints centred on the social provenance of advisors, and here the German and the English evidence converged. Henry (VII)'s advisors were thus of ill-repute and low standing (and gave correspondingly low and immoral advice), and so were des Roches and his allies. Peter des Rievaulx, Wendover for instance implied, was the illicit fruit of Peter's loins, and the stress Wendover and Paris put on the low social status of those killing the Marshal, for example, or dragging de Burgh from sanctuary, points in a similar direction. The bishop and his allies were, as we have seen, aliens both by birth and moral disposition, but they were also of low stock and breeding, and this was an accusation German observers, too, would have understood.

Exploring how the Marshal's and Henry (VII)'s rebellions were portrayed by the actors themselves, their antagonists, peers, neighbours and subjects, has revealed a number of important points about the ideological framework of politics. We have thus seen that observers experiencing rather different traditions of politics still used similar norms to assess political actions. We have also seen that abstract values could be given different meanings, depending on where an author wrote, or for whom. While, on the one hand, this has contributed to a more varied and complex picture of medieval politics, on the other, it has served to sharpen the differences between the political experience of thirteenth-century England and Germany. It is not, however, only the values, ideas and norms that have become clearer: we have also learned something about processes of communication, of the means by which the ruled could respond to the self-representation of the rulers. This has been particularly pronounced in the German case, where many chroniclers, while taking on board much of Frederick II's version of events, also introduced new elements, and where they were quite prepared to highlight different ideals and norms from those invoked by the emperor. In the case of Henry III, this process is more difficult to trace, but there, too, the chroniclers stressing stressed aspects of royal lordship (such as honour) which we have not found in royal acts of self-representation. We have thus before us reflections of political debates for which otherwise not much evidence survives. Our next step should thus be to highlight the means and mechanisms by which these debates were conducted, and the personnel participating in them. This, in turn, will allow us to say more about the public nature of medieval politics, and to move from a consideration of the ideals to one of the social reality of politics.

Part III
The Ways and Means of Politics

This section will focus, first, on the role of the public sphere in politics; second, on the means of political communication; and, finally, on the social context of politics. This perspective partly reflects the evidence and its limitations, and partly it is self-imposed. Chroniclers and other observers, even the actors themselves, clearly engaged with a wider public – hence the letters, mandates, and hence, in Germany, for instance, the surprising similarities between the imperial representation of revolt and the narrative record. Hence, too, the sometimes striking differences in the values evoked by different groups of observers or participants. While this may not be a political public in a modern sense, it should nonetheless alert us to the fact that in the Middle Ages, too, debates were by no means restricted to a small group of leading men. Our ability to trace that public is, of course, limited by the available evidence, that is, records of the royal and imperial administration, and the writings of educated clerics and (sometimes) laymen. Even so, sufficient evidence survives for us to be able to ask, first, how those who had an interest in politics, and who may even have participated in them, engaged with the political sphere, and, second, how political actors could utilise that public sphere.

In establishing the role of the public, we will engage with some of the processes of communication. This will bring us to the very heart of what distinguishes English royal from German imperial lordship. Henry III presided over an administratively and fiscally more sophisticated system of governance than Frederick II; he had access to a larger pool of officials, procedures and even means of recording and propagating his actions. To what extent did the undoubtedly more bureaucratic nature of English governance influence the ideals and conduct of politics? Did the fact that the English records tell us that Henry III preferred his wine to be enriched with rose and elderflower flavours,[1] or how much wine his court consumed on particular feast days,[2] change the way politics worked? The answer given by modern scholarship so far has been affirmative. We have, however, already seen that the reality of English and German politics was infinitely more complex: the bureaucratic dimension *did* influence ideals of royal lordship in England, but these ideals also included concepts, such as royal honour, more commonly associated with imperial lordship, and did so to a greater degree than in Germany. The question we need to address now is whether these distinctions dissolve as easily once we turn to the tools and mechanisms of political power. In doing so we need to be aware of the wider context of our subject matter. As we are dealing with structural features to a greater extent than ideologies, we need to remind ourselves of the degree to which both English and German politics were rooted in a wider European framework of political organisation and communication. There was only a limited number of ways in which thirteenth-century Europeans could organise a political public, address it and define its membership. To some extent, differences will thus be less clearly marked, but we will also be able to ask how two – within this broader framework – very different societies dealt with similar challenges, and what this, in turn, tells us about the nature of English and German and, by implication, Latin European politics in the thirteenth century.

Finally, we need to consider the social dimension of politics. Who was involved in politics, and what were the key mechanisms by which they were conducted? Other than kings and princes, who was involved? How could they influence the course of events? How and why did they matter? I will not be concerned with the administrators and officials we have encountered so far, for the simple reason that we already know they mattered in England, but not in Germany. Instead, I will focus on three particular groups, active both in England and Germany: townsmen, clergy and nobles. Townsmen were a relatively new group on the political scene of England and Germany. Urban movements had of course been a significant factor in Italian politics since the twelfth century, but in Germany, they only came fully to the fore in the early decades of the thirteenth, and it is during the 1230s that they began to penetrate the core of imperial politics. In England, the situation is more difficult to ascertain, but within a few decades of the Marshal's rebellion, the representation of boroughs at royal parliaments began to be formalised, and it is in the decades either side of 1233–4, too, that conflicts between citizens and lords of towns became more frequent and that they became a matter of concern to regnal as well as local politics.

That prelates, in turn, and members of the religious orders performed an important political function is one of the constants of medieval Europe. What form that role took varied of course, and it is in these variations, again, that important differences between realms emerge.

This brings us back to the self-imposed limitations mentioned earlier. There would, for instance, be little point in comparing English and imperial financial administration: the combined evidence for Frederick II's reign in Germany would probably fit on no more than a couple of pages of A4,[3] while just the edited (or calendared) evidence for Henry III's reign runs to about 20 volumes (with new materials still being found or edited). We would thus simply confirm something we already know (that Henry III had more administrators at his disposal). We need to compare aspects of politics which can be found in England and Germany alike, which, at the same time, would allow us to test established hypotheses about the nature of English and German politics. The public nature of politics clearly fits the bill, but it also ties the patterns this book seeks to explore more firmly to wider European phenomena.[4] How, then, were politics conducted?

7
Creating a Public

Politics were a public affair, and this public nature permeated the sources: charters, for instance, were aimed at informing a wider audience of a transaction.[1] Frequently, too, such documents reported a decision or agreement that had been reached in public, and the charter was an added means of verifying and confirming that decision. This is perhaps best exemplified by the various reissues of Magna Carta, which conveyed its contents to a larger audience in the expectation that that audience would hold the original partners to keeping an agreement. In 1225, for instance, Henry III had not only reissued and re-confirmed the Great Charter, but had also ensured that copies were distributed and publicised across the realm.[2] Similarly, when Frederick II confirmed Otto of Brunswick's elevation to the duchy of Brunswick, the audience to this act was by no means confined to those attending the Mainz *diet* of August 1235, nor was the act of elevation itself the only message this charter was meant to convey. Just as important was the image of emperor and princes acting in unison, and the idea and image of imperial lordship that Frederick was trying to convey: it was for this reason that Frederick had commanded Otto's elevation to be reported in works of history.[3] In both Germany and England, the issuing of a charter and the public context of the act were central to the diplomatic of these documents.[4]

This interdependence between public and written confirmation is superbly illustrated by a charter issued in 1234–5, confirming the succession of Duke Otto of Meran as lay advocate of the abbey of Benediktbeuren. After the death of Otto's father, the monks had approached Henry (VII) and his father to ask permission to elect a new advocate. That having been granted, they chose Otto, but only after the conditions under which the advocacy could be exercised were read out, and then publicly confirmed by Otto. These conditions, in turn, were listed, and were ratified, in a charter issued jointly by the duke, the bishop of Bamberg and the count of Meran.[5] The issuing of a charter was thus but one step in a lengthy process of confirmation, which repeatedly drew on its inherently public nature (involving at various stages the audiences of the royal and the imperial court, the abbey and its dependants, the entourage of both Duke Otto and the guarantors of the agreement, and any future readers of the agreement). The same applied to England, despite a more elaborate system of record keeping.[6]

The public nature of the act confirmed and of the reading of the charter that attest to this confirmation were one means by which a public could be created.[7] Other sources similarly reflected or anticipated a public. This was obviously the case with letters,[8] also, as we have seen, with chronicles and works of history. At the same time, they also depended on somewhat different, though still overlapping, audiences. Letters were frequently intended to be read out and to reach beyond the immediate recipients of the missive. This had been the case, for instance, with Henry (VII)'s letter to the bishop of Hildesheim, and Frederick II's various epistles about the misdeeds of his son. In England, many of these functions were performed by royal mandates like the one discussed in Chapter 6, meant to be read not only by the sheriffs to whom it had been addressed but also to local communities in shire and hundred courts. Letters were furthermore used to influence the historical record, and report current affairs. We have few examples for this from the early years of Henry's reign, and one of the most striking uses of letters as a means of communicating and creating a wider public are thus the various epistles sent by Earl Richard of Cornwall about his early years as king of the Romans and emperor-elect in 1257 and 1258, and recorded in a number of English chronicles and annals.[9] Such missives certainly overlapped with charters in being aimed at a future audience that did not itself witness events.

Yet there were fundamental differences, too. Most importantly, the public established by chroniclers and their audiences was not imme-diately constitutive of the political community of the realm.[10] These writings may have influenced the stance taken by individual abbots, and we should not ignore a process of communication between monastic houses, their neighbours and patrons (like the one we have surmised with regard to Richard Marshal, the *Margam Chronicle* and Roger of Wendover), and thus a further dissemination of information (and one that could be conscientiously utilised by political actors).[11] The audi-ence thus created was still fundamentally different from that recorded and addressed in charters and writs. It did not include the entourage, dependants and followers, the wide range of observers, political actors, petitioners and general hangers on, encompassing clerical and lay elites as well as a large section of the king's other subjects, that formed part of those occasions when charters were issued, and before or to whom they were read and addressed. It is with this wider, politically constitutive public, in turn, that this chapter is concerned.

I

This public could take various forms, and was addressed in several ways. The most familiar example, and one to which we will return in due course, were formal public assemblies, that is, parliaments or *diets*. Especially in the case of politically important actors, such as the king, leading magnates or prelates, large assemblies were not restricted to formally consultative occasions, but could include religious feast days, festive secular occasions and so on. Much of this had to do with the sheer size of the royal or imperial entourage. We do not know how large the imperial court normally was, although when Frederick Barbarossa celebrated his sons' knighting in 1184, Gislebert of Mons' list of the participants runs to three pages in the modern printed edition.[12] Reliable estimates have put the average size of the imperial court (once hangers-on are included, visitors, etc.) at close to 1,000 members during Barbarossa's reign.[13] The narrative sources do not give much information for the later period. Most of the chronicles which describe the great meetings of Henry (VII), for instance, simply mention that such an event had taken place.[14] All too frequently, we are informed that a particularly large gathering had taken place by a charter issued when the king's court visited a town, castle or palace.[15] About Frederick's German sojourn, the Cologne chronicles commented on the *multa turba* (large crowd) accompanying the emperor,[16] while the anonymous continuator of Godfrey of Viterbo embellished this with a colourful description of the exotic peoples and even more exotic animals in Frederick's entourage.[17] The *Annales Marbacenses* claim that 12,000 attended the Mainz *diet*,[18] and Caesarius of Heisterbach's account of the translation of St Elisabeth at Marburg in 1236, finally, claimed that several thousand witnessed the event.[19] While we have to be critical of these numbers, they may not be entirely unrealistic: Frederick's presence would have drawn a large crowd regardless of his son's rebellion, as this was the first time in fifteen years he visited his homeland. In combination with what we know about the twelfth century, an audience of several thousand seems not unlikely, but there is no way of knowing whether Henry (VII)'s court would have attracted similar numbers.

In England, Henry I's or Henry II's court in the twelfth century probably also numbered up to a 1,000 members.[20] For the thirteenth century, numbers are more difficult to ascertain, but that Henry III, in November 1236, ordered forty pounds of dates, six pounds of figs, four boxes of dried grapes, forty-eight towels and 'five or six packets of good ginger' to be delivered to Marlborough,[21] or that, in August 1238, he reimbursed Engelard de Cigogny for the 478 chicken which had been procured for the king's and queen's coronation,[22] may tell us something about the size of his court. The sheer presence of the court constituted a public, and one that frequently drew further crowds of petitioners, of magnates and princes, prelates and others by whose domains the court passed.[23] Wherever a ruler went, there existed a public.

The size of the royal court swelled even further on feast days or when marking particularly important events. Such events were not always organised by court officials: in 1231, for example, a feast to which Peter des Roches had invited the king and his court at Christmas marked Peter's return not only to England but also to the English political scene. Peter handed out such fine food and drink, such precious cloths, such treasures of gold and silver and of horses, that, in the eyes of the Dunstable annalist, the splendour of the occasion would have befitted the king's coronation.[24] Not only had the organisation of the king's Christmas festivities been the privilege of Peter's rival Hubert de Burgh,[25] but the sheer splendour of the occasion, the conspicuous display of the bishop's power and wealth, showed that he had not returned to England for a quiet retirement. It was for this reason, too, that Matthew Paris could describe the reconciliation between Peter's successor as bishop of Winchester and the king in 1238 as being symbolised by the fact that Henry III participated in a banquet given by his erstwhile opponent. More intriguingly, Matthew emphasises the public nature of this prandial peacemaking: the king's attendance was to show everyone that all transgressions had been forgiven, and that his friendship with the prelate was demonstrated to everyone at the meal.[26]

Nor was the political public in Germany confined to formal *diets* alone. One of the most famous *diets* of the High Middle Ages was that held by Frederick Barbarossa at Mainz in 1184, which celebrated the knighting of his eldest sons, and the planned marriage between the future Henry VI and Constance of Sicily. It was, however, also designed to mark the recently established peace with the Lombard League, the defeat of Henry the Lion, and as a forceful demonstration of imperial might.[27] Equally,

Frederick II's marriage aimed at celebrating the overthrow of his son and the full restoration of imperial power. Although the wedding took centre stage,[28] they were combined with the very public chastisement of the emperor's son and of Bishop Landulf; the knighting of Count Raymond of Provence at Hagenau in the winter of 1235–6 sought to settle the conflict between Raymond and his namesake, the count of Toulouse, and thereby demonstrate the reach of imperial authority even into the remote regions of Burgundy.[29] Similarly, the Mainz *diet* of 1235 was concluded by a particularly splendid feast in the fields outside the town.[30]

The line between public festivity and a formal imperial *diet* is more difficult to draw in the German case, partly due to the brevity of our sources, partly also due to the fact that Frederick II's appearance in 1235–6 was an event in its own right. As a consequence, and in combination with the challenge of Henry's uprising, many of the matters which would have been negotiated at *diets* like the one convened in Mainz in the summer of 1235, intruded into the general progress of Frederick II. From the moment he first set foot in Germany at Regensburg in spring 1235, overcoming his son's rebellion, the settling of various conflicts which had arisen during the revolt, and mustering the support of the princes, made it impossible to distinguish clearly between various types of public occasion. Nonetheless, there was an awareness that not every public feast was also an imperial *diet*: when summing up the various steps which had been taken to bring Duke Frederick back into the fold, for instance, the emperor implicitly distinguished between those meetings which had been occasioned by his presence (such as the wedding at Worms or the diet at Hagenau) and those to which a formal invitation had been issued.[31]

Holding an assembly or refusing to participate in one could be robust political statements. In 1223, for example, a number of rebels decided to hold a rival Christmas parliament at Northampton. When Henry's regents became aware of this, they issued orders for the king's court to celebrate Christmas at Northampton, too. According to the Dunstable annalist, the numbers in attendance were so great, no feast of comparable size had been celebrated either in King John's reign or afterwards during Henry's. Within five days, therefore, the rebels surrendered.[32] Such considerations may also have informed the banning of tournaments in England in September 1234,[33] as a means of pacifying the realm (by prohibiting the assembling of large groups of armed men), also as a means of preventing an illicit public gathering, outside royal control at a time of political crisis.[34] That reasoning also underpinned

Henry (VII)'s claim, made in his letter to the bishop of Hildesheim, that he had only opened proceedings against the margrave of Baden and the duke of Bavaria after advice from the princes of the empire, who had attended his court in unprecedented numbers.[35] Frederick II had similarly gone to considerable lengths to ensure that he would have a suitably large audience on arriving in Germany, and to witness the key stages of his sojourn. When Henry (VII) first approached his father at Wimpfen, he was told to come to Worms instead.[36] This may have partly reflected the fact that Wimpfen was in the Swabian heartland of Henry's uprising (and thus an area where he might have been able to find allies), but also, and perhaps more importantly, that at Worms a greater public could be ensured to witness Henry's submission and punishment. That greater public, in turn, not only witnessed these events but also, by its sheer size, conferred legitimacy unto and condoned the proceedings. Similar considerations had probably played their part in Henry III's demand that the Marshal submit in person and publicly to the king.[37]

The location of a gathering similarly mattered. In 1236, for instance, Henry III initially waited in the Tower while his magnates and prelates convened in London. This caused considerable unease among his subjects, who feared that they would not be able to receive a fair hearing for their complaints against one of the king's favourites. Henry III therefore moved to his palace of Westminster, where he could consult 'more honourably' with his men about the matters to be discussed.[38] Equally, there is some circumstantial evidence to suggest that the emperor's wedding at Worms was in part designed as reward for the citizens' stance against Henry (VII): when Frederick had first announced his impending visit to Germany in the summer of 1234, he had proposed to hold his returning *diet* at Frankfurt,[39] while the fact that his wife Isabella had been escorted to Germany by the archbishop of Cologne and had spent several weeks prior to the wedding as the archbishop's guest,[40] indicates that Worms may not initially have been the venue of choice to hold his nuptials.[41]

Refusing to attend a meeting, by contrast, was a sign of opposition. This explains why, according to Wendover, Henry III was both concerned and angry when Richard and other magnates refused to attend a meeting he had called to Oxford for June 1233. According to Wendover, he then sought to force them to attend.[42] This was the first in a series of attempts by the king to make the barons frequent his court. When, for instance, a third assembly was called to London in late July 1233, nothing could be decided, as Richard Marshal, Gilbert Basset and others rejected the summons. Henry therefore decided to call yet another gathering, this time at Gloucester, ordering the barons and prelates of the realm to bring their armed retinue. When Richard and his allies failed to attend yet again, the king publicly labelled them traitors, and ordered their lands to be seized.[43] This, in turn, was the ultimate beginning of the Marshal revolt. By refusing to attend the first meeting, the earl and his followers defied the king's authority. In their absence, not much could be done, and they had thus achieved at least part of their goal. Similar considerations, may be apparent in proceedings against the duke of Austria: it was, after all, only after the duke had been called to attend several successive *diets* that he was formally declared a contumacious vassal, and that military action was taken against him,[44] while, in 1232, Henry (VII) had been forced into humiliating submission to his father because he had refused to attend an imperial *diet* called the year before. Like the Earl Marshal, Duke Frederick had thus been able to stall proceedings against himself, and to thwart immediate action. However, like the earl, too, he faced the dilemma that by this stage even his attending court would have done little to assuage the emperor: he could delay, but not prevent the outbreak of hostilities. Like Richard, Duke Frederick faced an opponent who had demonstrated that common forms of political behaviour were no longer followed.

In the eyes of their accusers, the duke's and the earl's refusal to participate in successive *diets* only underlined the truth of the allegations made against them, the very allegations, moreover, which they thus publicly refused to answer. The refusal to attend was a clear token of protest and rebellion, as Richard Marshal had explained to the king.[45] It was also a response that could escalate a conflict further, and political actors normally preferred a more nuanced way of voicing criticism. When, also in 1233, Walter of Carlisle was arrested while seeking to flee England, Bishop Richard of London vociferously protested against the prelate's treatment. However, he did so in various steps, and he maintained his loyalty towards the king: he excommunicated those who had been involved in the attack, but then travelled to the king's court at Hereford, and even brought his knights and other armed followers with him, just as he had been ordered to do. However, once in the royal presence, he publicly, and in the presence of the king, voiced his anger, and repeated the earlier sentence of excommunication.[46] His fellow prelates were said to have done the same at a meeting later in the year in London, when they humbly (*humiliter*) requested (*rogabant*) that the king allow the rebels to be tried by their peers.[47] That is, criticism was voiced, but it was couched either in the form of humble (though still public) requests, or, as in the case of the bishop of London, it was combined with a demonstrative display of loyalty. Participating in a public meeting conveyed legitimacy on the person who held it, but acknowledging that legitimacy also brought with it opportunities to make demands or voice criticism.

Conversely, being denied a public was a clear sign of disfavour. This principle is most evident in the ecclesiastical sphere, with the punishment of interdict or excommunication,[48] but it also applied to politics and further contextualises Henry (VII)'s complaints about his treatment at the hands of Frederick.[49] The king's emissaries (and thereby the king) were denied the opportunity to voice their grievances in public, and the legitimacy of their concerns was publicly rejected (witnessed by members of the imperial court and those German princes or their agents visiting it). This mattered symbolically, as it visibly denied the rights and authority of those who held political power, and thereby also practically: by being denied a hearing, by being refused the opportunity to state their or their lord's case in public and – more importantly even – before an appropriate public, those who were denied access were also denied the possibility of finding allies, intercessors or supporters. This aspect was especially evident in the case of Henry (VII)'s attempted submission at Wimpfen. That, too, had been preceded by informal, public consultations (the king had sent emissaries to his father, who, however, had been sent away),[50] before Henry approached his father in person. Even then, though, he did not come on his own, but did so jointly with one of Frederick's closest allies: Herman of Salza, the master general of the Teutonic Knights.[51] Moreover, Herman's intervention might have set a precedent which, at Wimpfen, Fredrick would have sought to avoid, that is, that others, too, began to plead on the king's behalf.[52] By refusing to allow Henry into his presence, the emperor not only denied the legitimacy of his son's submission but he also denied him a public which might have argued on his behalf. That no similar interventions are reported from Worms may indicate that Frederick's response at Wimpfen had made evident the fact that he would not be swayed. Should there have been any doubts, the treatment inflicted on Bishop Landulf dispelled them for good.

When entering Worms, the emperor was greeted by a group of prelates singing the *Gloria*. Hiding among them was Landulf. This may well have been an attempt to use the public gathering of bishops as protection against Frederick's wrath but was combined with a faint claim to exercising Landulf's role as lord of Worms. That he did this in so subdued a manner needs little explanation: Landulf would have been aware that his previous support for the king was unlikely to endear him to Frederick.

At the same time, his display of loyalty, in the context of a very public and festive occasion, was also aimed at facilitating reconciliation. To no avail, as Frederick, on recognising Landulf, halted the procession, and refused to proceed until the bishop had left and taken refuge in the house of one of his canons.[53] What mattered was once again the public refusal of reconciliation.[54] That this was done in the presence of the prelate's subjects, and during an otherwise festive occasion, only added to Landulf's humiliation and loss of status.

The same principles applied in England. When Simon de Montfort fell from royal grace in 1239, this was made public by not inviting him to the queen's churching after the birth of Prince Edward,[55] while, according to Matthew Paris, Gilbert Marshal knew that he had fallen out of favour when the royal butler refused to let him participate in the king's Christmas feast.[56] That this was announced by one of Henry's domestics only underlined the loss of status and prestige, and the degree of Gilbert's disgrace. Similarly, Roger of Wendover constructed the Marshal's grievances around the denial of a public, although with a subtle distinction: as Richard had refused to attend several meetings of the royal court, it would have been difficult to portray him in the manner Henry (VII) had portrayed himself – the earl had excluded himself from the public, rather than having it denied to him. Roger's narrative therefore centred on the fact that the public the earl was offered was inappropriate (as it was dominated by des Roches' men), and that he was refused the one that he should legitimately have been able to address (one that consisted of the native prelates and barons of the realm). This was thus also a conflict over what kind of public constituted the community of the realm.

The public mattered: it provided an audience to which status could be demonstrated, before which legitimacy could be claimed and established, but also one through which important decisions could be ratified. There was a reason, after all, why important documents, like the 1235 land peace, were issued in the context of a large assembly, but this ratifying aspect was not limited to acts of legal reform, as the example of Otto of Brunswick's enfeoffment at Mainz demonstrates, or the frequency with which knighting, the formal ceremonial declaration of age, was combined with parliaments in England.[57] The presence of the politically active groups of the realm constituted and legitimised rule, too, and exclusion from it mattered. Differences between England and Germany were few in this respect. Even so, it is worth noting that denying access to a public in the case of Henry (VII) meant the audience of his father and the imperial court, and in Richard Marshal's that of a court which he and his followers would have deemed legitimate.

II

What, however, happened once a public had been convened? Gerd Althoff has distinguished three types of public deliberation for the tenth through to the twelfth century: the *colloquium publicum*, *colloquium familiare* and *colloquium secretum*,[58] that is, public consultation (in a large assembly); deliberations among those in the inner circle of a ruler or magnate; and confidential meetings outside the public gaze. I shall focus on the first of these, and only occasionally consider the other two. This does not mean that they did not matter or that they did not occur. In fact, we will be able to see quite clearly that they did – when, during a parliament or *diet*, several days elapsed between the public proceedings recorded by chroniclers, for instance, and final decisions being announced – but we do not normally know what happened during a *colloquium secretum* or *familiare*. This lies, of course, in the nature of these meetings. Sometimes, we glimpse the issues that might have been discussed. Richard Marshal's meeting with Friar Agnellus, for instance, would be a classic example of a *colloquium secretum*: it took place far from the public eye, treated sensitive matters and sought to prepare a more public meeting. In reporting Agnellus' encounter with the earl, Wendover also mentioned other meetings of a less secretive kind, but still addressing a highly restricted public: Agnellus referred, for instance, to private conversations he had with the king, or to exchanges between Henry and his familiars, in which the king expressed his desire to make peace with the Marshal. That the king made these statements where nobody but those who already knew his mind could hear him, would only have served to underline the sincerity of these promises.[59] Equally, Richard's attempts to break into the presence of the king to voice his demands,[60] point to the importance of those less public meetings: they allowed opinions to be voiced which otherwise might have been more difficult to convey. One complaint common to Wendover and other chroniclers had, after all, been that des Roches and his allies shielded the king from those who should have advised him. That is, the ability of the barons and prelates to influence royal decisions was limited to public gatherings of a more restrictive etiquette. The German evidence is less forthcoming, and this is one of the reasons why we will limit our coverage: we would lack a basis from which to compare the importance and significance of these meetings. All we can do is deduce from passing references that *colloquia secreta* and *familiares* mattered. Let us therefore turn to the *colloquium publicum*: what happened once a parliament or *diet* convened?

Important as these assemblies were, not much evidence survives as to what occurred at them. Wendover's narrative may be full of references to such gatherings, but even he rarely went beyond merely stating that they had taken place, and that either the earl or the bishops had complained to the king. In one case, he reports that des Roches had addressed the assembly on the king's behalf,[61] but gives little else in terms of how proceedings were conducted. The German evidence is even less conclusive. As far as Henry (VII)'s *diet* in the autumn of 1234 was concerned, for instance, which started his revolt, little is said by chroniclers apart from that it took place.[62] Similarly, in the case of Frederick II, one of the most significant stages of his return to Germany was the *diet* held at Regensburg in the spring of 1235.[63] However, the meeting's date does not survive, and we are dependent on the emperor's later letter of justification against the duke of Austria to find that, apparently, it had also been designed to receive the homage and fealty of the neighbouring princes (including the duke's).[64] The sources are usually silent about how this was done, in what order, and in whose presence.

This even applies to meetings as significant as that at Mainz in 1235. By far, the most detailed account of the *diet* is that in the *Chronica Regia Coloniensis* (Royal Chronicle of Cologne), extending to all of a paragraph in the modern edition: in August 1235, a most solemn *curia* was celebrated at Mainz, attended by all the princes of Germany. A general peace was sworn, old laws were confirmed and new ones issued, a German version of which was also put in writing and publicised to all; the crimes of the king against the emperor were made public, and Otto of Lüneburg was installed as duke and prince. On the day following Otto's enfeoffment, the *diet* concluded with a solemn crown-wearing and mass in Mainz cathedral, followed by a great feast which had been prepared in the meadows outside Mainz.[65] Similarly, the *Annals of Marbach* merely report that around 12,000 princes from various parts of Germany came to Mainz, that the emperor wore his crown, that Otto was made a duke at the advice of the princes, and that the emperor asked for an armed levy to accompany him to Lombardy.[66] This tells us a little more about the workings of an imperial *diet* than Wendover tells us about meetings of English parliaments or the royal *curia* (it mentions, for instance, the ceremonial context, about which the English chronicler are unusually silent), but it still says little about the specific proceedings at Mainz. To some extent, the charter evidence can be used to complement this picture, and the reference to the vernacular, Middle High German version of the *Reichslandfrieden* is worth noting, as is the fact that this had been done with the specific purpose of making the decrees of the *diet* public across the realm.[67] In the English case, the administrative sources can be used to reconstruct some of the more detailed preparations of parliaments, but the information on offer is still limited: when, in 1270, for instance, the citizens of Southampton were ordered to provide 200 tons of wine, 'as a parliament cannot be celebrated without good wine',[68] this tells us something about the intoxicating nature of late thirteenth-century parliaments, but not necessarily about how they worked and functioned. For that we depend on narrative sources. Nonetheless, if we are prepared to step outside the chronological focus of events immediately surrounding the rebellions of 1233–5, a number of suitably detailed narratives survive. I would like to focus on two of these, and we do not have to move far beyond the core of this study to find them: the first is a parliament convened in London by Henry III in January 1237, and recorded by Matthew Paris, the second a *diet* held by Henry (VII) at Frankfurt in February 1234, a few months before the outbreak of his revolt, and of which a (comparatively) detailed description survives in the *Annales Erphordenses*.

When Henry III celebrated Christmas 1236 at Winchester, he also issued a mandate asking the prelates and magnates of the realm to convene in London not long after Epiphany. The *parliamentum* thus called duly convened on 13 January 1237, attended 'by an infinite multitude of nobles, practically the whole of the community of the realm'.[69] Proceedings were opened by William Raleigh, 'a cleric and member of the king's household, prudent and well versed in the laws of the realm, who acted as mediator between the king and his nobles, so as to make public the wishes and demands of the king'.[70] Raleigh did in fact perform this function fairly regularly: in 1238, for instance, he led a group of royal emissaries to attend to council held by the papal legate to ensure that nothing was decreed that would be detrimental to the king's honour.[71] The king convened the assembly, but did not open it, nor did he personally propose what he wanted the assembly to agree: this was a task left to a member of the royal household. This may reflect common practice in early thirteenth-century English parliaments, and could thus contextualise Roger of Wendover's statement that Peter des Roches rather than the king addressed the barons in 1233.[72] This was not an innovation of Henry III's: several accounts survive of meetings of Henry II's *curia*, for instance, where the king similarly either stayed away from the meeting, or where it was one of the king's officials who spoke on his behalf and in his presence, and where the king himself did not speak until the meeting concluded.[73] This served a number of purposes: it underlined the ruler's special status, and underlined the distinction between him and his leading magnates, while at the same time highlighting the latter's special role in the administration of the realm (they consulted freely about the king's demands). Moreover, it allowed criticism to be voiced without attacking the king, by directing it at his officials instead, while also limiting the loss of prestige and standing of the king were his proposals turned down. In 1237, for instance, Gilbert Basset was said to have advised the king to send another representative to meet with the barons, and he was said to have done so because he was one of the few barons siding with the king.[74]

That Gilbert was chided for his statement by Richard de Percy, and that the resulting debates extended the meeting by another four days,[75] also indicates that a parliament's decisions were by no means a foregone conclusion. In 1237, this partly reflected the subject matter: the king needed money to pay for his sister's dowry, and the barons and prelates were thus asked to agree to a tax of a thirtieth on moveable property. In fact, as John Maddicott has shown, most of Henry's parliaments did not result in the grant of financial levies requested by the king: between 1232 and 1257, he received only twice (in 1232 and 1237) the tax he requested, twice he was granted a feudal aid, and was turned down nine times.[76] Moreover, it seems that these royal demands had come as somewhat of a surprise: according to Matthew Paris, the barons had flocked to London in such large numbers because they expected that the matters discussed would relate to 'the empire or other urgent matters', that is, to the ongoing conflict between Frederick II and the Lombard League (which also involved a sizeable English contingent).[77] It thus comes as no surprise that Henry was turned down: the king, some of the participants complained, kept asking for money – here a twentieth, there a thirtieth, another time a fiftieth – but had little to show in exchange. He was easily duped, and not once, for instance, had he expelled an enemy of the realm, however small and insignificant, or installed fear in him, and he never expanded the borders of his kingdom, but kept reducing them.[78] This raises questions about the reliability of Matthew's report. That he had William Raleigh argue for additional taxation because those who had been in charge of the royal treasury were incompetent and that the king was thus penurious should alert us to the fact that Matthew modelled these events so as to criticise the king both directly and indirectly. The complaints made by the barons were in fact familiar themes in his writings, and may well reflect his concerns rather than those of the magnates. At the same time, what matters here is not whether Matthew's rendering of baronial complaints is accurate, but that complaints were made, debates conducted and royal requests rejected. That not all of this was said publicly and in the king's presence, and that discussion was an integral element of the proceedings, is also indicated by Matthew's statement that, after the king's demands had been heard, the barons withdrew to a less public location to discuss the matter.[79] This opened the next stage of proceedings: the demands made of the king.

According to Matthew, Henry became agitated once he realised the opposition his requests had encountered, and thus sought to regain the barons' favour by offering a solemn reissue of Magna Carta, and by renewing the sentence of excommunication which, in 1225, Stephen Langton had issued against all those who violated the Great Charter.[80] This concession filled the hearts of his subjects with joy, and their minds miraculously turned towards the king. After it had furthermore been agreed that the earl of Warenne, William Ferrers and John fitzGeoffrey join the royal council, a thirtieth was granted. This levy was, however, agreed upon in stages – first by the prelates, then, rather grudgingly and not without murmurings, by the lay magnates – and had further conditions attached to it, or at least so Matthew claimed: the clergy were only prepared to consent if the king promised not take the advice of foreigners who were enemies of the realm, and if he instead relied on the counsel of his native subjects.[81] We may assume that Henry III had not conceded the reissue of Magna Carta at the spur of the moment – despite Matthew's statement that his consent was both unprompted and voluntary – but that it had been the result of further consultations of which, however, no evidence survives. As such, and with the difficulties inevitably involved in using Matthew Paris' testimony duly noted, a basic structure emerges, indicative of how parliaments worked: they followed a royal summons, but the monarch did not himself take the lead in conducting the proceedings. He may have attended part of them,[82] although there is also some evidence to suggest that he may have stayed away from the meeting altogether. These gatherings moreover worked in several stages: a public hearing of the king's petitions, followed by separate, less public consultations among the participants, and there was a clear expectation that the king's demands could be rejected, or that they could be amended by his subjects. Much of this, it is worth reiterating, reflects the somewhat unusual subject matter of the 1237 parliament: this was a parliament about taxation, and this was by no means typical.

Matthew's account of a parliament taking place in April 1236 in London, although less detailed, may thus give us a taste of what parliaments normally were about. Apart from customary complaints about the king's patronage of aliens, it was also decided that all sheriffs would be replaced by men motivated by a love of truth and justice, not riches and wealth; the king of Scotland sent emissaries to demand that his ancestral lands be restored, but a decision was postponed; furthermore, Richard Siward was advised by the king to go into exile as Henry would not be able to protect him against the anger of the king's brother, Earl Richard (whose estates he had plundered in 1233–4); while Ralph fitzNicholas and other royal councillors were removed from office.[83] The 1236 parliament thus discussed the administrative reform of the realm, possibly responding to common grievances, and also the conduct of relations with the kingdom's neighbours, and the settlement of feuds and disputes among those at court.[84] Some of the issues mentioned by Paris probably required baronial consultation, not necessarily to agree the kings actions, but in order to legitimise them (as they would then have been undertaken with the advice and counsel of his nobles), and to demonstrate the king's concern for the welfare of the realm (by removing corrupt officials and thus upholding the principle of fair and even justice). Similar considerations had probably underpinned proceedings at the king's Pentecost court of 1233 at Gloucester, where several barons were knighted, and where it was announced that, for the first time in almost in many years, itinerant judges would tour Cornwall.[85] The 1236 parliament was thus perhaps more representative of the kind of issues discussed at parliaments, but this does not mean that we can dismiss as atypical the structure and order of proceedings Matthew reported for the 1237 gathering.

A key aspect of these meetings was their admonitory function: they were not designed to rubber stamp royal decisions, but were venues of deliberation and true debate. As such, they were also markedly different from the pattern Gerd Althoff has established for the workings of public communication in general, and the one Timothy Reuter has traced for assemblies between the tenth and twelfth century, where debate and dispute were frowned upon as violating rules designed to present a smooth façade of public concord.[86] As far as thirteenth-century England is concerned, the volatile nature of parliaments can hardly come as a surprise: for those participants, who were not members of the monarch's inner circle, his officials or close relatives, this was the chief opportunity to participate in the governance of the realm. The narrative record is thus filled with councils, gatherings and parliaments being used to criticise the king or his ministers, or to force actions upon him. In late 1233, for instance, Wendover described a parliament as having been called to London so that the king would make true his promise that he would take the advice of his barons in reforming the realm. The meeting was convened specifically to hold the king to account and to enforce his earlier concessions. In the end – and this highlights the still considerable power of the monarch – he did not allow the magnates to offer their counsel, and it was thus left to the bishops to complain about des Roches' regime.[87] It was ultimately the initiative taken by the ecclesiastical elite, too, which, during a parliament in the spring of 1234, brought about des Roches' fall from power: the bishops publicly threatened to excommunicate the king should he not remove the aliens from his council.[88] This does not mean that the magnates normally just stood by: when in 1238 Richard of Cornwall rebelled about the marriage of his sister Eleanor to Simon de Montfort, Matthew Paris claims that the barons attended a parliament at Westminster fully armed so that, if necessary, they could force the king to comply.[89] That is, there was a clear expectation that the magnates would regulate and oversee, and if necessary correct the king's governance.[90] Armed threat may have been one way of doing so. Another, and perhaps more practical means was to use public gatherings to exert control over the composition of the royal council, of the men who had regular access to the king, and who ought regularly to be consulted by him. The remit given to the barons selected in 1237 is thus worth noting: they were made to swear that they would not be swayed by gifts or anything else from giving the king 'sound advice for the better of the realm'.[91]

At the same time, Roger and Matthew may have attributed to the assembled prelates and barons a greater willingness to challenge the king than they did in reality possess or claim. To some extent, Wendover and Paris ascribed to those attending parliaments the kind of influence they thought these gatherings should have possessed, and the kind of aggressive oversight the chroniclers felt the barons, knights and clergy should have exercised. The same writers, after all, also record numerous meetings and gatherings where protest was muted, and where participants were afraid of criticising the king openly. Luke of Dublin, for instance, was repeatedly singled out by Wendover for his courage in publicly criticising de Burgh's treatment,[92] while one measure of the Marshal's fortitude was that he alone among the magnates spoke out against des Roches. In 1236, the barons had been afraid of meeting the king in the Tower, and this does not conform to Matthew's image of them being prepared to use arms should Henry be reluctant to do their bidding. Similarly, that approaching the king by force, rashly or in too insistent a manner – as Richard Marshal, for instance, was said to have done in 1233 – was a sign of extraordinary courage, may indicate that Paris and Wendover may have allowed their ideals to form their representation of the reality they claimed to record. We should not let ourselves be duped into underestimating the king's power.

While magnates and prelates were dependent on public assemblies to participate in the running of the realm, and to exercise and demonstrate their status as the kings' leading subjects, Henry, too, relied on these gatherings to gain legitimacy for his actions and to win the support of his barons. It was, however, also a lesson which Henry III was slow to learn. Many of his initiatives over the next two decades – his abortive invasion of Poitou in 1242–3, for instance, the Gascon campaign of 1253–4, or the ill-fated Sicilian Business of the 1250s (which centred on the attempt to make his son Edmund king of Sicily) – were undertaken either without or against the advice of his subjects, and it was this lack of consultation that often brought about the king's failure and defeat. It was ultimately, too, what forced the king, in 1258, to accept a far greater degree of baronial oversight and control than had been envisaged even by his most ardent opponents during the crisis of 1233–4.[93] Matthew's statement that in 1237 a number of earls were elected to act as permanent advisors to the king may thus have been written under the impression of these and other events, including, for instance, the crisis of 1244,[94] but they certainly reflected more widely held grievances against the king's reluctance fully to involve his barons in the governance of the realm. What this also indicates, however, is the still considerable power exercised by the king. There may have been the expectation that the king would be held to account, but in reality the monarch exercised sufficient power to set aside, ignore or overrule the opinions of his barons and prelates.

III

How does all this compare to the German experience? Let us begin by highlighting the differences, some structural, others rooted in the very different political situation of 1234–5. Among the former stands out that the issue so central to the 1237 parliament would never have arisen in Germany: there was no general taxation to be raised. An emperor could expect the kind of personal service which started the conflict with Duke Frederick (when the latter refused to attend the Regensburg *diet*), or the provision of troops and armed men – according to the *Annales Marbacenses*, one of the items discussed at the 1235 Mainz *diet*.[95] Similarly, when the emperor first announced his intention of returning to Germany, in the summer of 1234, he explained to the archbishop of Trier that he intended to call a *diet* to Frankfurt for June 1235, and the business that was to be conducted there: he would be accompanied by a papal legate to dispose of affairs relating to the Holy Land and the affairs of Christendom.[96] Furthermore, while in England, from about 1160 at the latest, a changeable but identifiable group of people had emerged who ought to attend parliaments and participate in these general assemblies,[97] the situation in Germany was considerably more fluid. Individuals were certainly invited to attend *diets* – as Frederick had stated explicitly to the archbishop, as we have seen in the summons issued *generaliter et communiter* to the German princes for the 1235 Mainz *diet*, or the fact that Duke Frederick's refusal to attend imperial *diets* was deemed an affront against the imperial majesty – but it also seems that the composition of this group varied considerably.

Sometimes this was a matter of geography: crossing the Alps to attend an imperial *diet*, for instance, like the one which Henry failed to attend at Ravenna in 1231, was an endeavour which by the thirteenth century few German princes were willing to take upon themselves.[98] In other cases, special grants and privileges had been issued that exempted individuals from attending *diets* outside a particular region (as in the *Privilegium Minus*, allegedly granted to the dukes of Austria by Frederick Barbarossa in the twelfth century).[99] Quite often the composition of an imperial *diet* was thus dependent on where it was held, and this irrespective of the subject matter discussed. While Frederick II may thus have been able to get even the dukes of Lorraine and Saxony to meet him on his progress from Regensburg to Nuremberg (in far away Franconia) in 1235, when he convened a *diet* in Vienna in 1237 to confirm the election of his second son, Conrad, as king of the Romans, the witness list to the document consisted almost exclusively of south German princes and prelates.[100] This made *diets* like the ones at Mainz stand out all the more for the fact that they represented the universality of the German princes. When Matthew Paris used similar language to describe events at Westminster in 1237, he referred to the number of participants, especially those who were not magnates, and only implicitly to the fact that they had flocked to London from all corners of the realm. What constituted the community of realm in the empire, by contrast, was all too often defined by the location of its meeting. Furthermore, when, in 1234 and 1235,

Frederick II repeatedly stressed that the empire was ruled jointly by princes and emperor, this was not necessarily an invitation to the kind of debate which Roger of Wendover and Matthew Paris put at the centre of English parliaments. In fact, by the time the Mainz *diet* convened, Frederick had amply demonstrated that he would not allow his decisions to be changed or challenged. To some extent, the role of the princes was to fulfil the tasks which the emperor entrusted them with and to carry out the duties he instructed them to perform. This was also an attitude, however, that was rooted in the circumstances of 1235: unlike the king of England, Frederick had overcome the recent rebellion, and had done so with noticeable ease, and unlike his brother-in-law, the emperor had thus every reason to construct the *diets* and festivities of 1235 as an exuberant celebration of imperial power. Once the emperor returned to Lombardy, German politics, too, returned to normal.[101]

To define the normality of German politics, we must look back from 1235, not forward; Conrad IV's powers were more limited even than those granted to Henry (VII),[102] and were soon curtailed further by the emperor's second excommunication in 1239 and the subsequent transformation of German imperial politics. We face the added difficulty that the narrative sources do not allow us to paint a detailed picture of imperial politics during Frederick's early reign. Certainly, as far as the evidence for his grandfather Frederick Barbarossa is concerned, the role of an emperor in conducting imperial *diets* was rather more limited than that of an English king in conducting parliaments. He may have presided over events in person, but the evidence also suggests that the lead in making decisions was taken by his noble subjects, not the emperor.[103] There are, of course, dangers in trying to draw conclusions for the thirteenth century by relying on descriptions from the twelfth. Let us, therefore, step down one level from the *diets* presided over by the emperor to those presided over by his son.

In February 1234, Henry (VII) held a *diet* at Frankfurt which had been convened to deal with grave matters indeed. Six months earlier, Conrad of Marburg and some of his companions had been murdered.[104] Unsurprisingly, this had caused outrage at the papal court, and the king and the archbishop of Mainz (in whose diocese the friar had been killed) had been ordered to find and judge those responsible. The Frankfurt meeting was attended by numerous princes and prelates, also by several monks and representatives of religious orders (our source specifically singled out Cistercians, Dominicans and Franciscans), and other religious.[105] The meeting was opened by the king, who accused the bishop of Hildesheim of having been the friar inquisitor's all-too willing henchmen. The prelate rejected any such claims (he had, under pressure from Conrad, signed many people with the Cross, but had afterwards quickly absolved them from their vows), and the meeting soon divided, with the clergy convening separately from the king and the princes.[106] Henry (VII)'s lack of empathy for the late friar was widely shared: one unnamed participant was said to have suggested that Conrad's remains be disinterred and burned. At the same time, the friar also had numerous supporters among those assembled, and the meeting descended into acrimony. Matters were not helped by the fact that some of those who, the previous year, had been accused of heresy by Conrad, interrupted the meeting, leading to such tumultuous scenes that those pleading for Conrad took flight.[107] The individuals in question were probably the count of Sayn, one of the most prominent of Conrad's victims, and those who had been accused of being behind the friar's killing.[108] How exactly the shuffle was resolved we do not know, but four days later the king led a procession of all the princes and prelates attending the *diet* to the fields outside Frankfurt, where judgement was passed. Nor do we know how that judgement had been reached. That four days had passed between the *diet's* commencement and its conclusion, suggest, however, that it had been the result of both arduous and non-public negotiations. The count of Sayn, accompanied by eight bishops, twelve Cistercians, a dozen Franciscans, three Dominicans, as well as several Benedictine abbots and other clergy, in addition to numerous secular lords, 'publicly and confidently' cleared himself by oath.[109] Subsequently, the count of Solm confessed under tears that he had only admitted to being a heretic in fear of death, but, with no legitimate accusers present, he, too, was granted the right to clear himself by oath.[110] Settling the issue of Conrad's murder was not, however, the only issue discussed: among others, the citizens of Erfurt and the archbishop of Mainz brought their dispute over the extent of the archbishop's rights in the town before the royal court.[111] Dealing with Conrad's murder was an important point, but only one among several.

Just as imperial *diets* would not have dealt with issues of taxation, so English parliaments did not deal with heresy: not since 1166, when Henry II had a group of heretics branded, stripped naked and left to die in the cold.[112] Even so, enough evidence survives for basic parallels to be drawn and differences to be outlined. That, unlike in 1235, disputes erupted, conforms to a pattern familiar from the somewhat better documented meetings of the twelfth century. Similarly, how the king's role was described merits attention. Henry may have opened the proceedings, but he also acted at the behest of his subjects, first by convening the meeting, and secondly, in passing judgement: the *Annales* explicitly state that the king passed judgement jointly with secular and spiritual princes.[113] The king shared in the passing of judgements, and to some extent followed the guidance of the princes, but it was also the king who conveyed legitimacy onto that decision. Partly due to the subject matter, this was not a case of Henry presenting his demands, and his subjects discussing them, but it is also an image that ties in with the way Henry and Frederick, too, portrayed their actions. Ruling the empire was a collective undertaking, and the ruler could not act without the advice and counsel of the ruled. This is perhaps one of the key differences between imperial *diets* and English parliaments: in the latter case, although the ruler may not have received what he hoped for, the initiative still rested with him. In the former, the emperor (or the king of the Romans) acted in a more pronouncedly passive fashion (he responded to the demands of his subjects and at their behest). Even if this was a matter of a convention more than actual practice – and the example of Frederick II in 1235 should alert us to the degree to which an emperor could set the agenda – that even the Mainz *diet* was described in these terms indicates that it reflected fundamental principles of how the political order of the realm should be structured (and thus mirrors what we have seen in previous chapters). There was an emphasis on joint government, but without disempowering the king: royal or imperial legitimisation was still needed, and only the ruler by his presence and assent could convey legitimacy onto the proceedings.

There was another important difference. In England, parliaments existed alongside other fora of public debate and communication. In particular, as we have seen, county courts played an important role in disseminating decisions, though not perhaps in confirming and legitimising them. Nonetheless, they were integral to the functioning of the realm, its governance and administration.[114] This is evident, for instance, in the fact that Magna Carta was distributed across the realm, with the specific mandate that it be read out in the shires,[115] and like provisions were made in Henry III's mandate discussed in Chapter 6. Similar mechanisms seem to have existed in towns, and are best documented, although mostly from the 1250s, in London. In 1253, for instance, prior to the king's departure for Gascony, the citizens were ordered to assemble outside St Paul's, to swear fealty to Prince Edward;[116] in March 1265, a new oath of fealty to the king was sworn by the mayor and aldermen of London in the Church of St Paul, to be followed by every Londoner over the age of twelve in a public assembly of their ward;[117] and in 1265, a royal mandate that Magna Carta was to be confirmed and conformed to was read out to the assembled Londoners in the guildhall.[118]

No such devolved publics seem to have existed in Germany. This reflected the nature of imperial governance, and the fact that an emperor and king did not preside over a similarly elaborate apparatus of administration. Well into the fourteenth century, a new king could thus not order his subjects to perform oaths of fealty in his absence to his officials, but had to ensure himself of the loyalty of his subjects by touring the realm. Even then, the fealty he received was that of the leading princes, with little provision made for that of their subjects. Similarly, because there were no grants of taxation to be collected, no imperial judges to perambulate the realm and no subdivisions like counties and hundreds to control or administer, there existed little need for formalised gatherings relating to matters imperial on a local and regional level. Of course, public consultation did take place. It was not, however, necessarily concerned with regnal affairs, but with those of a particular principality or town. These gatherings were certainly addressed by the emperor but were so because of their local function, in order to gain or reward political support against local opponents (like Bishop Landulf or King Henry in the case of Worms), not because they played an identifiable part within the community of the realm at large (and we will return to this point in Chapter 9). Chroniclers portrayed imperial lordship as one step removed from local affairs, partly because this reflected the reality of imperial politics.

IV

The time has come to offer a more detailed analysis. In the Marshal's case, the royal court and the public which parliaments provided for it were both the starting point of the conflict, and where it was ultimately resolved by the public dismissal of des Roches and de Rivallis,[119] and the equally public reconciliation accorded to the surviving rebels.[120] In Germany, by contrast, imperial *diets* were often but one stage in the conflict, appealed to once local means of resolving it had been exhausted, but from which it was also returned to one or more of the parties involved. This distinction should not be drawn too rigidly – there were cases in England, too (as we will see in the next chapter), that involved the king and his court as but one step in a prolonged local dispute. Nonetheless, the basic difference remains. In Germany, bringing a case before the king was a means of gaining legitimacy and support. Turning that added legitimacy, or a sentence passed by royal

judges, into political reality was, however, something left to the parties
themselves, and their neighbours and peers (and to a far greater degree
than in England).[121] In the case of Worms, for instance, Frederick may
have allowed Bishop Henry to revoke the charters he had granted,
but it was still left to the bishop to turn that judgement into reality.
This pattern was broken only rarely, and only in the most excep-
tional of circumstances: when Henry moved against the duke of Bavaria,
or Frederick II against that of Austria. Both stressed, however, that
their involvement had, first, been a last resort, laid upon them by
the common counsel of the princes, and, second, one that had been
undertaken because the dukes had committed crimes against both their
honour and that of the empire. Imperial action derived its legitimacy
from the public sanction of the princes, as much as those of the
princes derived theirs from that of the king or emperor. That legitimacy, in turn, was conveyed and expressed in a public meeting of
the ruler and his subjects. This is not to say that emperors had no
means of influencing the course of debates: rulers could clearly take
the initiative. Comparing the ultimate outcome of the *diet* with Henry's
recorded opening statement (when he accused the bishop of Hildesheim
of having too willingly done the friar's bidding), we can see both
that he got his way, also, that his opening statements foreshadowed
(and probably reflected) the consensus of the assembled princes and
prelates.

In this context, Professor Althoff's tripartite division of gatherings may
indicate one means by which that consensus could be formed, although,
rather ironically, it is in the English, not the German sources, that
we find evidence for *colloquia secreta* and *privata*. We should certainly
not over interpret the evidence: just as much as Matthew Paris had
not been privy to all the discussions at Westminster in 1237, so the
Annales Erphordenses had only limited information about the less public
part of proceedings at Frankfurt. Much of the image emerging is probably idealised, in the sense that chroniclers represented these gatherings how they think they should have, rather than how they had been
conducted. At the same time, as far as Germany is concerned, there
also is a remarkable overlap between how Frederick and his son defined
imperial lordship, and how *diets* seem to have functioned. There was
a marked emphasis on the collaborative and joint nature of decision-
making. Equally, though, and as in the case of the narrative sources,
we can see different perceptions and ideals come to the fore. While
Henry's involvement (perhaps because it was reported under the shadow
of his deposition) was thus described in almost non-committal terms,

most chroniclers also applauded Frederick when he took decisive action: the *Annals of Heiligenkreuz* thus dwelled on how he disposed and ordered matters of secular justice, destroyed numerous castles, doing justice to everyone and punishing evildoers irrespective of rank,[122] while the *Annals of St Ruprecht* in Salzburg also commented favourably on Frederick's efforts at doing justice by destroying illicit castles and banning evildoers.[123] There was little mention of consensus politics in what these chroniclers deemed an exemplary exercise of imperial duties. Similarly, we have seen how a number of Middle High German poems emphasised the need for decisive imperial governance, for strong lordship and the ruthless maintenance of law and justice. Even if we take into account that some of this praise may be indebted to established conventions of describing good kingship, the contrast with how political actions were otherwise described is nonetheless striking, and may indicate that, as much as in the English case, ideals of political power were born out of disillusionment with the reality of its exercise.[124]

In both England and Germany, the public assembly mattered as the visible expression of the community of the realm. It was the chief tool by which to legitimate political actions. *Diets* and parliaments were both deeply rooted in the political structures of the respective realm, and thus expressed quite different concepts of a ruler's authority and function. That these frequently reflect reality only to uphold an ideal against which that reality could be judged and found wanting, is something we need, of course, to keep in mind, but it is not something that fundamentally undermines the plausibility of the image painted in this chapter. To begin, English kings were granted a greater ceremonial role in the conduct of parliaments than emperors, but that did not necessarily denote greater control. Quite to the contrary: largely because of the very real power Henry III had, his government and his officials were more likely to be exposed to criticism than Frederick II or Henry (VII). Equally, that imperial *diets* were constructed as an exercise in consensual lordship did not mean that the emperor could not force his will upon the princes. The means by which public was constructed, the role it performed and how it worked in practice thus reveal fault lines within the respective political communities of Staufen Germany and Plantagenet England, not unlike those we have encountered before. This is evident in the more formalised nature of the English gatherings, and their increasingly circumscribed membership; in the more fluid composition of the imperial *diet*; and in the business conducted at either, and their relationship with other types of public assembly or gathering. All this also highlights how difficult it is to maintain the easy distinctions that have charac-terised much modern scholarship on Staufen Germany and Plantagenet England, and this will become even more pronounced once we turn to the means by which this public was addressed, and by which it took part in this process of communication.

8
Addressing the Public: Rituals, Gestures and Charters

We have seen how the size of a public mattered, as did the location in which it gathered. But how was this public addressed? Answering this question brings us to the core of the differing traditions of English and German historical scholarship. Among historians of Angevin and Plantagenet England, greater emphasis is commonly placed on the tools and mechanisms of royal administration, and relatively little attention has been paid to how these formed part of a process of political communication. In the context of rebellions, for instance, the primary focus has been on nature and the importance of financial and bureaucratic reform to rebels.[1] In Germany, by contrast, scholarship has increasingly focused on what Gerd Althoff has termed 'symbolic forms of communication',[2] that is, on ideas, concepts and claims conveyed largely through gestures, ceremonies and rituals,[3] rather than (though not necessarily to the complete exclusion of) the spoken or written word. This has served to exacerbate and deepen a perceived gulf between German and English politics: the one administrative–bureaucratic,[4] the other concerned with issues of honour and ritual.[5]

The reality of medieval politics was, of course, more complex.[6] The following will thus not rehearse those arguments, and will instead focus, first, on how symbolic actions were used in England and Germany, and, second, on their relationship with other means of political communication. There is, after all, a tendency among historians of medieval political ritual to argue that ritual and administrative, legal and fiscal procedures were somehow antagonistic, and to do so with the assumption that ritual was slowly, gradually and inevitably replaced by written forms of communication.[7] There, too, the following will propose, medieval reality was more complex than modern scholarship

130

would sometimes lead us to believe. How, then, did public communication work, and what was the relationship between written and symbolic forms of communication?

I

Reading accounts of public meetings, one immediately notices the emphasis on gestures, forms of address and behaviour. These were not isolated or incidental episodes, but frequently form part of the overall moral message a text sought to convey. In Wendover's case, for instance, those criticising the king, resisting him or seeking to intervene on others' behalf, are described as acting humbly, pleadingly or soberly, while Peter des Roches, Geoffrey de Marsh and others behaved callously, secretively, or driven by anger. In 1233, for instance, shortly after the coup against de Burgh, the bishop of Winchester is described as accusing the bishops who objected to his measures (*apud regem accusabat*),[8] while the earl Marshal first approached the king courageously (*audacter*), but then humbly requested that Henry restrain the excesses of des Roches (*humiliter rogabat*).[9] That is, in his behaviour towards and in the presence of the king, the earl already revealed an inner disposition indicative of his more noble and sincere motives. Similarly, when, in October 1233, the king convened a parliament at Westminster, the bishops requested humbly (*humiliter rogabant*) that he make peace with the barons,[10] while, in April 1234, Edmund Rich, too, approached the king courageously (*audacter*) to move him against Peter des Roches.[11] When, by contrast, the bishops of Salisbury and London protested against de Burgh's abduction, the king, *iratus*, swelled with anger, ordered the local sheriff to besiege the church and not allow provisions to reach de Burgh.[12] The Marshal, furthermore, always acted in public, before witnesses, and remained sober, polite, yet insistent that right be done by him and others.[13] Moral rectitude manifested itself in its public nature and perfidy in its secrecy: when sending letters to Ireland claiming that the Marshal had been found guilty of treason, des Roches and his men secretly affixed the royal seal to their forgery.[14] Men like the Marshal acted like truly faithful subjects: they approached Henry humbly, openly and politely; they acted courageously, knowing that their actions were morally justified. Peter des Roches and his allies, on the other hand, acted deceitfully, secretively and treacherously, and thereby also revealed their depraved motives and perfidious character. The demeanour of political actors revealed their true inner moral make up.[15]

In the German case, the narrative sources are less detailed, but emphasise similar points. They thus draw an implicit distinction between the serenity of Frederick's actions, and the panic, fear and cruelty of Henry (VII) and his supporters: Henry feared the arrival of his father and was motivated solely by fear;[16] seeing that he had no supporters in Worms, Henry became enraged and agitated beyond measure.[17] Once the king's partisans beheld the emperor's might, they thus became fearful and disturbed, and flocked to side with Frederick.[18] Equally, the duke of Austria was driven by stupidity and intolerable arrogance,[19] and he was characterised as someone unable to control his emotions: he was a harsh man (*severus homo*), cruel and strict in his justice (*in judicio districtus et crudelis*), greedy (*cupidus*), someone who instilled terror among his neighbours and subjects,[20] and unable to restrain his libido.[21] The emperor, by contrast, acted *debita honore*, with due respect;[22] he did stern but fair justice.[23] None of these examples does, of course, amount to the detailed description of behaviour we have encountered in the English sources. Even so, the principles underpinning them are very similar: those who were driven by emotions, who allowed them to be expressed too strongly and did so publicly, also committed morally damnable political acts.

Encounters between political agents were moreover guided by a series of behavioural norms, not unlike those we have encountered in an English context. Imperial charters thus emphasise the humility of those who approached Frederick to have their grants confirmed,[24] while Henry (VII), too, had stressed that his envoys had approached the emperor in a most humble and respectful manner (by prostrating themselves at Frederick's feet).[25] Conrad of Fabaria, who provides one of the most detailed accounts of a career at the imperial court (that of the abbot of St Gall), similarly stressed the importance of proper behaviour: during the meeting of the imperial court at Ravenna in 1231, for instance, the emperor greeted all those present in a manner befitting princes, but especially so the abbot, thus expressing the latter's special status.[26] That, during the mass concluding the Mainz *diet* of 1235 the princes remained standing in the emperor's presence may indicate similar norms of behaviour,[27] as may the fact that in May 1236, out of respect for the emperor, and so as not to delay him unnecessarily, the body of St Elisabeth was disinterred three days earlier than originally planned.[28] That encounters between groupings or individuals of different social status were guided by rules defining what was appropriate and inappropriate behaviour is, of course, not surprising. What matters, however, is that because this behaviour was displayed in public, it confirmed and strengthened the political structures of the realm: hence the regularity with which those who conformed to these norms were also those who acted righteously, while those who violated them all too often also acted in a sly, depraved or tyrannical manner.[29]

We should not, however, assume that this principle worked automatically. For those of good moral standing, too, could violate behavioural norms, but then they did so in order to underline their moral uprightness – as, for instance, Richard Marshal or the bishops did when courageously confronting the king in 1233–4. A different manifestation of this phenomenon can be observed in Germany. When in 1235 Henry (VII) finally submitted to his father, his self-abasement (he fell on his knees and sought to kiss the emperor's feet) indicated perhaps most clearly and visibly that his rebellion had failed. Just as important, however, was Frederick's breaking of the rules: he turned away his son, and did not allow him near his person.[30] Equally, that the emperor, on entering Worms a few weeks later, refused to proceed until after Bishop Landulf was no longer among the prelates greeting him, was a break with protocol: he acted full of anger and revenge. Henry's and Landulf's offence was such that it could not be forgiven, and their treatment has to be viewed in combination with the events at Worms and Mainz, which aimed to make public the punishment inflicted upon those who had betrayed the emperor, and to highlight the rewards awaiting those (like the citizens of Worms and the duke of Brunswick) who had remained loyal.[31] At the same time, as Theo Broekman has argued, contemporaries found Frederick's treatment of his son so difficult to grasp that they had to invent crimes to justify the king's humiliation and incarceration.[32] This interpretation is further strengthened by the striking fact that it was not until a few decades later that Frederick's handling of his son's rebellion was criticised by German observers, too. The breach of protocol was noted, but it was still endorsed.

What Rees Davies has called the 'theatre of politics',[33] the spectacle surrounding political events, was a constitutive element of politics. This was partly a matter of numbers – as we have seen, such occasions often involved audiences in the hundreds and thousands, and the acting out of what had been decided was one means by which that audience could be reached, and its backing received. Hence the insistence of Henry III, as conveyed by Agnellus, that Richard submit publicly, and Frederick II's decision to receive his son's submission only at Worms, before a larger audience. This public nature was especially important in the case of acts that confirmed, restored or established legal status: the audience, by its presence, was called upon to witness and confirm and, if necessary, enforce a decision. Moreover, while the written confirmation of these acts did, of course matter (and we will return to this point), it was through their enactment, the spectacle surrounding their confirmation and conclusion, that a large section of the politically significant could be reached. This was one of the reasons why knightings, for instance, were normally combined with parliaments and other public gatherings,[34] as had been the case with Gilbert Marshal in 1234.

Similarly, Gilbert's reconciliation changed his legal status (from outcast to familiar of the royal court), and, because it was so widely recorded, can serve as an example for some of the more complex elements that constituted a process of ritual communication. The rebels arrived to attend a *colloquium* called specifically for this occasion to Gloucester, where they were received with the kiss of peace, and restored to the ranks of the king's familiars and members of his household.[35] That they were received with the kiss of peace mattered – in fact, the *Annals of Dunstable*, for instance, stressed that the rebels were restored not only to their reputation, lands and all possessions (*famam, terras et possessiones universas*) but also (*insuper*) that they received the *osculum pacis*.[36] This was the final confirmation that no ill will rankled with the king, that they had been forgiven their past actions, and would now be able to hold the position of power which they had previously and unjustly been denied.

While the act of legal restitution mattered, it was the public kiss of peace that sealed the newly established concord. More importantly, and this brings us back to the display of emotion in acts of public communication, there was no indication of the grudging reluctance with which, infamously, Henry II had been reconciled to Thomas Becket, and which, to later observers, foreshadowed the archbishop's martyrdom.[37] Henry III extended his peace willingly and without hesitation. Furthermore, as part of the proceedings Gilbert Marshal was knighted by the king, installed as earl of Pembroke and showered with honours and gifts.[38] Proceedings lasted six days, a sign of the solemnity of the occasion. Gilbert's reconciliation thus publicly expressed his restoration to favour (and specific care had been taken to ensure a public of suitable size and composition), and it confirmed his status and standing within the realm (hence his being given many gifts and honours). This set-up was by no means unusual: when, in 1238, Simon de Montfort was reconciled to Richard of Cornwall, the barons of the realm had assembled with an armed entourage to treat the conflict between the two (which had arisen from Simon's secret marriage to Richard's sister). Simon publicly submitted to Richard and, at the request of various intercessors and offering many gifts, received the kiss of peace from the king's brother.[39] Acts of closure consisted of a written document, and a public ceremony publicising and confirming the act. More importantly, both were constitutive of its validity. An act of reconciliation would hardly have been effective if it remained secret (although exceptions, as Agnellus' offer to the Marshal illustrates, were, of course, possible), while much of the point of patronage was to make public the proximity of a political agent to the source of power and patronage, thereby to demonstrate his standing in relation to his peers, and to advertise his ability to secure grants, privileges, gifts and honours for himself and his men.

When, in 1238, the clergy of Oxford were reconciled to the papal legate, this restoration of concord was embedded in a series of ritual acts. The exact order and nature of these acts had been the subject of lengthy and detailed negotiations, and thus reveals another feature of symbolic communication. While some of the clergy involved were imprisoned, others had to assemble at a place three days distant from Oxford, and wait to be taken back into Cardinal Otto's favour. This left the details of their submission and reconciliation to be worked out (Matthew Paris, our main source for these events, did use *elaborare* to describe the process): the scholars were to assemble at St Paul's, about one mile from the legate's residence. They were to be accompanied by the English prelates (who were to walk on foot), and were to walk from St Paul's, bareheaded and without cloaks, to the bishop of Carlisle's residence (where Otto was staying). On getting there, they were to beg humbly for forgiveness, and were to be reconciled to the cardinal. This they did, and Otto not only lifted the interdict on Oxford but also issued a letter which confirmed that they had been forgiven, and that no infamy would arise from their actions.[40]

Details mattered: the distance to be travelled by the Oxford scholars, for instance, aimed to publicise their crime and contrition, and their humble appearance signified both the punishment they had suffered (appearing in the traditional guise of penitents) and their feeling of repentance. That they were accompanied by the English bishops mirrored the specifics of the situation – the scholars had, after all, attacked the entourage of a papal legate, thereby shaming their ecclesiastical superiors – and a role frequently performed by the English prelates: that of both intercessors, and of guarantors of settlements.[41] Otto, in turn, had his honour and status restored, and this restoration derived from the public humiliation and contrition on the part of the Oxford clerics. Their reconciliation with the legate was thus constructed as an elaborate quid pro quo. Moreover, the public act of reconciliation mattered more than its written confirmation: in the eyes of Matthew Paris, at least, Otto's epistle was little more than an afterthought, a gesture that added to the spirit of reconciliation without being constitutive of it.

This confirmatory element was equally evident in Germany. In 1234, for instance, the Frankfurt *diet* settled the question of how to pursue Conrad of Marburg's killers with a public procession, attended not only by the men allegedly behind the murder, but also the victim's brethren.[42] A similarly elaborate process of reconciliation was chosen at Worms in 1233, when Bishop Henry confirmed the privileges which, only a few years before, he had asked the emperor to repeal.[43] This process of confirmation was a drawn out one, testified to by a number of letters and charters. We thus have a copy of King Henry's letter, in which he urged the citizens to agree to a settlement, thereby safeguarding both his honour and that of the bishop,[44] as well as charters by the commune, the cathedral chapter and the king confirming the details of the agreement.[45] Just as important, however, was the symbolic enactment of this concord: bishop and townsmen assembled at Neuhausen outside Worms, where the citizens met the prelate on foot, and kneeled before him. Once the sentence of excommunication had been lifted, they returned to Worms, where they were soon joined by the bishop. The prelate then called together the citizens and, with all the clergy and townsmen present, the new town regiment was chosen. The consuls, in turn, vowed to act in consultation with the bishop, while he swore to maintain the town's liberties.[46]

The Worms example matters because it points to the complex relationship between written and non-written forms of communication. The ritual of confirmation, for instance, went beyond the text of the actual agreement. The authority of the bishop was symbolically restored (the townsmen submitted to him in public), and subtle variations in status continued to be maintained: when the consuls performed their oath of loyalty to the bishop, for instance, they had to do so themselves, while the bishop performed his oath not in person, but through one of his chaplains. We may also assume that the citizens' initial submission had deliberately been chosen to take place outside Worms. Otherwise, it would have signified a higher degree of episcopal authority than the citizens might have been willing to accept (by meeting outside the town walls, the bishop's spiritual authority was symbolically separated from his temporal lordship over the town). Equally, the agreement itself was ritually confirmed and enacted in Worms, at the bishop's behest (who addressed the citizens from a stage [*stega*]), symbolising both the bishop's authority and the restoration of concord. The ritual made public, confirmed and to some extent modified – and we will return to this – the restoration of concord between prelate and commune.

These examples also seem to confirm a basic premise of Gerd Althoff's work on ritual: such acts were the result of careful negotiation and planning, with every part of the ritual act pre-arranged and debated.[47] An example is the debate about how the citizens of Milan were to submit to Frederick Barbarossa in 1162 – what clothing they had to wear, whether they wore sandals, shoes or came barefooted and so on – and another is Frederick Barbarossa's reconciliation with Pope Alexander III in 1178.[48] Similar considerations played their part in London in 1238. Equally, the carefully choreographed reconciliation of the citizens of Worms and Bishop Henry in 1233 seems to suggest some more careful planning preceding its public performance. Failing to plan such acts could, after all, have disastrous consequences, as Henry (VII)'s failed submission in 1235 illustrates: with his act of public self-abasement he had sought to force the emperor's hand, and in 1235 Frederick was not willing to suffer attempts at blackmail, be they political, emotional or ritual. Equally, that Bishop Landulf was among the prelates greeting the emperor on entering Worms presupposed a degree of forgiveness which Frederick was not inclined to offer. Planning and negotiating a ritual act was one means by which success could be secured.

We have, however, encountered numerous incidents where acts of symbolic communication were used spontaneously, without prior arrangement or negotiation. That they did not always trigger the hoped for response thus underlines the importance of advance negotiations, but we should also keep in mind that actions were performed as a means of protest, of stating claims and of rejecting symbolic claims made by others, and that the main point of these acts was thus to have that objection heard and registered, without necessarily expecting that it would succeed. In fact, simply stating a claim could be enough. The repeated attempts by archbishops of York, for instance, to have their crosier carried before them in the province of Canterbury, thereby rejecting Canterbury's claim to primacy, and the equally frequent excommunication of the prelates by their superiors in Canterbury were hardly the result of extended negotiations, though they still allowed both parties to state their claims.[49] Ritual could be counteracted in other ways, too: by refusal to participate, or doing so grudgingly, as when, in April 1234, the English bishops assembled to hear mass at St Albans, and most of them sat away from des Roches.[50] These instances, too, were not pre-arranged and pre-negotiated.

Ritual and symbolic behaviour did not trigger an automatic response. Their effectiveness was dependent on context: they mattered as a means of communication, as a tool by which more complex concepts and agreements could be conveyed. By acting in a prescribed manner – for instance, by approaching the ruler humbly – those who did so certainly acted politely, but they also expressed the moral validity of their actions not only to those whom they approached but also, and perhaps more importantly, to those who witnessed that approach. Whether this triggered the hoped for result depended on a series of factors external to the act itself: the standing of the actor, his ability to inflict sanctions if his advances were refused, the expectations of the audience, and so forth. In some cases, especially when much hinged on a successful confirmation, matters had to be arranged beforehand, but there also were numerous cases when acting without prior arrangement either conformed to established precedent, was a risk worth taking, or the only option available. In fact, the majority of the cases we have been able to trace fall within that latter category: the approaches made by the Marshal and others, Hubert's clutching of his crucifix when taken from sanctuary, Peter de Rivallis appearing in clerical garb when asked to give account for his time in office, the behaviour of the count of Sayn at Frankfurt in 1234, and so on. Not all of them failed because they had not been negotiated in advance (the ability to ignore such gestures mattered, as Henry (VII)'s and Landulf's case illustrates), and a few of them succeeded despite a lack of advance negotiation (like Edmund Rich's approach to the king, or those causing a ruckus at Frankfurt; even Hubert was transformed from a fallen favourite into a martyr of justice and piety). That public acts of reconciliation mattered in a German context is thus hardly surprising, but how much they did in England certainly is. This also raises the question what the relationship between ritual and other forms of communication was. If they mattered as much in England as in Germany (and perhaps even more so), what was the relationship between symbolic and other forms of communication?

II

The relationship between symbolic and written forms of communication was symbiotic: one rarely worked without the other. When Bishop Henry was reconciled to the citizens of Worms, for instance, the public act of reconciliation would have had little effect, had it not also been based on a written document that clearly outlined the division of authority between bishop and commune. That compact, in turn, derived its validity from the fact that its clauses were recited and confirmed ritually and publicly. Similarly, when Duke Otto of Meran was confirmed in his claim to the advocacy of Benediktbeuren, the process of validation went through several stages, not unlike those at Worms.[51] Oral and written confirmations were equally necessary for the duke's election to become valid.[52] To these examples might be added a phenomenon explored by Claudia Garnier, who has traced a tendency in thirteenth-century Germany to produce written accounts which outlined exactly how a ritual confirmation of peace agreements had to be performed.[53] Similar agreements are difficult to find in England, partly perhaps because conflicts would have been conducted through different avenues (such as the royal courts), but the basic principle applied (hence perhaps also Cardinal Otto's separate written confirmation of his reconciliation with the Oxford clerics).

In other circumstances, ritual could be used to modify the contents of written agreements.[54] We have, for example, already noticed that the offer made to Richard Marshal by Agnellus entailed very different messages to be conveyed to different audiences. While on the one hand Richard was to throw himself at the king's mercy, thereby publicly confirming the illegitimacy of his actions, he was privately guaranteed safety of life and limbs.[55] There was, equally, a marked difference between the public reconciliation of the king and Richard's partisans, and the guarantees actually offered to the latter. As far as the narrative sources were concerned, reconciliation was whole and complete: the rebels were restored in all their possessions.[56] The records of the royal chancery paint a more varied picture: when, a few weeks after the formal reconciliation, Henry ordered the sheriff of Wiltshire to return several of Gilbert Basset's domains, Henry emphasised that Gilbert had approached his court 'to plead for our mercy'.[57] Similar statements had been made in the safe conduct issued to the rebels – they had come to seek the king's grace.[58] This may, of course, reflect chancery conventions, rather than the king's sentiments, but it does chime with the insistence we have encountered previously that those who wanted to be reconciled to the king had first to seek his forgiveness. This was not a matter merely of language, though, but also of content: the rebels' restoration was far from complete. Although Gilbert Marshal was assured that the king's anger and indignation would cease, and although he was granted all of his inheritance in England, Wales and Ireland, this restoration came with strings attached. The castle of Striguil (i.e. Chepstow), for instance, of central importance for the control of the Welsh marches and the earldom of Pembroke (and one of his family's most expensive and favourite castles), was given into the hands of Edmund Rich for safekeeping, and that at Dumas into those of Lucas of Dublin, where it would remain during the king's pleasure – a sour pill, even though it was sweetened with the promise that Henry would not claim the castles for himself. Gilbert and his brothers, furthermore, had to promise that they would not seek vengeance against those who had killed the Marshal.[59]

Lawrence and Edmund had, of course, been instrumental in bringing about this reconciliation, and their stewardship may thus have been a means of limiting Gilbert's ability to follow in his brother's rebellious footsteps while at the same time assuring him that these parts of his inheritance would not be used against him or his dependants. Even so, Gilbert was deprived of some of the most prestigious parts of his inheritance. Moreover, he fared well in comparison with some of the other rebels: Hubert de Burgh, for example, while being pardoned for his flight and outlawry, lost all those lands which had not come to him by inheritance. That is, in exchange for an unspecified but strictly limited sum, he would have to return all lands formerly in the royal demesne, including Montgomery castle and others, 'quit of the said Hubert and his heirs forever.' In addition, Hubert had to swear solemnly that he would not sue to be reinstated as justiciar.[60] Considering that Hubert's wealth and standing had largely depended on his ability to monopolise royal patronage, his restoration to full favour still deprived him of the means by which he had been able to secure and build his basis of political power.[61] This hardly amounted to the exultant terms of reconciliation used by the Dunstable annalist.

We do not possess detailed descriptions of how this ritual reconciliation had been enacted (apart from the kiss of peace, the many gifts received, and Gilbert's knighting and enfeoffment), but the impression it gave to those witnessing it was of a more wide-ranging and complete settlement than had actually been offered. It may also have been the case that the promise of a new start was to be made both politically and symbolically: within a few weeks of Gilbert's enfeoffment, Henry's new government embarked on what Nicholas Vincent has described as a programme of moral reform, clearly distancing itself from the practices of both de Burgh and des Roches.[62] Combined with Henry's very public display of grief at the news of Marshal's death, and the soon to follow expulsion from court of des Roches and his henchmen, this offered the opportunity to bring symbolic closure to the events of the past few years. Under these circumstances, a public display of forgiveness would have been difficult to avoid. This would also explain the carefully balanced restoration of lands evident in the administrative sources:

the more closely associated with the Marshal, the more generous the terms of peace. Hubert could thus hardly have expected a full restoration of his properties, given that his regime as much as des Roches' had been responsible for the abuses which the new government was now so keen to end. In short, then, the administrative evidence seems to contradict what we know about the symbolic elements of the 1234 reconciliation only if we fail to view them as part of a larger whole. What mattered were the promise of a new start, and the restoration of full royal authority. Both the ritual and the administrative context of Gilbert Marshal's enfeoffment stressed this point, but they emphasised different parts of this message, and did so to different audiences.

Bishop Henry's reconciliation with the townsmen of Worms followed a similar pattern. There, too, the symbolic element – with its emphasis on the prelate's hierarchical superiority – modified the written agreement. Henry's standing and *honor* were maintained, while also granting the townsmen a level of autonomy which previously he had been reluctant to condone. There also were, however, important differences. While in Worms part of the process included a public reciting of the agreement itself, with the exception of the 1225 reissue of Magna Carta, no similar reciting of written agreements is recorded in the English sources. This points to more profound differences, as does the detail with which the Worms *Chronicon* reported the symbolic context of the agreement, while, at the same time, studiously avoiding to record the text itself: in Germany, it seems, the procedural context of an act of confirmation was sometimes given greater weight than the actual content. This raises questions about the relative importance of symbolic and written forms of communication. Was this, though, a specifically German phenomenon?

The degree to which Roger of Wendover and other chroniclers ignored the fiscal and administrative apparatus of royal lordship remains striking. The Marshal rebellion, for instance, was portrayed as a conflict that pitched aliens against the *homines naturales*, and very little was said about the intricacies of royal administration, or the bureaucratic and legal lead up to the revolt. That much of the rebellion centred on the validity of royal charters, the king's ability to revoke or amend earlier grants, barely registered. This does not mean that chroniclers were not interested in administrative materials or procedures: Matthew Paris, for instance, produced a whole appendix of documents to his *Chronica Majora*, and Wendover even included the text of Magna Carta,[63] the Forest Charter,[64] the mandate confirming the appointment of twenty-five barons to oversee the Great Charter's enactment,[65] and the letter patent to the sheriffs ordering that the Charter be publicised and abided by.[66] Similarly, later in the thirteenth century, the Provisions of Oxford of 1258, one of the key documents leading up to the Baronial Wars of 1263–5, survive in the *Annals of Burton*,[67] rather than the royal archives. Clearly, chroniclers were aware of the importance of legal documents, but reported and recorded administrative processes only once they deemed them sufficiently important. This marked an important shift from the twelfth century, when cartulary like chronicles had been far more common.[68] The exception to this rule was local disputes: when, in May 1229, Henry III visited Dunstable, the prior humbly petitioned him to restore peace between the monks and the town.[69] The king appointed a commission to investigate and propose a compromise. Although that settlement was accepted by the citizens' representatives, the citizens themselves rejected it, and the case was thus brought before the royal courts.[70] The quarrel soon escalated, including attacks on the abbot's fields and horses, and the citizens threatening to sell their lands and settle elsewhere. Successive attempts by royal officials, including the chancellor and justiciar, to resolve the issue failed, and it was not until another party – John, the archdeacon of Bedford – got involved that a settlement could finally be reached: in exchange for a payment of £100, the prior conceded the citizens their privileges, and peace was restored.[71] The parallels with some of the cases Henry (VII) had to tackle are intriguing, as are the differences (approaching the king in England was an opening salvo, rather than something to be done after all other means had been exhausted). What matters in the present context, though, is what it tells us about the kind of administrative process chroniclers tended to record. The Dunstable case shares with the majority of those that they fell outside the normal workings of royal bureaucracy: this was not a case that resulted in a clear and unanimous victory, but a laboured compromise, defying even the king's authority. The stages by which it had been reached, and its contents thus needed recording. Similar reasons may have played their part in the recording of documents like Magna Carta, the Provisions of Oxford or the Laws of Merton: they fell outside the normal procedures of royal administration of justice (and we will return to this point).

This also marks a contrast with the German experience, although one that played itself out on a different level. The 1235 *Reichslandfrieden*, for instance, exactly the kind of document English chroniclers would have copied, does not survive in the chronicles and annals. Nor do charters and documents, and, as in England, the cartulary like texts of the twelfth century became less fashionable.[72] At the same time, considerable time was spent on describing the procedural context of agreements and privileges, or at least on stressing its importance, and this focus was by no means limited to works of history alone. Henry (VII) had sought to legitimise his uprising by painting a clear contrast between his own scrupulous adherence to legal norms, and his father's wilful disregard for them. The emperor may have felt a similar need to justify his treatment of the king with reference to clear legal norms (hence the lengthy middle sections of the *Reichslandfrieden* dealing with the treatment to be meted out to rebellious sons), and he also did so in his proceedings against the duke of Austria.[73]

This focus is even more pronounced once chronicles and annals dealt with conflicts and disputes on a local level, and it is there that differences with the English experience are most pronounced. We have already seen how, at Worms, the *Chronicon* emphasised the various steps leading to the settlement with Bishop Henry. Equally, one of the issues discussed at the 1234 Frankfurt *diet* had been the clash between the archbishop of Mainz and the citizens of Erfurt. Unlike in Worms, the conflict had emerged not over town governance, but the extent to which the archbishop could demand military and fiscal aid.[74] The Dominican chronicle of Erfurt followed the proceedings in considerable detail and while, similarly to Worms Chronicle, it failed to record the exact content of the agreement,[75] it nonetheless emphasised the procedural aspects of successive attempts to resolve the conflict, including the names of those who guaranteed the final agreement.

The reasons for this emphasis are manifold. It certainly reflects the geographically more limited focus of thirteenth-century German historical writing. That restriction was not, however, one of fashion, convention or literary preference alone, but echoed fundamental political structures of the late Staufen empire. These included the emperor's prolonged absence, but also the role which the king, for instance, was meant to perform (i.e. acting as an authority at least one step removed from that with which parties in conflict normally engaged). To some extent, in relation to Erfurt and Worms, the prelate performed a function resembling that of the king in England, and the charter granted by Bishop Henry that of Magna Carta. The charters which the bishop of Worms was or was not willing to confirm thus mattered more than the *Reichslandfrieden* or the procedures Frederick II applied in dealing with the duke of Austria (which is why the latter were recorded in Austria and Bavaria, but rarely elsewhere). This still does not explain, however, why the confirmation of the charter was recorded, but not its content, nor does it explain why such emphasis was put on the public confirmation of these agreements. A more developed system of record keeping on a communal level may be one explanation. More importantly, though, public acts of confirmation offered greater security for the continuing validity of written documents.

The monks of Benediktbeuren, for instance, combined a whole series of mechanisms, including acts of public and oral confirmation, with the charter confirming and recording these just one in a series of steps by which the duke's authority was bestowed, confirmed and curtailed. As in the case of Worms, particular emphasis was placed on the duke promising to respect customary restrictions on his authority, that he did so before a range of audiences, and after having recited these restrictions.[76] There were good reasons for this emphasis on the public and voluntary confirmation of privileges: in Germany, charters were revoked with remarkable ease. As the Worms *Chronicle* had emphasised, by the time the conflict with Bishop Henry had erupted, the townsmen had been in possession of several charters confirming their liberties, issued by both the emperor and Henry (VII), and confirmed by the bishop, too. The prelate, though, felt that they violated both his honour and that of his Church, and therefore decided to appeal directly to the imperial court, demanding that the privileges be revoked.[77] In this he succeeded. More importantly, what caused chagrin at Worms was not that the emperor had annulled his own grant, but that Henry had requested that he do so. While Frederick merely did what he was meant to do, the bishop treacherously sought to curtail the freedom of his flock.

This is not to say that charters had no validity: that Henry (VII) had complained that Frederick kept revoking or amending his charters suggests he set some store by them. Similarly, in November 1234, Frederick explicitly restored those grants which he had previously made to the margrave of Baden, and of which he had been deprived by Henry (VII): they remained written guarantees of promises and confirmations of gifts.[78] Equally, charters could not be revoked at a ruler's whim: when, in the *Reichslandfrieden* of 1235, Frederick rescinded all grants from the imperial domain made since his father's death in 1197, this could only be done because the *diet*'s decrees had been issued with the full support and at the behest of the princes; when Duke Frederick of Austria was deprived of his imperial fiefs, this was done after judgement had been passed by the princes; and even in 1231, the Worms *Chronicon* was eager to stress, the citizens' privileges were revoked only after lengthy discussion during an imperial *diet*, with the consent and at the advice of the princes. Even so, just because a privilege had been issued in writing did not mean that its validity was guaranteed. When, in November 1234,

Frederick issued to the archbishop of Mainz a privilege which, only three years before, he had issued to the commonality of the German princes, and when he did so to reward the archbishop's loyalty, this implies that individual confirmation of a general grant was still deemed necessary,[79] as does the fact that the citizens of Erfurt had their rights confirmed both by the emperor (in July 1234)[80] and his son (in September 1234).[81] The more confirmations and the more frequent, the better.

Let us be careful, though, about what this means: we are not talking about the arbitrary overturning of legally valid promises, some form of incipient absolutism. Rather, the ease with which charters could be revoked, or the desire to have multiple confirmations, normally reflected little more than the somewhat haphazard realities of imperial administration and political organisation. There was no central archive against which grants could be checked, and the majority of the surviving imperial charters thus confirmed earlier grants, made out by a ruler's predecessors (which did not mean that written documents lost validity on the grantor's death, but simply that an up to date record of claims was needed). What this also signified, and more importantly so, was that charters were often issued at the recipient's request, with the necessary documentation presented to the imperial court for confirmation. While this does not explain all the cases in which Frederick revoked his own charters (when, in 1238, for instance, he annulled the privileges which, only two years before, he had granted to the citizens of Worms, this reflected a rapprochement between bishop and emperor, and changing political priorities on Frederick's part, rather than the messiness of his chancery),[82] it highlights a general pattern, and one that further contextualises Henry (VII)'s complaints to the bishop of Hildesheim: much depended on the ability to make one's case before the court, and hence also the rush with which both the citizens of Erfurt and the archbishop sought to have their case heard at Frankfurt.[83] The Germans were not victims of imperial administration, but sought to use it to their own advantage: hence Bishop Henry's decision to have the townsmen' privileges rescinded just as Frederick was turning his attention to what he considered the evils of communal movements in Germany.[84]

All this bring us back to the question why an act of settlement, especially its ritual context, was recorded, but not the terms of the settlement itself. The problem was not that the written document was difficult to access – in most cases it was not – or that it did not matter – it clearly did (hence the need to have it revoked or amended) – but that it provided an insufficient guarantee on its own. The public restoration of concord, by contrast, bound all the parties involved into upholding what they had agreed, and did so at least in part because of the number of witnesses. Similarly, that this ritual confirmation avoided any display of pressure, and that it emphasised the voluntary nature of the act, ruled out the option of claiming that it had been consented to by force. Bishop Henry's participation was thus at least in part designed to prevent him from playing a similar trick on the townsmen again. It was perhaps for the same reason that those who had brought about a settlement, who had negotiated a compromise and had overseen its confirmation, were listed by name: both the Worms and the Erfurt sources stressed the role of the count of Leiningen and the king, and of the landgrave of Thuringia and the clergy of Erfurt respectively. Arbitrators also acted as guarantors of an agreement, and could be called upon if either party violated its terms.[85] Concluding a settlement in public thus added yet another level of security. The charter mattered, but recording the steps by which it had come about, who had negotiated it, and how it had been confirmed, protected its content. In the Worms case, we may assume, the problem was not that the charter had been difficult to access (in fact, it survives to the present day), but that means had to be found of holding Bishop Henry to abiding by its clauses, of ensuring that he would not seek to revoke or have cancelled out again what he had endorsed so willingly and publicly. If necessary, the historical record or the witnesses could be called upon to come to the townsmen's aid.

Let us return to the English example. We have seen that the procedural context of public agreements mattered more in Germany than in England, and we have also seen why. At the same time, we should remind ourselves that in England, too, charters alone were not always and not necessarily safeguard enough. While few of the chronicles refer to the revocation of royal grants as a factor in the Marshal rebellion – in fact, only the much later *Flores Historiarum* claim that the dispossession of Gilbert Basset had anything to do with the revolt, while Wendover makes only a passing reference to des Roches declaring invalid a charter which Hubert claimed protected him against prosecution, and the section in Bracton's *De Legibus* safeguarding royal charters was a later interpolation [86]– the administrative sources paint a different picture. Let us use the dispute over the manor of Upavon (which we have touched upon in Chapter 2) as example, which had pitched Gilbert Basset, a relative of the Marshal, against Peter de Maulay, an old companion of des Roches. The manor had been held in Norman escheat: after the loss of Normandy in 1204, those magnates who held lands both in Normandy and England were forced to choose between Phillip Augustus, and their English king. Many decided to forfeit their

English estates, and these lands were then used to reward the king's followers and partisans in England. Most commonly, lands were held under the proviso that they would be returned to the lawful heir of these lands, if they returned to England. The specific case of Upavon was, furthermore, tied up in the rivalry between des Roches and de Burgh: having been a close dependant of the bishop of Winchester, Peter de Maulay found himself dispossessed in 1229, when the manor was granted to Gilbert Basset by royal charter. In 1233, however, the king decided to reopen the case, and granted the estate to Peter de Maulay.[87] As in the German case, royal charters could be amended and revoked to reflect changing priorities at court. Similar pressures, too, applied: in the Upavon case, the problem was not so much that Basset was dispossessed (after all, it could be argued that de Maulay had been unlawfully disseized), but the wider political context within which the property changed hands. For the Marshal, this meant that he was no longer capable even of protecting his own dependants and relatives. More generally, it pitched leading members of the aristocracy against des Roches and his allies, exacerbated already existing tensions, and thus replicated, on a much wider scale, the problems faced by Richard Marshal. That de Burgh had only some of his estates restored in 1234, should also warn us against exaggerating the longevity of royal grants – the former justiciar's dispossession was legitimised, irrespective of earlier privileges that had protected him from prosecution or dispossession.

At the same time, the more elaborate bureaucratic and judicial apparatus at the king's disposal also put greater restraints on him: property transactions and royal grants were easier to trace, the procedures by which lands could be claimed and administered were more clearly delineated and more easily followed. It would have been almost impossible, for instance, for the prior of Dunstable to play the kind of trick on his townsmen that Bishop Henry had played on those of Worms. Equally, even if he had wanted to, Henry III would have found it very difficult to emulate the emperor's 1235 Mainz decree and simply revoke all grants that had been made since 1216: there was already an in-built safeguard limiting the validity of grants made during his minority (hence the need to reissue Magna Carta in 1225), while the judicial apparatus of royal lordship was more clearly separated from the royal person than had been the case in Germany. It also explains why the symbolic confirmation of administrative documents was less frequently recorded in England: there were other and more effective ways of securing one's rights and possessions. The public ritual accompanying acts was only relied upon when the normal processes of royal administration and justice would have been insufficient – for instance, when the king or those close to him were party to a dispute, or when the legitimacy of the process itself was in doubt. In those cases, the public restoration of concord mattered, and it mattered for the same reasons as in Germany: it bound those who agreed to a settlement as much as those who were witness to it.

III

Symbolism mattered because it allowed messages to be conveyed more succinctly and to a larger audience than could be reached by written communication alone. It expressed status, proximity and influence, but also moral character, ideas and values. It did not always work: messages might be disputed or rejected, and, like any means of communication, it was dependent on outside factors – the political clout of those performing it, for instance, their standing with the audience and so on. It was also just one among several means of communication. In some cases, written documentation proved more effective, but this did not mean that we should assume a clear dichotomy between something archaic and numinous (ritual) and something modern and rational (written communication). Both were used depending on their usefulness and likelihood of success. The relationship between the two was symbiotic, and one could be used to reinforce, but also to qualify the other.

Nor, as we have seen, was it necessarily the case that ritual mattered more in Germany than England. As far as the narrative sources are concerned, symbolic actions were given greater weight by English chroniclers than their German counterparts. This had, of course, something to do with the relative length of their writings, but cannot be explained solely by Wendover's or Paris' more loquacious nature. Equally, that German chroniclers spent relatively more space on describing the procedural aspects of politics did not reflect a more legalistic outlook. Rather, it echoes the differing structural features of the respective realms, as well as basic conventions of historical writing. Each group of chroniclers focused on very different levels of political action, and for very different audiences. In England, the audience for which Wendover, for example, wrote, is difficult to ascertain, but seems to have included primarily his own community and its patrons, and his writing was intended to provide a general account of regnal politics, of the affairs of the realm as a whole. This also determined the amount and the kind of information he had at his disposal, and, as we have seen in the previous chapter, frequently led to an idealised depiction of how events should have unfolded rather than necessarily how they did unfold. Equally, chronicles with a more limited geographical horizon – such as the *Margam Chronicle* or the *Annals of Dunstable* – still focused to a considerable degree on regnal affairs. The kind of events they did report were thus, furthermore, frequently those that had been designed to reach a wider audience and which, for these purposes, relied to a greater degree on ritual and symbolic acts of communication.

A similar phenomenon can be observed in Germany: the way local events (or those with local significance) were reported differed greatly from the way regnal affairs were described. We thus have somewhat formulaic accounts of Henry (VII)'s rebellion, indebted in equal measure to conventions of describing tyrannical lordship and the image Frederick II had painted of his son. Once local events were reported, by contrast, the historical record played a function as part of communal political and sometimes legal memory, a point of reference for the conduct and resolution of conflicts and disputes. Hence the comparatively detailed descriptions of events at Frankfurt in 1234, at Erfurt, or at Worms, of their public nature, and the emphasis on listing by name those who had brought about or who were to guarantee these settlements. This does not rule out an idealising function, as the Worms *Annales*' account of the citizens' loyalty to the emperor has demonstrated, but these accounts still served as part of an aide memoire for future use.

Approached in this manner, accounts of public communication also reveal something about underlying political structures. In the German case, we have yet another piece of evidence for the more fragmented and localised nature of political power, also for the continuing importance of imperial and royal authority. The latter has become particularly evident in the role played by written communication and documentation: charters might be overridden more easily if not accompanied by public acts of ritual confirmation, but they still required royal or imperial endorsement. This even applied to such instances as the Duke of Meran's role as advocate for the abbey of Benediktbeuren, where there had been no dispute, but where it was still deemed necessary to have the clauses of the appointment verified by the imperial court. In England, both the greater power of the king and the correspondingly stronger constraints on that power have become apparent: here, too, charters could be overridden, revoked or ignored, but the framework within which this could be done was increasingly limited by the professionalised nature of royal administration, and by the need to consult over the workings and practices of that administration. All this, furthermore, points to the final chapter of this book: we have discussed the ideals by which politics were judged, the venues within which politics were conducted and the means by which ideals, actions and settlements were communicated. In the process, we have seen how politics were not a concern for rulers, princes and prelates alone, but how they involved a larger section of society. It is to this wider social dimension of politics that we will now turn.

9
Townsmen, Clergy and Knights: the Public in Politics

We have considered the values by which actions were judged, and the role and function of the public as political events unfolded. That public has so far remained a shadowy body, a witness to events, but not a participant in them. This does not do justice to the reality of medieval politics, and this chapter is therefore intended to take a wider look at the personnel of politics, and the means these men had at their disposal. Who were they? How did they react, who were not themselves party to a conflict? What means did they have at their disposal? What, finally, does this add to our understanding of medieval politics, and what does it tell us about the differences and parallels between Staufen Germany and Plantagenet England?

I

Our reconstruction of events is inevitably dependent on the interests, prejudices and concerns of those who took it upon themselves to report them. The following cannot offer a comprehensive picture of the social dimension of medieval politics, but it can compensate for this by a greater depth of analysis. There will, for instance, be very little that can be said about the role of women. This is partly the case because in 1234–5, both Frederick and Henry III lacked a spouse (the former a widower, the latter still a bachelor), and one of the most common avenues into exploring female political agency, the role of the queen or empress,[1] is thus not available to us. In addition, though, our mostly clerical authors often lacked the access or the incentive to explore the role which women could, for instance, play within extended family networks. Henry (VII)'s queen thus makes no appearance in the record (except in rumours that the king was planning to divorce her). That this was not necessarily an accurate reflection of reality is suggested by Roger of Wendover's claim that, in 1233, Richard Marshal refused to attend a parliament because his sister (who was married to the king's brother) had warned him of des Roches' machinations.[2] Equally, the duke of Austria's mother played a major role in bringing about her son's downfall: her flight from the ducal court first to the king of Bohemia and then the emperor seems to have triggered proceedings against the duke,[3] and Frederick II was later to claim as one of the duke's many crimes that he had dispossessed and expelled his mother, and would even have imprisoned her, had she not been able to escape to Prague.[4] All this provides tantalising glimpses of women's political role, or their part in the moral discourse of politics (as someone to be protected and honoured), but glimpses are all we will be able to retrieve.

Gender roles and gender perspectives limit the evidence at our disposal, and so do social norms. Some groups thus provided a convenient shorthand for moral values, or they are used to voice truths which thus became common and self-evident. When Wendover described the Marshal as being killed by a rabble carrying pitchforks, was it a moral indictment of the earl's opponents, or an accurate reflection of the practices of warfare in thirteenth-century Ireland?[5] Or was it both, and, if so, how can we draw the line between historical fact and its literary application? Similarly, when Matthew Paris had the blacksmith, commissioned to produce the chains for de Burgh's imprisonment, offer a long list of the former justiciar's deserts, this may indicate a surprising awareness of high politics among thirteenth-century artisans,[6] but it may also be a rhetorical figure used to highlight the injustice of de Burgh's treatment, recognised as such even by the king's most common subjects. There is no way of knowing, and the best we can therefore offer is a reasonably plausible picture about some of the groups involved in the conduct of politics, and about some of the roles they were said to have performed. On this occasion, I would like to focus on three of these: townsmen, clergy and nobles, each representing a different strand of contemporary political society, and each highlighting some of the underlying structures defining English and German politics in the thirteenth century.

II

That townspeople played a prominent role was by no means peculiar to the thirteenth century, at least not with regard to such major settlements and commercial centres as London or Cologne.[7] The 1230s were also a period of transition, and equally so in England and Germany. It is also a development which, in an English context at least, has so far not attracted the interest of many historians. These were years when not only increasing numbers of towns were founded, or where small market places assumed the privileges and rights of towns, but also when the political role of cities within the realm began to change. This manifested itself, for instance, in an increasing number of conflicts between towns and their lords or neighbours (such as the ones at Dunstable), and also with a more formalised political role, which began to take full shape within the decades after 1233–4.[8] This echoed developments in Germany: within a few decades of 1234–5, with the partial exception of Cologne, the kind of privileges the men of Worms had secured for themselves in 1233 had become fairly common. Similarly, the political role of towns had begun to change: in 1256, for instance, the Rhineland towns took it upon themselves to oversee the election of a new king,[9] and after 1273, Rudolf of Habsburg was increasingly dependent on the support and backing of towns not only to establish his grip on the throne but also to equip and finance his governance of the Empire.[10] We are thus able to paint a snapshot picture of a period of profound political change, still rooted in the practices of the twelfth century, but already pointing to those of the fourteenth.

Townspeople mattered because of the size of their populations and the wealth in their coffers. They provided part of the public without which, as we have seen, politics could not be conducted. This was especially pronounced in England, where London and the Londoners assumed a far greater importance than the citizens of any single German town. While the townsmen of Erfurt, Cologne, Worms and so on certainly mattered, no single urban centre dominated politics to quite the same degree, nor did the peripatetic nature of German kingship allow for one town or city to assume as central a function. London's political role expressed itself in a variety of ways: the Londoners had been listed by Wendover among those who, in 1232, contributed to the fall of de Burgh by accusing him of having one of their citizens hanged without trial.[11] When in 1238 the conflict between the king and his brother Richard erupted, Matthew Paris singled out the citizens of London as among those urging the king to adopt his brother's stance – presumably, because they carried particular weight with the king.[12] This political weight was rooted in the townsmen's proximity to Westminster, the centre of Henry's financial and juridical administration, and also in their sheer number, and processions and assemblies of the Londoners thus formed an integral element of English politics.[13] They could thus be used both to strengthen royal control, and to undermine it. After Hubert de Burgh escaped from prison, for instance, Henry had been planning to order the mayor of London to arm his citizens in pursuit of de Burgh. According to Wendover, the earl of Chester warned against this, as an armed mob might then decide to side with de Burgh.[14] This may, of course, be a statement not dissimilar to that of Matthew Paris' blacksmith (even those close to the king saw the injustice of de Burgh's imprisonment), but it also echoes the fact that the Londoners played a very real and palpable political role, as they had done in 1216 (when they had welcomed Prince Louis of France) and were to do again in 1264 (when they supported Simon de Montfort and the rebels).

As far as other towns are concerned, communal identity seemed to define itself through proximity to the king, and did so to a larger degree and more frequently than in the metropolis. The evidence is, however, fragmentary. In 1234, the citizens of Cardiff gave hostages to the Marshal. This may have resulted from a lack of choice but may indicate royalist tendencies.[15] Equally, the men of Bristol were so keen to intercept Hubert de Burgh that they sent a fleet to prevent him and Richard Siward from crossing the Severn: this may have had more to do with existing rivalries between the citizens and the Marshal, than with their stance towards the king.[16] The evidence from the *Annals of Winchester*, associated with the cathedral chapter, but still taking a strongly communal stance, is a little clearer. Their entry on the events of 1233–4 is rather laconic, and also stands out for its mutedly royalist stance: it simply records that de Burgh had been deposed and imprisoned, and replaced by Peter des Roches and de Rivallis, but there is little of the invective we have encountered in other sources. Similarly, while most chronicles describe Edmund Rich as having forced the king into submission, the Winchester annals inverted this and gave the episode a significant twist: the archbishop pacified all those who were against the king. It was not Henry who had to be brought back into the fold, but his opponents. Similarly, the initiative for des Roches' dismissal was said to have rested with the king, not his subjects. This is, in fact, and unsurprisingly for a history produced in the wider environs of Peter des Roches' own see, followed by a lengthy account of an attack by Richard Siward on the bishop's stable, and his subsequent excommunication and reconciliation – the latter, intriguingly, emphasising that peace was restored between the Church and the *civitas* of Winchester.[17] The text is too short and fragmentary, and too much in need of a critical investigation of its themes and provenance, to draw far-reaching conclusions. Nonetheless, while perhaps not fully supportive of des Roches, the

Annals of Winchester were certainly not critical of the king. Not Henry, but the Marshal's followers had to be brought to heel; not the archbishop of Canterbury, but the king had decided to dismiss des Roches from office (viewed, at least implicitly, as a good thing); and those crimes that were recorded were those of the Marshal's allies. All this at least seems to imply that in Winchester, loyalties, unusually, lay with the king, not the barons, and may thus also contextualise the (much later) remark by the *Annals of Oseney* that in the revolt Winchester (together with London and Oxford) belonged to the king.[18]

The impression of Winchester's royalist tendencies is strengthened further once we look at later entries. In 1243, for instance, the king sought to resist the installation of William Raleigh as bishop of Winchester, and could rely on the full backing of the townsmen, who refused to let William enter the town.[19] Similarly, when the feast in celebration of Edward the Confessor's translation in 1268 descended into turmoil (with the men of London and Winchester squabbling over who should provide the king's butler), the Winchester annals still represent this éclat in a manner that highlighted their traditional loyalty to the king (unlike, it is implied, the fickle Londoners).[20] We are, however, also fortunate in having at our disposal a relatively detailed narrative source, and this may assign undue significance to the men of Winchester. Annoyingly, Arnold fitzThedmar's chronicle of the sheriffs of London barely dealt with the events of 1233–4,[21] while the citizens of Cardiff, York or Bristol have left no similarly detailed record. Even so, we can see how communal identity was formed in relation to the king, and how it sought to appropriate proximity with the royal court in relation to rivals both local (the Winchester annalist implies there was antagonism between des Roches and the citizens, for instance) and elsewhere (as in 1269).

This complexity should alert us to the fact that internal politics could lead to a rapid change of allegiance, and to fronts emerging which appropriated existing tensions in the realm at large, rather than originating in them. This had been the case at Oxford in 1238, for instance, where opposition to the papal legate blended with lingering rivalries from the Marshal's revolt, and long-standing enmities between the university clerics, the bishop and the townsmen.[22] It would be impossible to deduce from these events a simple reading of political sympathies or attitudes. The Oxford riots are thus a useful reminder, too, that the political role of townsmen was often exercised not in relation to the affairs of the kingdom at large, but those between a town and its immediate lord. This may have been one of the factors underpinning the often-volatile relations between the Londoners and the king, and may also explain some of the difficulties which the bishops of Winchester experienced in their dealings with the townsmen. Such conflicts also dominated much of German politics during the 1230s. In fact, some of the problems which, in 1229, the monks of Dunstable had with the town's inhabitants were not at all unlike those facing Landulf in Worms, or the archbishop of Mainz in Erfurt, nor was how the king handled them. They also provide a warning example for how quickly local rivalries could become a matter of regnal politics. The dispute between the prior and the citizens went before the royal court (when Henry happened to visit Dunstable), but to no avail: the king appointed a commission to investigate matters, but its proposed solution to the conflict was rejected by the townsmen.[23] They did not reject the king's arbitration because they deemed his government to lack legitimacy, but because they were holding out for a better offer. Their refusal to abide by royal arbitration certainly had negative consequences: Henry III, quite obviously, was unable to settle the case, and the king's inability to pacify conflicting parties at court was in fact a recurrent theme with chroniclers. It was, however, born out of specific local needs, rather than because of the citizens' stance on matters of significance to the crown.

There was, though, one important difference between towns in England and Germany. In theory at least, and with the possible exception of Durham, all English towns were subject to the king, and it was up to the monarch to grant communal privileges and oversee them. In practice, local lords or bishops did, of course, exercise considerable control, at times rivalling and occasionally surpassing that of the ruler. In Germany, by contrast, towns were confronted with a variety of lords, and towns were founded as frequently by princes and prelates as the king – in fact, some major German towns, such as Munich, Freiburg or Berlin had emerged as princely foundations. In these cases, the emperor exercised limited authority, although he could seek to utilise internal tensions to his own benefit (hence his support for the citizens of Worms against Bishop Landulf). Other towns, by contrast, the so-called imperial cities, were directly subject to the emperor, and consequently exercised considerable control over their own affairs. In exchange, they had to provide services, both fiscal and military, and also received protection from the emperor. Free imperial status, while coveted and desirable as the thirteenth century drew to a close, also brought with it risks: pawning imperial cities to princes became a common tool of royal finance. At the same time, while we should be aware of these fundamental differences, we should not exaggerate them, especially not with regard to the period under consideration here. In the 1230s, the main difference between the English and German cases was one of degree rather than substance: German townsmen, too, defied the authority of their lords, and sought to safeguard their privileges by maintaining proximity to the king. Many of the conflicts which Henry (VII) had been asked to intervene in thus originated in disputes between ecclesiastical lords and their urban subjects – like those between the men of Erfurt and Worms and their prelates, or, though less well documented, between the men of Frankfurt or Oppenheim and their lords.[24] Similarly, in 1234, the refusal of the citizens of Worms to aid Henry (VII) stemmed less from loyalty towards Frederick II, than opposition to Landulf.[25] Matters were further complicated by the fact that the emperor's attitude towards towns was pronouncedly hostile. At best, they were granted privileges grudgingly, and only after the citizens had abased themselves in a manner befitting the majesty of both the emperor and their immediate lord.[26] Their political role was meant to be passive, providing a festive backdrop to the proceedings, as the Rhineland towns did during the progress of Isabella Plantagenet along the Rhine to Cologne, where she was paraded before the citizens before being escorted to one of the archbishop's palaces,[27] or during the imperial entry into Worms.

The limited role of towns extended to more formal pronouncements of royal policy. The *Confoederatio cum principibus ecclesiasticis* (alliance with the ecclesiastical princes) of 1220,[28] for instance, had largely curtailed the autonomy of German towns at the expense of their princely lords and neighbours, and many of these clauses were repeated in the *Constitutio in favorem principum* (Constitution on behalf of the princes) of Henry (VII) of 1231,[29] Frederick II's *Statutum in favorem principum* (statute in favour of the princes) of 1232[30] and the *Reichslandfrieden* of 1235.[31] In fact, while an older tradition in German historiography sought to establish a contrast between Henry (VII) as a friend of urban movements, and Frederick II as their inveterate opponent,[32] the contemporary evidence paints a more confusing picture. Both father and son, for instance, sought to strengthen the compromise reached at Erfurt in 1234.[33] Whatever support towns were able to receive depended on the position and influence of their lords and neighbours. Both Henry and Frederick thus on occasion revoked communal privileges, or granted them again if they had fallen out with a lord or town.[34] That is, the degree of autonomy they were willing to grant was dependent on the wider political gains they might therefrom derive.

Once we look beyond the immediate question of dealings between communes and the king or emperor, towns exercised a degree of autonomy far exceeding that of their English counterparts. Part of this had to do with the political structures of the empire. The conflict between the archbishop of Mainz and the citizens of Erfurt, for instance, had originated in the refusal of the townsmen to provide troops for the 1233 campaign against the duke of Bavaria.[35] In 1234, Henry III may have contemplated arming the Londoners, but this was highly unusual, as townsmen would not normally have provided a regular contingent of royal troops.[36] The rights demanded by the towns extended well beyond what English communes might have deemed worth fighting for: among the privileges which the citizens of Worms had to surrender again in 1238, for instance, was the right to mint their own coinage.[37] Towns were capable of rejecting, delaying or appropriating for themselves the privileges of their often ecclesiastical lords. They could also play a political role independent of either the king or their lord: the men of Erfurt, by refusing to provide troops, not only undermined the authority of the archbishop but also that of the king, while, as we have repeatedly seen, the townsmen of Worms were quite capable of choosing their allies according to the gains they hoped to make from them. They were not the passive bystanders as which they appear at Worms, or during Isabella's wedding procession.

This complex role also had repercussions for the performance of public acts of self-representation, or for the holding and organisation of *diets* or parliaments. Towns were a convenient location for the latter, partly because of their economic function (by being more easily able to accommodate several thousand visitors), but their inhabitants could also scupper, mould and influence the proceedings of these meetings. We have seen that to be the case in the conflict between Richard of Cornwall and Simon de Montfort in 1238 or that between the papal legate and the men of Oxford later that year. Similarly, during the early 1230s, the fall of Hubert de Burgh was attributed to the hostility of the Londoners, and there was perhaps a reason why the Marshal refused to attend parliaments or meetings of the king's court in London. In Germany, the evidence is more fragmentary, but we should remind ourselves of the – admittedly futile – pleas by the men of Worms on Landulf's behalf, or the speed with which Henry (VII) was removed, first, into the safety of the duke of Bavaria's lands, and, second, far away from the Alsatian heartlands of his revolt and their numerous towns and urban settlements. The location of the great acts of imperial self-representation during Frederick's sojourn should also be noted: they took place in places like Regensburg (the old ducal capital of Bavaria), Nuremberg (a centre of Staufen power, but one outside Henry's sphere of influence) and Worms (where the citizens' loyalties were self-evident), where Frederick was unlikely to encounter resistance or his son to find much sympathy. That the great *diet* of 1235 took place in Mainz, rather than, as announced the year before, Frankfurt, may, of course, reflect the turmoil of Henry's revolt, and it may have been a reward for the archbishop, who, once a loyal supporter of the king, quickly threw in his lot with the emperor,[38] but it may also indicate a degree of suspicion about the loyalties of the men of Frankfurt (who were too frequent and late recipients of the king's largesse).[39] Towns and communes may not have been accommodated within the formal structure of imperial politics, but they still exercised a clear and palpable influence over them.

The reality of communal power also differed from the ideology of royal and imperial lordship. Neither English nor German chroniclers, for instance, assigned towns much of a role in establishing the moral and political norms against which they judged the events they recorded. Like the rulers, they accorded townsmen at best a passive role. They figured as victims of Henry (VII)'s tyranny, which manifested itself in demands for hostages, or as a convenient means of voicing self-evident truths critical of the king (indirectly, for instance, in the earl of Chester's fear that arming the Londoners would result in them supporting de Burgh), but they did not themselves warrant coverage as political actors. This did, of course, reflect the reality of early thirteenth-century politics (even a passing glance at, for instance, the chronicle accounts of Rudolf of Habsburg's reign or that of Edward II will indicate how much the situation was to change). It perhaps also reflected the concerns of mostly clerical members of communities which were at odds with townsmen (true of Winchester, for instance, Dunstable or Cologne, but with the important exception of Worms), or in houses either sufficiently distant from urban settlements (Marbach, Wendover, Margam, etc.) or with urban settlements of limited significance (St Albans). The events we are dealing with here occurred in a moment of transition, a period of profound change, and this is reflected in the imagery of politics as much as its practice.

III

Chronicles do, however, deal in considerable detail with clerical and secular elites, and there a more complex image emerges. Let us begin by looking at the role of bishops. We have already seen how (even without des Roches) prelates played a profoundly important role during the Marshal rebellion. Next to Richard Marshal, much of the criticism of the regime had been voiced by the bishop of Salisbury or Lucas of Dublin, who had pleaded on the Marshal's or de Burgh's behalf, had excommunicated those attacking de Burgh and had repeatedly pleaded with the king to mend his ways and dismiss his ministers. Finally, the revolt had been concluded when the new archbishop of Canterbury, Edmund Rich, threatened to excommunicate not only the king's ministers but the monarch, too. Wendover's annals in particular are littered with instances of opposition voiced by the episcopacy.[40] Equally, though, it is worth noting that bishops and prelates remained at the royal court, and continued to provide services as demanded, even after the earl and others had left it in protest.[41] They did so not out of fear, but, first, in order to perform the duties which the Marshal had also claimed for himself (providing truly loyal counsel), and, second, to fulfil one of their most basic functions: to admonish, chastise and correct the king.

Standing up to the king was, in fact, the sign of a saintly prelate, and two of des Roches' most fervent opponents – Lawrence of Dublin and Edmund Rich – were later venerated as such. When, a few years after Edmund's death, Matthew Paris composed his *Life of St Edmund*, he stressed Edmund's resistance to royal encroachment on ecclesiastical liberties, and even portrayed the archbishop's journey to France in terms of political exile, but he also emphasised the saint's success in arbitrating and settling political conflicts, as interceding with the king and returning him frequently to the path of righteousness.[42] By then, this was already part of a long tradition: the theme of political exile had been stressed by the hagiographers of Thomas Becket, who, in turn, had looked back to St Anselm,[43] while the ability to win the king's ear, even against his wishes, the courage to counteract and change royal actions, had been a prominent theme in the cult of St Hugh of Lincoln.[44] This should be read not as rejecting royal power (Becket remained the rare though influential exception), but as reflecting the moral relationship between spiritual and secular authority. It was a prelate's duty to admonish, reprimand and correct those in power.

This role was not limited to hagiographical texts: earlier in the twelfth century, William of Malmesbury had constructed an image of royal lordship that depended on the moral supervision and instruction of rulers by their ecclesiastical subjects,[45] and this theme continued to permeate the historiography of Norman and Angevin England. In the thirteenth century, Stephen Langton, St Edmund's predecessor but one, had taken a similar line, even before his appointment to the see of Canterbury. While he was still a master at the University of Paris, he espoused a view of royal lordship which stressed the limitations of royal authority, and which apportioned responsibility to maintaining and enforcing these limitations to the clergy.[46] Similarly, once in England and once formally enthroned as archbishop, Langton, to use David d'Avray's words, 'had the opportunity to turn his thoughts into action in the world of real politics.'[47] He did so, first, by lending his backing to those who, in the years preceding 1215, sought to codify the limitations of royal authority,[48] and, perhaps more importantly, by taking the lead role in establishing the 1225 reissue of Magna Carta as the benchmark against which royal government continued to be measured for most of the thirteenth century, and as the tool by which resistance – including that of Richard Marshal – continued to be legitimised.[49] This is not to say that bishops always and willingly challenged their kings, but that, in 1233–4, the English prelates who did so acted within an established tradition of providing moral and political oversight over the king and his officials.

There is also little about this that was unusual: moral guidance and instruction had been an integral part of the role of bishops and ecclesiastical leaders since the inception of an organised Church. It had been one of the planks on which the theory of ecclesiastical supremacy emerging since the eleventh century had been built, and a means by which that supremacy could be expressed and applied. In fact, as John Baldwin and others have demonstrated, similar ideas had been espoused in scholastic debates from at least the second half of the twelfth century.[50] Even so, there remains an often stark contrast between theoretical precept and political reality. The degree to which English bishops implemented these moral precepts, the degree to which they formed part of the ethos of episcopal leadership in thirteenth-century England remains striking, and is, in fact, one of the key areas where the political culture of thirteenth-century England differed from that of contemporary Germany.

Prelates played an important political role in Germany, too. From 1257 onwards, a college of electors began to emerge, whose duty it was to choose an emperor-elect, and nearly half its members were churchmen (the archbishops of Mainz, Cologne and Trier), and even before then, bishops had played their part. Henry (VII)'s first guardian had been Archbishop Engelbert of Cologne, while the chief recipient of Frederick's epistles had been the archbishop of Trier; Henry had turned to the bishop of Hildesheim for support; and those leading the campaign against the duke of Austria after the emperor's departure in 1237 had been the bishops of Bamberg, Passau and Freising.[51] Nonetheless, there is little indication that prelates assumed a similarly prominent role in admonishing and correcting royal actions. The sole exception to this rule is a short comment in a later thirteenth-century history of the archbishops of Trier, which reported that Henry (VII) had been persuaded by the bishops to surrender before his rebellion got out of hand.[52] Princely opposition towards Henry had been voiced primarily by the secular princes, with the episcopacy divided in their allegiance (although mostly supporting Frederick), while the few incidents of intercession reported in the chronicles do not compare to the English examples we have encountered. In May 1235, for instance, Herman of Salza, the master of Teutonic knights, was the only named individual to have pleaded Henry's case with the emperor (although the continuator of Godfrey of Viterbo claimed that others in Frederick's encourage also pleaded for the king).[53] When Frederick, on entering Worms a few weeks later, was met by a procession of bishops, including Landulf, and refused to proceed as long as the bishop of Worms remained present, protest was voiced not by the prelates present (whose reaction was not recorded), but the citizens.[54] In the first case, protest was voiced by one of the emperor's closest allies, and in the other by those who, having suffered at Landulf's hands and on Frederick's behalf, had every reason to remain hostile to the prelate, but who through their intercession must therefore also have hoped for greater success. In Germany, princes of the Church were not meant to play the part of a ruler's most loyal and critical friend to quite the same degree as their English counterparts.

Anecdotal as this evidence may be, it nonetheless highlights the more limited role of bishops in the politics of Staufen Germany. A similar picture emerges from historical writings: in the eyes of their biographers, few German bishops were distinguished by their opposition towards royal action. They might well resist imperial advances, but then such episodes were normally embedded in a more general narrative about resisting encroachments of a see's lands, rights and privileges, and were not specifically directed at the emperor.[55] The Cistercian monk Caesarius of Heisterbach's *Vita* of Engelbert of Cologne provides a case in point: it followed the model of the Becket corpus in presenting the archbishop as a martyr for the liberty of the Church, but Engelbert's martyrdom was inflicted not by the emperor, but the archbishop's relatives in a dispute over family lands.[56] If bishops excelled and merited the odour of sanctity, it was because of their emphasis on pastoral care, or because they resisted those more immediately a danger to them and their flock (princes and neighbours). Partly perhaps because German bishops exercised more secular authority than their English counterparts (being, in many respects, indistinguishable from their lay counterparts), moral guidance and leadership seem to have been directed more commonly at their subjects and immediate neighbours, not the emperor.

At the same time, matters may have been slightly different in the case of the king of the Romans. When Frederick wrote to the archbishop of Trier in the summer of 1234, he not only announced his intention of visiting Germany the following summer, but also, and very specifically, asked the prelate to admonish and guide Henry towards the proper exercise of kingship.[57] Similarly, much of Henry (VII)'s letter to the bishop of Hildesheim can be read as revealing an image of episcopal authority not unlike the one we have encountered in England: to admonish and plead with the emperor, and to make him return to the proper way of dealing with his son. Bishop Conrad was expected to perform the very role for which Roger of Wendover and Matthew Paris had praised the archbishop of Canterbury.

As far as the emperor was concerned, there was, however, an institution which did perform functions not unlike those of the English prelates: the papacy. Both pope and archbishop conveyed the legitimacy to rule on their respective ruler by presiding over the installation ceremony, and both, to some extent, derived therefrom a right to spiritual and moral oversight. This was, in fact, one of the key elements in the writings of papal reformers from Gregory VII in the eleventh-century onwards.[58] We should also notice the picture of the relationship between Frederick II and Pope Gregory IX painted by the latter's hagiographer: the pope was regularly represented as offering guidance to Frederick, acting as a spiritual friend and mentor, who used spiritual sanctions against Frederick only after all other means of correction had failed. More importantly, Frederick's lapses were political as well as moral. As in England, punishments and reprimands were offered in a spirit of friendship, of loving yet stern admonition.[59] This offers a more complex picture of the German bishops: they were caught in a complex web of obligations and expectations, of roles, demands and duties; they were secular lords, princes of the empire, spiritual leaders of their own communities, who owed obedience and counsel to both king and emperor, and who, to some extent, competed with the papal court in performing their admonitory functions.

Equally, the pope, like the archbishop of Canterbury, to some extent compensated for his lack of palpable political power by a renewed claim to moral and spiritual authority and oversight. That moral authority, in turn, was dependent on the moral make-up of those who sought to exercise it. Hence the emphasis with which, later in the thirteenth century, Matthew Paris, for instance, maligned the public demeanour of Archbishop Boniface of Savoy,[60] and with which, in the context of 1233–4, Wendover and others outlined des Roches' immorality. The latter in particular presents us not only with a clear contrast between the bishop of Winchester and the Earl Marshal, but also between the prelate and his episcopal colleagues. The Earl, Lucas of Dublin, Edmund of Canterbury and the bishop of Salisbury performed a function it should have been des Roches' duty to perform, and they acted from a superior plane of mortal rectitude. This moral dimension of episcopal involvement in politics also defined how other members of the clergy could participate in the affairs of the realm.

The evidence is too fragmentary to allow us to say much about canons, parish priests or even most monks. An exception has to be made, though, for the Friars, and members of the military orders. The political role of the Friars in England has so far been described largely with reference to the 1250s and 1260s, when John of Darlington acted as the king's confessor, when various Friars sided with the barons against the king, and circumstantial evidence suggests that the thought of the Franciscan Adam Marsh, for instance, influenced the political actions of Simon de Montfort in taking over the leadership of the baronial reform movement.[61] Little work, by contrast, has been done on this earlier period. Within roughly a decade of their arrival, the Friars had begun to play a prominent political role, hardly less significant than that of the prelates. They usually acted as intermediaries, as envoys and emissaries, not (with one exception) as party to the conflict. Their role was that of a moral arbiter, trusted by both sides, which could voice opinions and criticism that others could not, or that was to be heeded more easily if voiced by a friar.[62] One of the defining moments in the conflict between Henry and the Marshal was a speech by a humble Friar during the June 1233 parliament at Oxford. Before the assembled barons and prelates, the Dominican preached that peace could not be restored as long as Peter des Roches and his nephew remained among the king's councillors. The context of this episode is worth noting: this was one of the meetings which the Marshal had refused to attend, and it was after hearing the friar, Wendover claims, that many urged the king to seek reconciliation with Richard and his partisans.[63]

As in similar cases, we should maybe not take this to be an accurate report of the Dominicans' involvement in English politics: what mattered was that someone from an order renowned for its piety, religious fervour and moral uprightness chided Henry III, and that, although he was able to sway the barons, his advice went unheeded by the king. Moreover, these were warnings from the member of a religious order to which Henry had extended his patronage almost as soon as they had arrived in England, and the king's generosity continued to be bestowed upon the order.[64] Wendover's episode about the meeting between Agnellus and the Marshal also gains meaning in this context. Although the Friar's speech has to be used with caution, the *Flores Historiarum*, in a passage interpolated in Matthew Paris' revision of Wendover lists the Dominicans and Franciscan as those whom, jointly with the bishops and other members of the clergy, the Marshal had sent as his emissaries to speak out against Henry's actions.[65] Similarly, the *Tewkesbury Annals* claim that, in April 1234, Edmund Rich had sent bishops and friars to both the king and the Marshal, in an attempt to restore peace between the king and his magnates.[66] That is, both parties drew on the Friars in equal measure, and, more importantly, their services were also called upon by those who sought to resolve the conflict. Dominicans and Franciscans were considered best suited to perform this task.

These were early days for the Friars, and they still basked in favour among Benedictine and Cistercian monks who render contemporary events (and who would take a considerably more hostile view once the mendicants became more firmly established).[67] Equally, as recent arrivals on the political scene they were able to play a prominent role, since they had not yet aligned themselves with political factions (and had been patronised in equal measure by the king, des Roches and de Burgh, with Gilbert Marshal among the first significant lay patrons).[68] Like the bishops, the Friars derived their political authority from being perceived as standing outside the chief political divisions of the realm, and thus compensated with moral authority for what they lacked in political, economic or military clout. At the same time, the later development of their political role (in particular the support for de Montfort and the rebellious barons) points to the degree to which that neutrality changed, and the extent to which they, too, adopted the role of being to the king a critical friend.

This political role was unlike anything the friars exercised in Germany, where Dominicans and Franciscans make at best a passing appearance during these years. In 1234, for instance, they were singled out as among the participants of the Frankfurt *diet*, but then this was an event linked to the recent murder of Conrad of Marburg. At best, we might be able to surmise that they were already firmly integrated into German political society, as they were said to have intervened on the count of Sayn's behalf when he was accused of heresy. That the *Erfurt Annals*, compiled in Erfurt's Dominican convent during the 1260s, normally side with the townsmen when in conflict with the archbishop, may point in a similar direction. Otherwise, they hardly appear, and they certainly do not appear as confidantes of either the emperor or the duke of Austria or Henry (VII). At best, they make an indirect appearance in 1236, when Frederick wrote to Brother Elias, the then master general of the Franciscans, about his participation in the translation of St Elisabeth of Marburg, an early friend and supporter of the Dominicans and Franciscans, and one of the earliest examples for their impact on lay spirituality.[69] However, this document was also self-consciously fashioned as an expression of the emperor's piety, and assiduously avoided making reference to political events, instead focusing on the glory of the saint and the events of her translation. As in England, the political role of the Friars only developed fully during the final decades of the thirteenth century; but there was an important difference. Whereas in England, they easily slipped into an established tradition of clerical authority being called upon to chastise, admonish and correct the king, in Germany they came to prominence though not as kingmakers, so nonetheless as a group which was relied upon to mediate between the ruler and his subjects: Rudolf of Habsburg's bid for the throne would have been more difficult to pursue without the Friars' active support.[70] In fact, so prominent was their role in backing Rudolf, that a representative of Ottokar of Bohemia, Rudolf's chief rival for the throne, argued that the surest sign that peace and public order had been thrown into disarray was that there were too many friars 'mendicanting' about.[71]

Moreover, in the 1230s, the Friars faced competition from another religious order, closer to Frederick II: the Teutonic Knights.[72] This was partly related to the wider international politics of Frederick II – the Knights played an important role in the emperor's efforts in the Holy Land,[73] and even in his government of Sicily.[74] It also reflected an international role, frequently performed by members of the military orders. In England, for instance, Henry III frequently used Hospitallers and Templars in conducting diplomatic missions, or for financial transactions.[75] Similarly, Wendover reports rumours that Hubert de Burgh's treasures were kept by the London Templars.[76] Unsurprisingly, this was a function which, in Germany, fell to the Teutonic Knights. One of the emissaries escorting Isabella Plantagenet from England was thus a member of the order,[77] and the same individual would later repeatedly be sent to England in negotiations over Isabella's dowry.[78] Much of this, too, had to do with the influence which Herman of Salza, the master of the Knights, had with Frederick, and it was Herman, too, who had sought to exert this influence when Henry (VII) submitted at Wimpfen. Nor was this the first time Herman had acted as intercessor and go-between: he repeatedly did so in dealings between the emperor and the papal court, even after Frederick's second excommunication of 1239.[79] At least in this respect, his role resembled that of the Friars in England.

While the political role of the clergy and Friars thus reveals important structural differences between Germany and England, it also shows several shared features. Most importantly, the duty to provide moral and spiritual guidance. How successful such efforts were depended, of course, on regnal traditions, and on circumstances. Similar functions could also be exercised differently in relation to different groups: most importantly, while English prelates were praised above all for their willingness to chastise and criticise the king, in the imperial case this was largely a matter for the pope. When Henry (VII) thus asked the bishop of Hildesheim to plead on his behalf with the emperor, this was not to be a case of criticising Frederick's governance (which was what the English prelates did with Henry III), but to act as an intercessor, a morally and spiritually reputable go-between. Similarly, when unnamed bishops convinced Henry to submit to his father, they did so not as an exercise in administering moral chastisement, but as intercessors who pleaded for Henry to seek his father's forgiveness before it was too late (and Herman of Salza similarly acted as intercessor, not critic). It was in relation to the king (as opposed to the emperor), or in conflicts between nobles and towns and their neighbours and peers, by contrast, that the question of moral guidance came more fully to the fore. This moral dimension was equally evident in the case of the friars: they were considered to be of morally higher authority and hence more likely to be heard, or at least to speak with a morally more authoritative a voice than others. The ability to conform to and abide by ethical norms of political power mattered.

How successfully such ideals could be turned into reality was matter of context, and of the individuals involved. Henry III, for instance, would have found it very difficult to do anything but abide by the demands of his prelates. By the spring of 1234, des Roches had manoeuvred himself and his king into a corner from which only the bishop's dismissal would allow the king to escape. Even so, Henry's willingness to do just that enabled him to redeem himself morally and politically, show his adherence to basic norms of political behaviour, and thereby limit the political damage caused by the Marshal's uprising. In Germany, by contrast, Frederick was at the height of his power, and Henry's uprising presented him with an opportunity to press through claims which on other occasions would have been considerably more difficult to have accepted by his German subjects. He had no need to show mercy, and while he accepted the prelates' duty of providing moral guidance (by instructing the archbishop of Trier to offer it to the king), it was something that was needed not by the emperor, but his son.[80]

IV

What about the secular elites? In Henry (VII)'s case, the princes appear as victims or fellow-villains, rarely as agents. This reflects the specific circumstances of 1234–5: Frederick's return was an event that overshadowed the role played by anyone else, with the exception of his eldest son. It also reflects the limitations of the evidence, which by it very nature stressed the importance of ecclesiastical princes and institutions, but it is also in ecclesiastical archives that many of the documents and letters survive which we can use to complement the accounts of chroniclers. We may assume, for instance, that the archbishop of Trier was not the only one who had been told about Frederick's planned visit, but none of the copies made out to secular recipients are extant. The same goes for Henry's letter to the bishop of Hildesheim. In addition, events like the *diet* at Regensburg in early 1235 must have been announced some time in advance. That by April princes from as far afield as Saxony and Lorraine had assembled near Nuremberg indicates that Frederic's progress may have been accompanied by preparations (including the issue of summons) of which little record survives, as well as the degree to which he could count on the backing of his princes.

Frederick's arrival in particular and the role of the princes in his progress were among those cases where the theory of imperial lordship overlapped with its reality: the empire could not be governed without the involvement of the princes, and this also manifested itself in the frequency with which they were cited as the driving force behind royal actions: by Henry (VII) to justify his campaign against the duke of Bavaria, by Frederick II to legitimise those against his son, or the duke of Austria, but also the *Reichslandfrieden* or Otto's enfeoffment with the duchy of Brunswick.[81] The role of the princes extended to the more mundane business of imperial government: when Frederick or his son revoked charters, they proclaimed to do so only at the advice and counsel of their leading subjects. Naturally, this reflected the realities of imperial politics, but this was not all there was to this issue: as we have seen, Frederick sought to use this accepted principle to impose a deeper involvement of the princes in imperial affairs, and for himself a stronger control over the princes. Many contemporary observers had somewhat different expectations about how the relationship between ruler and princes should be structured. This alerts us not only to the clash of expectations at the heart of imperial politics, but also the degree to which the reality of politics could trigger and seek to mould very different ideals of politics.

In Richard Marshal's case, the role and function of the barons may have been the principle over which he went to war, but the magnates were also curiously absent from the conflict itself, or its conduct. This was partly due to divisions among them; that de Burgh had been handed over to Richard of Cornwall, William of Warenne, William Ferrers and Richard Marshal for initial safekeeping may thus have been a sign of their support for the king.[82] Similarly, the earl of Chester and others, including even the Bigod earl of Norfolk,[83] refused to lend Marshal their backing, which suggests that the fronts between the king and his barons were by no means drawn as clearly as Wendover and others imply.[84] References to the barons are normally vague and unspecific: Wendover might claim that they left the court, but he does not name those who did (which matters, as he normally went to considerable lengths to identify by name those who stood up against des Roches). Certainly, few of the earls were coming forth to side with the Marshal, and this generally passive role (though not necessarily one supportive of the king) compares unfavourably with that of the bishops and Friars.

The Marshal rebellion is, however, useful in highlighting the importance of the middling and lower ranks of the aristocracy, who, after all, were the ones who frequently drove the conflict. Men like Richard Siward had done their best to escalate the revolt, while the earl's ultimate demise had been the work not of the king's agents, but of the Marshal's entourage. In the German case, the role of these men is more difficult to ascertain. Henry had certainly drawn on the services of various *ministeriales* – most importantly perhaps Anselm of Justingen, who had been sent to Lombardy to negotiate an alliance with the communes.[85] Similarly, as Karl Borchardt has demonstrated, Henry (VII)'s strongest support was among the *ministeriales* of Franconia, although there, too, his rebellion had been embedded in a series of already ongoing conflicts.[86] This was not the only time that *ministeriales* played a leading role in the events of these years: their alleged oppression at the duke of Austria's hands had been one of the reasons why Frederick II had him outlawed and deprived of his fiefs.[87] Unsurprisingly, the *ministeriales* were also those who most eagerly flocked to the emperor once he moved against the duke, and the ones on whom (rather than the princes) much of the military campaign against the duke rested.[88] Knights, members of a magnate's affinity, or *ministeriales* mattered for very similar reasons: they were dependent upon their own immediate lord for patronage, protection and support, but because of this could also force actions upon him.

Wendover's report about the exchange between Geoffrey Marsh and Richard prior to the earl's death conveys, as we have seen, some of the ideals upheld by the Marshal (or at least believed to have been upheld by him), and it reflects some of the basic pressures he found himself exposed to: shying away from battle was behaviour unbecoming of the son and heir of William Marshal. This was, though, more than simple goading, and reveals a fundamental dilemma: by the time Richard came to England, he had spent most of his life in France, and thus arrived as an alien and newcomer, who still had to earn the loyalty and respect of his father's and brother's entourage and followers.[89] That he found himself pushed into the role of a champion of the English aristocracy against alien fortune seekers is not without its ironies, but is also, first, not untypical of English politics (vice Simon de Montfort a generation later), and, second, only added to the need for Richard to prove his mettle before the wider Marshal affinity. His room for manoeuvre was curtailed not only by des Roches and others monopolising access to royal patronage, but also by the need to demonstrate to his own men that he still had the means to secure rewards for them. Similar pressures had applied to Henry (VII): Frederick's refusal to grant him the authority to acquire a following of his own, and to reward, protect and aid his dependants, was, as we have seen, a key factor in bringing about his revolt. Equally, Henry III's problems ultimately originated in the need to accommodate those who in the past had loyally served him and his family: des Roches as well as de Burgh, and those who had been expelled from Poitou after its loss to Louis VIII in 1224. This also underlines the stress on loyalty as a political virtue in the English sources: good and loyal service brought with it the expectation of suitable rewards, but what constituted loyal service remained a matter of debate. Frederick's emphasis on obedience and loyalty points in a similar direction, and together these examples outline the variety of demands and expectations, of ideals and norms by which participants in politics were expected or claimed to be guided.

Neither emperor nor king, neither the barons and princes nor the prelates and townsmen acted in a vacuum, and their responses, attitudes and actions have to be viewed in relation to those of the men on whom they depended to exercise their power and who depended on them in turn. While this may, at first sight, seem fairly obvious, it also has far-reaching implications, and one aim of this book has been to outline the complex relationship between the ideals and the reality of political power in England and Germany, and of the multitude of expectations, norms and harsh realities that conditioned political actions. It is only by extending coverage to a wider public, some of it not even formally deemed to have a say in the affairs of the community of the realm, that these tensions and contradictions become apparent, and that we gain a proper understanding of the complexity and richness of medieval politics and political society. Only then will we also be able to appreciate why contemporaries ascribed certain functions to some actors, but not to others. Equally, though, without the broader structural and ideological framework of politics outlined in previous chapters we will not be able to grasp properly the social context of politics, the interplay and mutual dependence of ideal and reality, of norm and action.

Conclusion

The Marshal's and Henry (VII)'s revolt have allowed us to trace several factors essential for understanding how medieval politics worked. These include the imperial nature of English as well as German royal lordship; the use of violence; the importance of honour, or the stress on joint governance and a desire for strong kingship respectively; and the role of the public. We were dealing not with two disparate political systems, but with two realms that used surprisingly similar tools and mechanisms, and that invoked surprisingly similar ideals to counter very different challenges. Such parallels include, for instance, the importance of ritual and public communication; the variety of political actors, by no means limited to those who were numbered among those whose opinion had to be taken either by rulers or chroniclers; and, perhaps most importantly, surprisingly similar values and norms of political behaviour: Henry (VII)'s justification of revolt was almost interchangeable with that of Richard Marshal. This is not to say that the two were identical, and the role of England and Germany within their respective empires may serve as a case in point: England formed the political and fiscal heartland – without which the other domains under Henry's rule could not be secured – of an Angevin Empire that still stretched from the Pyrenees to Ireland. Germany, by contrast, although important in symbolic and political terms, was neither the primary focus of imperial politics nor its chief source of funding or manpower. At the same time, these differences were by no means as pronounced as modern scholarship has so far argued.

In the case of England, for example, we have seen how important ritual was, and that it fulfilled functions superficially similar to those of rituals in Germany, and also that contemporaries stressed different aspects, and that they employed symbolic actions within a somewhat different set of values and norms. What was different was thus not that rituals were used in one realm, not the other, but that they were used in relation to a differently ordered set of norms, and in response to differences in the structural framework of politics. To put this in less abstract terms: while English and German observers would have stressed the importance of collective governance, of stern justice, and the protection of those who could not protect themselves, they ranked these norms differently, assigned these functions to different sections of the elites (with German princes, for instance, performing many of the functions assigned to the English king), and in response to different practices of government (the stress on public behaviour and symbolic action in England could thus have been a reflection of the more elaborate administrative apparatus at the king's disposal). Equally, that German observers stressed Frederick's willingness and ability to practise stern justice by executing evil doers, and destroying illicit castles, and that they thus expressed a desire for a more authoritative exercise of imperial power, reflected the specific circumstances of late Staufen imperial politics. Hence, in Germany, the importance of confirmatory ritual, the stress on the voluntary nature of concessions and agreements, performed before as broad a range of witnesses as possible, was much more pronounced, while in England the focus was on ritual as a means of evaluating the moral character of political actors.[1] A similar phenomenon emerged with regard to the tools of politics: the political public mattered in England and Germany alike, but how it constituted itself, met, conducted its debates and what it did debate, differed and reflected the specific traditions and conventions of either realm. We are normally dealing with shades of difference, not clear and identifiable contrasts, with variations on common themes, not altogether different tunes.

It is thus not only in modifying established views of English and German politics that studying these revolts has taught us something. Just as important is the complex nature of political debates that has emerged. There was, for example, a considerable gulf between the ideals invoked by rulers, and those highlighted by their literate subjects, and an otherwise complicated relationship between the norms and the practice of politics. The former was perhaps more pronounced in Germany (with Henry (VII)'s and Frederick's highlighting of honour largely ignored by their subjects), but even in England, we have encountered at least very different interpretations of what basic principles meant in practice. This should warn us against limiting consideration of medieval political ideals to the pronouncements of rulers alone. While we will never be able to gain an insight of how the great mass of Englishmen and Germans thought about regnal affairs, these clashes nonetheless matter in allowing us to trace fault lines along which the political and ideological structures of these kingdoms developed. Ultimately, no ruler was able to ignore this chasm for long, as he remained dependent on the financial and military support of the very people who doubted, criticised or rejected his actions. In the German case, this led to an attempt to find alternative sources of strong governance (either by a rise in communal movements or in wary yet closer, and often fatal, co-operation with neighbouring princes) and in England to the rupture of the Baronial Wars of Reform in 1258–65 and a tradition of resistance, however polite and muted, to royal demands.

We have also seen how the ideals and norms evoked by rulers and ruled alike had a complex relationship with the reality of politics. On a most elementary level, observers seemed to stress as desirable the very things they did not have: in England, a collaborative form of governance that restrained not so much the king, as his choice of advisors, and in Germany, an emphasis not on the *honor imperii*, but the effective and ruthless keeping of the peace. This cannot be reduced to just a feeling that the grass was greener on the other side: in fact, if German chroniclers knew about England at all, they were horrified at the rebelliousness of the English, and the tyranny of their kings,[2] while English observers remarked on the 'furious insanity' of the Germans, and their bellicose nature.[3] Rather, it reflected the reality of politics: the identity, the moral disposition and the actions of those who ran the king's administration mattered more in England than in Germany, and it was for this reason that their appointment had to be controlled, and that their probity and honourable nature had to be demonstrated publicly and repeatedly. In Germany, on the other hand, the fragmented and comparatively more violent nature of imperial politics mattered: there was a reason, after all, why the pacification of the realm remained a chief duty of emperors and would-be emperors long after similar norms had either disappeared from or had been relegated far down a list of formulaic promises, in the pronouncements of rebels and would-be kings in England, for instance, or Castile.[4]

Furthermore, these differences reveal just how little most chroniclers knew about the reality of politics outside their own immediate locality and community. While it would be odd to expect chroniclers in even the more remote parts of England or Germany to know how imperial or royal administration worked, when most academic historians today do not even know how their own institutions are run, it is still striking that even men like Matthew Paris, who had unprecedented access to documents of the king's administration,[5] cared to report very little about the processes that had caused them. This may partly have been because he deemed it too mundane a subject, but perhaps also because what mattered to him and his audience were not the processes of royal government, but the results of its actions and the motivation of its agents. In the German case, the matter was a little different: administrative procedures mattered, but, as we have seen in the conflict between the citizens of Worms and their prelates, they formed only one part in a far larger and more complex machinery of government. They could too easily be overridden, depending on the influence of one party or another, and thus had to be used in combination with other tools. All this matters for reasons very similar to those we have just considered: as ignorant of or uninterested in the procedures of government a ruler's subjects might be, their support was still needed for government to function, and for a ruler's acts of self-representation to work. Rulers and magnates alike had to conform to ideals of power that were often in clear opposition to the reality of politics. This tension was another factor driving the political development of England and Germany, and one that merits closer attention by modern historians of the European Middle Ages.

Chroniclers may only have been one part of a far larger public, but they frequently reflected, amplified and disseminated the views of their peers, patrons and neighbours. It was this public nature, moreover, that makes the dichotomies we have just outlined so important for the functioning of political exchanges. We are not, of course, dealing with a public in the post-enlightenment sense, but we have also seen how rulers were dependent on this wider public, and how that public could, by a variety of means, restrain, mould and challenge royal and baronial, princely and imperial actions. This could be straightforward debate and criticism: even if we have to be wary of relying too much on Matthew Paris, that several days could elapse between various public stages of a parliament indicates the degree of debate. Certainly, that this also applies to the *diets* of Henry (VII) tells us that these debates and criticisms were not a peculiarly English phenomenon. Equally, subjects could use public meetings to petition their rulers, they could absent themselves, participate reluctantly, stress certain elements in the public proceedings over others and so on. It was partly because of this public nature, moreover, that those who, in theory at least, were not part of the political elites could influence the course and outcome of political actions. They could disrupt or ignore, and also, through their presence, legitimise and make possible elaborate public constructs of political consultation and symbolism. That, finally, even the political elites were by no means a homogenous group, that even the clergy, for example, contained different groups performing different functions, drawing on different means of influencing politics, and at times voicing quite different concerns, only serves to underline the complexity of politics and political exchanges in this period.

This book does not claim to have offered a comprehensive account of medieval politics. There are, in fact, numerous areas we have not considered at all. On a most elementary level, this study has aimed to offer a snapshot of things were at a particular point in time. Whether similar structures were in place a generation earlier or later will have to be the subject of another investigation. Equally, how matters may have changed over time, and what drove that change, would have been questions beyond the scope of this study. What we have offered, however, is a more complex image of medieval politics than the one we hitherto had available to us, and one that, it is hoped, will be relevant beyond its geographical and chronological focus. This book has argued for a move away from a strictly administrative view of English kingship, and for a more decentralised view of German politics (by looking at responses to, rather than formulations of, imperial acts of self-representation, for instance, and by giving greater weight to the relationship between ritual and administrative practice). It has, furthermore, argued for a broader, comparative take on medieval political history. After all, only by setting England and Germany against each other has it been possible to delineate what was specific about either, and what they had in common. Wider issues have thus emerged that can only be explored from a similarly comparative basis. This is not to suggest that we should all become comparativists, but one wonders, for instance, how England or Germany fare in comparison with the Iberian realms, with those of Scandinavia, or Central Europe. How did the even more fragmented nature of royal power in Bohemia, for instance, or Hungary, influence discourses of political legitimacy? How did the specifically Iberian concerns of the reconquest influence the norms and how the ways and means of politics? Similarly, how does the place of England and Germany within the Angevin and the Holy Roman Empire respectively compare to that of Sicily, for instance, within the Angevin Empire that began to emerge in the Eastern Mediterranean from the late thirteenth century, or with that of Barcelona within the wider lands of the crown of Aragon in the thirteenth? Moreover, what does this tell us about wider European developments and structures? Even if we do not all go down the comparative route, an awareness of developments and phenomena outside our area of expertise can open up fruitful paths of enquiry.[6] In the English case, it would thus be possible to ask questions about ritual, for example, which, in a German context, the evidence would not allow us even to pose. The wealth of administrative sources makes it possible to trace the organisation, planning and frequency of certain acts much more reliably than the narrative record would allow, while the wealth of detailed narratives makes it possible to discuss reception and perception, the working and functioning of such acts.

This book has also argued for a more complex view of political processes and debates. It thus forms part of a wider trend – exemplified by Samuel Cohn's study of medieval popular revolt in the later Middle Ages, with its emphasis on the frequency of popular protest,[7] and one already suggested by Timothy Reuter, who viewed debate and conflict as a defining features of the political public from the thirteenth century onwards.[8] We have certainly seen the degree to which debate and criticism, in a variety of forms and guises, were essential elements of thirteenth-century politics. This may reflect the richer source base for the period after 1200, but on its own this seems too simplistic an explanation. Certainly, the degree to which assemblies and *diets* became more institutionalised and formal manifestations of the political community of the realm mattered,[9] as did the rise of new political players and actors, explored in the final chapter of this book. We certainly cannot write the political history of either England or Germany, or, I suspect, any other medieval European kingdom or community, without making stronger reference to the variety of political actors, their concerns and the means at their disposal for voicing them.

All this, furthermore, had repercussions for the use of the various tools we have outlined, for the significance and effectiveness of bureaucratic processes as much as acts of ritual self-presentation, and also for the ideals, norms and values that continued to guide politics and political actions. These differences and debates must not be mistaken for such simplistically modern categories as class conflict or a bourgeois public, but nonetheless need to be taken more seriously and have to be given greater weight by historians. That many of these debates were conducted within the elite strata of society also means that we have to recognise more fully the fragmented nature not just of society at large, but also its leading groups.

This, finally, complicates the way we can deal with norms and values, their symbolic expression and effectiveness, while at the same time, we should avoid exaggerating differences. Even in the German case, where the rejection of imperial ideas of governance was more pronounced, this did not mean that they were rejected outright: their most visible expression (honour) was ignored, but several of its elements survived, but remoulded to fit the existing concerns, and the somewhat different priorities, of the ruler's subjects. In England, equally, we are not dealing with different ideologies of governance, but with different interpretations and weightings of an established canon of political virtues. The resulting image may be more complicated, but because of that it is perhaps also truer to the reality of politics not just during the 1230s, but the thirteenth century in particular, and the high Middle Ages in general.

Notes

Introduction

1. Henry's regnal number is conventionally put in brackets to distinguish him from Emperor Henry VII (r. 1308–13).
2. In 1273, 1281, 1287, 1291, 1292, 1298. *Constitutiones 1198–1272*, no. 196.
3. *Constitutiones et Acta Publica Imperatorum et Regum, 1273–98*, ed. J. Schwalm, MGH Leges (Hanover, 1904–6), no. 284. For the contemporary context see B. Weiler 'Image and "reality" in Richard of Cornwall's German career', *EHR* 113 (1998), 1111–42, at 1138–41.
4. R. Huscroft, *Ruling England, 1042–1217* (Harlow, 2004) provides perhaps the best survey. See also the articles collected in *English Government in the Thirteenth Century*, ed. A. Jobson (Woodbridge, 2004), which, while providing an excellent and important survey of the bureaucratic, fiscal and juridical mechanisms of power, also confines itself to just those.
5. A case most eloquently made by Timothy Reuter, though largely with reference to the tenth to twelfth century: 'The medieval German *Sonderweg*? The empire and its rulers in the high Middle Ages', in *Kings and Kingship in Medieval Europe*, ed. A. Duggan (London, 1991), 297–325; repr. in his *Medieval Polities and Modern Mentalities*, ed. J.L. Nelson (Cambridge, 2006), 388–412.
6. 'The pilgrimages of the Angevin kings of England, 1154–1272', *Pilgrimage. The English experience from Becket to Bunyan*, ed. C. Morris and P. Roberts (Cambridge, 2002), 12–45, at 40.
7. See, for instance, T. Reuter, 'Modern mentalities and medieval polities', *Medieval Polities*, 3–18.
8. *Das europäische Mittelalter im Spannungsbogen des Vergleichs: Zwanzig internationale Beiträge zu Praxis, Problemen und Perspektiven der historischen Komparatistik*, ed. M. Borgolte (Berlin, 2001); *Building Legitimacy. Political Discourses and Forms of Legitimacy in Medieval Societies*, ed. H. Kennedy, I. Alonso and J. Escalano (Leiden, 2004).
9. Which is not to deny the validity of this approach, of which Tim Reuter has been a most accomplished practioner. See, for instance, his 'Assembly politics in the West from the eight century to the twelfth', in *The Medieval World*, ed. P. Linehan and J. Nelson (London, 2001), 432–50; repr. In his *Medieval Polities*, 193–216; 'Die Unsicherheit auf den Straßen im europäischen Früh- und Hochmittelalter: Täter, Opfer und ihre mittelalterlichen und modernen Betrachter', *Träger und Funktionen des Friedens im hohen und späten Mittelalter*, ed. J. Fried, Vorträge und Forschungen xliii (Sigmaringen, 1996), 169–202; repr. and transl. in his *Medieval Polities*, 38–71.
10. Notable exceptions are James Given's classic *State and Society in Medieval Europe. Gwynedd and Languedoc under Outside Rule* (Ithaca, 1990); M.T. Clanchy, 'Did Henry III have a policy?', *History* 53 (1968), 203–16; T. Reuter, 'The making of England and Germany, 850–1050: points of comparison and difference', in *Medieval Europeans. Studies in Ethnic Identity*

and National Perspectives in Medieval Europe (London, 1998), 53–70; repr. in his *Medieval Polities*, 284–99; S. Reynolds, 'How different was England?', *TCE* vii (1999), 1–16.

11. M. Jones and M. Vale (eds), *England and her Neighbours 1066–1453: essays in honour of Pierre Chaplais* (London, 1989); B. Weiler and I. Rowlands (ed.), *England and Europe in the Reign of Henry III (1216–1272)* (Aldershot, 2002); D. Matthew, *Britain and the Continent 1000–1300. The Impact of the Norman Conquest* (London, 2005).

12. D. Crouch, *The Birth of Nobility: Social Change, 950–1350. Constructing Aristocracy in England and France, 900–1300* (Harlow, 2005). This is not to say that by comparing England and the German parts of the Holy Roman Empire we are dealing with two realms that had little or no contact – especially for the thirteenth century, this was blatantly not the case: J.P. Huffman, *Family, Commerce and Religion in London and Cologne. Anglo-German Emigrants, c. 1000–c. 1300* (Cambridge, 1998); B. Weiler, *King Henry III of England and the Staufen Empire, 1216–1272* (Woodbridge, 2006).

13. A view that has been criticised before: Reuter, 'Modern mentalities'; Reynolds, 'How different'. In an Anglo-French context, the historiographical models developed by Nicholas Vincent and David Crouch should be noted: N. Vincent, 'Conclusion', in *Noblesses de l'espace Plantagenêt (1154–1224)*, ed. M. Aurell (Poitiers, 2001), 207–14; D. Crouch, 'Les historiographies médievales franco-anglaises: le point du départ', *Cahiers de la civilisation médiévale* xlviii (2005), 317–25.

14. J. Ehlers, *Die Deutschen und das europäische Mittelalter. Bd. 3: Das westliche Europa* (Berlin, 2004); idem (ed.), *Deutschland und der Westen Europas im Mittelalter* (Stuttgart, 2002).

15. Certainly a criticism to be made of some of the contributions to Ehlers, *Deutschland und der Westen*.

16. Reuter, 'German *Sonderweg*'.

17. Reuter, 'Modern mentalities', 17.

18. In lieu of a very rich literature see, most recently: G. Althoff, *Die Macht der Rituale. Symbolik und Herrschaft im Mittelalter* (Darmstadt, 2003); H. Krieg, *Herrscherdarstellung in der Stauferzeit. Friedrich Barbarossa im Spiegel seiner Urkunden und der staufischen Geschichtsschreibung* (Ostfildern, 2003); J. Schwarz, *Herrscher- und Reichstitel bei Kaisertum und Papsttum im 12. und 13. Jahrhundert* (Cologne and Vienna, 2003); K. Görich, *Die Ehre Friedrich Barbarossas. Kommunikation, Konflikt und politisches Handeln im 12. Jahrhundert* (Darmstadt, 2001).

19. Althoff, *Macht der Rituale*. Many of his key articles have been reprinted in his *Spielregeln der Politik im Mittelalter. Kommunikation in Frieden und Fehde* (Darmstadt, 1997).

20. Görich, *Die Ehre*; 'Ehre als Ordnungsfaktor. Anerkennung und Stabilisierung von Herrschaft unter Friedrich Barbarossa und Friedrich II.', *Ordnungskonfigurationen im hohen Mittelalter*, ed. B. Schneidmüller und S. Weinfurter (Ostfildern, 2006), 59–93.

21. Somewhat intriguingly, most of the relevant work has been published either by German historians, or by historians of Germany. See, for instance, K. van Eickels, *Vom inszenierten Konsens zum systematisierten Konflikt. Die englisch-französischen Beziehungen und ihre Wahrnehmung an der Wende vom*

Hoch-zum Spätmittelalter (Stuttgart, 2002); K. Görich, 'Verletzte Ehre? Richard Löwenherz als Gefangener Heinrichs VI.', *Historisches Jahrbuch der Görres-Gesellschaft* cxxiii (2003), 65–91; Timothy Reuter, '*Velle Sibi Fieri in forma hac.* Symbolisches Handeln im Becketstreit', Althoff (ed.), *Formen und Funktionen*, 201–25; repr. and transl. in his *Medieval Polities*, 167–91. See, however, A. Chaou, *L'ideologie Plantagenêt. Royauté arthurienne et monarchie politique dans l'espace Plantagenêt (xii–xiii siècles)* (Rennes, 2001); D. Carpenter, 'Henry III and the cult of Edward the Confessor', *EHR* (forthcoming); idem, 'The meetings of King Henry III and Louis IX', *TCE* x (2005), 1–31; N. Vincent, *The Holy Blood. King Henry III and the Westminster Blood Relic* (Cambridge, 2001); idem, 'The pilgrimages'; B. Weiler, 'Knighting, homage and the meaning of ritual: the kings of England and their neighbors in the thirteenth century', *Viator* 37 (2006), 275–300; idem, 'Symbolism and politics in the reign of Henry III', *TCE* 9 (2003), 15–41.

22. Reuter, 'Modern mentalities', 15; Vincent, 'Conclusion'.

1 To be king in name as well as deed: the revolt of Henry (VII) in Germany (1234–5)

1. *Acta Imperii Inedita saeculi XIII et XIV. Urkunden und Briefe zur Geschichte des Kaiserreichs und des Königreichs Sizilien*, ed. E. Winkelmann, 2 vols (Innsbruck, 1880–5; repr. 1964), nos. 470, 642.

2. *Acta Imperii Selecta. Urkunden deutscher Könige und Kaiser. Mit einem Anhange von Reichssachen*, ed. J.F. Böhmer (Innsbruck, 1870), no. 303.

3. See most recently: M. Lower, *The Barons' Crusade. A Call to Arms and Its Consequences* (Philadelphia, 2005), 19–21, 38–41, 159–64; for a more positive view: H.M. Schaller, 'Die Frömmigkeit Kaiser Friedrichs II', *Das Staunen der Welt: Kaiser Friedrich II. von Hohenstaufen 1194–1250, Schriften zur staufischen Geschichte und Kunst* xv (Göppingen, 1996), 128–51; R. Hiestand, 'Friedrich II. und der Kreuzzug', *Friedrich II: Tagung des deutschen Historischen Instituts in Rom im Gedenkjahr 1994*, ed. A. Esch and N. Kamp (Tübingen, 1996), 128–49; although limiting its coverage to the actual crusade still useful: B. Hechelhammer, *Kreuzzug und Herrschaft unter Friedrich II. Handlungsspielräume von Kreuzzugspolitik (1215–1230)* (Ostfildern, 2004).

4. B. Weiler, 'Frederick II, Gregory IX and the Liberation of the Holy Land 1231–9', *Studies in Church History* xxxv (2000), 192–206.

5. Hechelhammer, *Kreuzzug und Herrschaft*, 211–23; M.A. Aziz, 'La croisade de l'Empereur Frédéric II et l'Orient Latin', *Autour de la Première Croisade*, ed. M. Balard (Paris, 1996), 373–8; W. Stürner, *Friedrich II*, 2 vols (Darmstadt, 1994–2000), ii. 130–68.

6. In 1231, for instance, he promulgated the *Liber Augustalis*, or the constitutions of Melfi, which sought to codify the legal practice of the kingdom of Sicily [*Die Konstitutionen Friedrichs II. für das Königreich Sizilien*, ed. W. Stürner, M.G.H Leges (Hanover, 1996); for an English translation see *The Liber Augustalis or Constitutions of Melfi Promulgated by the Emperor Frederick II for the Kingdom of Sicily in 1231*, transl. by J.M. Powell (Syracuse: Syracuse University Press, 1971)], while in 1232–4 he began to take a more active interest in the affairs of the kingdom of Burgundy [*Layettes du Tresor*

de Chartes, ed. H.-F. Laborde and A. Teulet, 4 vols (Paris, 1863–1909), no. 2309; J. Chiffoleau, 'I ghibellini de regno di Arles', *Federico II e le città italiane*, ed. P. Toubert and A. Paravacini Bagliani (Palermo: Sellerio, 1994), pp. 364–88].

7. Weiler, *Henry III of England* 60–7; Stürner, *Friedrich II*, ii. 266–75, 286–96.
8. This follows the more traditional reading proposed by Stürner, *Friedrich II*, 296–309; C. Hillen, *Curia Regis. Untersuchungen zur Hofstruktur Heinrichs (VII). 1220–1235 nach den Zeugen seiner Urkunden* (Frankfurt am Main, 1999), 214–36; P. Thorau, *König Heinrich (VII.), das Reich und die Territorien. Untersuchungen zur Phase der Minderjährigkeit und der 'Regentschaften' Erzbischof Engelberts I. von Köln und Herzog Ludwigs I. von Bayern (1211) 1220–38*, Jahrbücher der Deutschen Geschichte: Jahrbücher des Deutschen Reichs unter Heinrich (VII.), Teil I (Berlin, 1998), pp. 202–27; T. Broekmann, *Rigor Iustitiae. Herrschaft, Recht und Terror im normannisch-staufischen Süden (1050–1250)* (Darmstadt, 2005), 260–368, has suggested a conflict of political cultures as a driving factor of Frederick's response. Although, as we will see, this was certainly one element, it does not invalidate the reading proposed here.
9. See L. Shepard, *Courting Power: Persuasion and Politics in the Early Thirteenth Century* (New York, 1999), for a recent case study.
10. Stürner, *Friedrich II*, i. 231–5; G. Baaken, 'Die Erhebung Heinrichs, Herzogs von Schwaben, zum Rex Romanorum (1220/1222)', G. Baaken, *Imperium und regnum. Zur Geschichte des 12. und 13. Jahrhunderts. Festschrift zum 70. Geburtstag*, ed. K.-A. Frech and U. Schmidt (Cologne, Weimar and Vienna, 1997), 289–306.
11. As had been the case with Otto I and Otto II, Conrad II, Henry III, Henry IV, Henry V, Conrad III, Frederick Barbarossa. For a convenient overview of the twelfth century, see U. Schmidt, *Königswahl und Thronfolge im 12. Jahrhundert* (Cologne and Vienna, 1987), 109–21, 167–93, 225–60.
12. In many ways, this was a problem not unlike the one which had faced Henry II in England after 1170, when he had his son Henry crowned king, but with the important difference that, in theory at least, Henry (VII) could exercise real political power in the heartlands of the Staufen Empire. *Le Recueil des Historiens des Gaules et de la France* xvi (Paris, 1814), pp. 643–8.
13. W. Stürner, 'Der Staufer Heinrich (VII.) (1211–1242): Lebensstationen eines gescheiterten Königs', *Zeitschrift für Württembergische Landesgeschichte* 52 (1993) 13–33.
14. H. Flachenecker, 'Herzog Ludwig der Kelheimer als Prokurator König Heinrichs (VII.)', *Zeitschrift für Bayerische Landesgeschichte* 59 (1996), 835–48; Hillen, *Curia Regis*, 147–62.
15. K.A. Frech, 'Ein Plan zur Absetzung Heinrichs (VII): die gescheiterte Legation Kardinal Ottos in Deutschland 1229–1231', *Von Schwaben bis Jerusalem: Facetten staufischer Geschichte*, ed. S. Lorenz and U. Schmidt (Sigmaringen, 1995), 89–116; P. Thorau, 'Die erste Bewährungsprobe Heinrichs (VII.)', *Der Staufer Heinrich (VII.). Ein König im Schatten seines kaiserlichen Vaters* (Göppingen, 2001), 43–52; Stürner, *Friedrich II.*, ii. 170–4.
16. *Constitutiones 1198–1272*, no. 155.
17. *Constitutiones 1198–1272*, no. 170.
18. *Constitutiones 1198–1272*, no. 316.

19. Stürner, *Friedrich II.*, ii. 302–9; Hillen, *Curia Regis*, 214–36; Broekmann, *Rigor Iustitiae*, 284–90; *Annales Neresheimenses*, MGH SS 10, 23; *Annales Placentini Gibellini*, MGH SS 18, 470.

20. *Annales Marbacenses qui dicuntur (Cronica Hohenburgensis cum continuatio et additamentis Neoburgensibus)*, ed. H. Bloch, MGH SSrG sep. ed. (Hanover and Leipzig, 1907), 96.

21. *Acta Imperii Inedita*, no. 470; *Acta Imperii Selecta*, no. 334.

22. *Acta Imperii Inedita*, no. 642.

23. *HB* iv. 531–3. On the bishops see: E. Freiherr von Guttenberg, *Das Bistum Bamberg. Erster Teil*, Germania Sacra: Zweite Abteilung – Die Bistümer der Kirchenprovinz Mainz 1 (Berlin and Leipzig, 1937), 164–70; A. Wendehorst, *Das Bistum Würzburg. Teil 1: Die Bischofsreihe bis 1254*, Germania Sacra Neue Folge 1: Die Bistümer der Kirchenprovinz Mainz (Berlin, 1962), 211–17.

24. Hillen, *Curia Regis*, 214–36; K. Borchardt, 'Der sogenannte Aufstand Heinrichs (VII.) in Franken 1234/35', *Forschungen zur bayerischen und fränkischen Geschichte: Festschrift Peter Herde*, ed. K. Borchardt and E. Bünz (Würzburg, 1998), 53–119.

25. *Urkundenbuch zur Geschichte der Babenberger in Österreich. Vierter Band. Zweiter Halbband. Ergänzende Quellen 1195–1287* ed. O. Freiherr von Mitis, H. Dienst, C. Lackner and H. Hageneder (Vienna and Munich, 1997), no. 1198.

26. *CM*, iii. 319.

27. *Annales Marbacenses*, 98.

28. Broekmann, *Rigor Iustitiae*, 272–8; B. Weiler, 'Reasserting power: Frederick II in Germany (1235–6)', *Representations of Power in Medieval Germany, 700–1500*, ed. S. MacLean and B. Weiler (Turnhoult, 2006), 241–70.

29. B. Keilmann, *Der Kampf um die Stadtherrschaft in Worms während des 13. Jahrhunderts*, Quellen und Forschungen zur hessischen Geschichte 50 (Darmstadt and Marburg, 1985), 47–80.

30. *Gotidfredi Viterbensis Continuatio Eberbacensis*, MGH SS 22, 348; *Annales Wormatienses*, in: *Quellen zur Geschichte der Stadt Worms*, ed. H. Boos, 3 vols (Berlin, 1886–93), ii. 146–8.

31. Keilmann, '*Der Kampf*', passim.

32. *Ryccardi de Sancto Germano Notarii Chronica*, ed. C.A. Carufi, RIS NS (Bologna: Niccola Zanichelli, 1936–8), p. 190.

33. *Annales Erphordenses fratrum praedicatorum*, in: *Monumenta Erphesfurtensia saeculi xii., xiii., xiv.*, ed. O. Holder-Egger, MGH SSrG sep. ed. (Hanover and Leipzig, 1899), 89.

34. He had first announced his imminent arrival to the German princes in January 1235: *RI*, no. 2075.

35. *Annales Marbacenses qui dicuntur (Cronica Hohenburgensis cum continuatio et additamentis Neoburgensibus)*, ed. H. Bloch, MGH SSrG sep. ed. (Hanover and Leipzig: Hahn, 1907), p. 96.

36. *Annales Scheftlarienses Maiores* MGH SS 17, p. 340.

37. *RI*, v, no. 2096.

38. *Chronicon Ebersheimense*, MGH SS 23, 453.

39. *Continuatio Eberbacensis*, 348.

40. *RI*, v, no. 2098.

41. Hillen, *Curia Regis*, pp. 214–19; Stürner, *Friedrich II.*, ii 302–9; G. Wolf, 'Wimpfen, Worms und Heidelberg. Einige Bemerkungen zum

Herrschaftsende König Heinrichs', *Zeitschrift für Geschichte des Oberrheins* Neue Folge 98 (1989), 471–86.

42. *Continuatio Ebersbacensis*, 348.

43. *Annales Moguntini*, MGH SS 17, 2; *Annales Sancti Trudberti* MGH SS 17, 293 (which does not mention Sicily, but simply has Henry taken captive and sent *in exilium*, as do the *Annales Maiores Zwifaltenses*, MGH SS 10, 59); *Annales Sancti Georgii in Silva Nigra*, MGH SS 17, 297; *Continuatio Sancrucensis II*, MGH SS 9, 638; *Annales Ottoburani Minores*, MGH SS 17, 317; *Annales Stadenses Auctore Alberto*, MGH SS 16, 362; *Continuatio Lambacenses*, MGH SS 9, 558; *Annales Sancti Rudberti Salisburgenses*, MGH SS 9, 786.

44. *Chronica Regia Coloniensis*, 271; *Constitutiones 1198–1272*, no. 329.

45. This summarises an argument, made in more detail, in Weiler, 'Re-asserting power', 246–68.

46. A. Buschmann, 'Landfriede und Verfassung. Zur Bedeutung des Mainzer Reichslandfriedens von 1235 als Verfassungsgesetz', *Aus Österreichs Rechtsleben in Geschichte und Gegenwart. FS Ernst C. Hellbling* (Berlin, 1981), pp. 449–72.

47. *Constitutiones 1198–1272*, no. 197.

48. E. Boshof, 'Reich und Reichsfürsten in Herrschaftsverständnis und Politik Kaiser Friedrichs II. nach 1230', *Heinrich Raspe – Landgraf von Thüringen und römischer König (1227–1247)*, ed. M. Werner (Frankfurt/Main, 2003), pp. 3–27, at 10–11.

49. F. Hausmann, 'Kaiser Friedrich II. und Österreich', *Probleme um Friedrich II.*, ed. J. Fleckenstein (Sigmaringen, 1974), pp. 225–308 (pp. 242–56); H. Dopsch, K. Brunner and M. Weltin, *Österreichische Geschichte 1122–1278. Die Länder und das Reich. Der Ostalpenraum im Hochmittelalter* (Vienna, 1999), pp. 189–94; Stürner, *Friedrich II*, ii. 263–6.

50. *Urkundenbuch Babenberger*, no. 1198.

51. *Chronica Regia Coloniensis*, 271.

52. J.P. Huffman, 'Prosopography and the Anglo-imperial connection: a Cologne ministerialis family and its English relations', *Medieval Prosopography* 11 (1990), 53–134.

53. Weiler, *Henry III*, 72, 82–3.

54. Hillen, *Curia Regis*, 95–7; Borchardt, 'Der sogenannte Aufstand'. On the *ministeriales* more generally see: B. Arnold, *Medieval German Knighthood, 1050–1300* (Oxford, 1985), 209–25; J.B. Freed, *Noble Bondsmen. Ministerial marriages in the archdiocese of Salzburg, 1100–1343* (Ithaca, 1995), 189–99. Similarly, one of the crimes Duke Frederick of Austria was said to have committed was to attack imperial *ministeriales*, that is, the emperor's dependants, and thereby he also attacked the honour of the empire. *Urkundenbuch Babenberger*, no. 1198.

55. M. Morris, *The Bigod Earls of Norfolk in the Thirteenth Century* (Woodbridge, 2005) provides an illuminating case study.

56. B. Arnold, *Princes and territories in medieval Germany* (Cambridge, 1991); idem, 'Emperor Frederick II (1194–1250) and the political particularism of the German princes', *JMH* xxvi (2000), 239–52.

2   The Marshal rebellion in England (1233–4)

1. *CM*, iii. pp. 321–4.

2. The most detailed modern narratives of the revolt and its background are those by N. Vincent, *Peter des Roches: an alien in English politics 1205–1238*

(Cambridge, 1996), pp. 337–9, 375–428, 438–40; D. Carpenter, *The Struggle for Mastery. The Penguin History of Britain 1066–1284* (London, 2003), 312–17; M.T. Clanchy, *England and Its Rulers 1066–1307*, third edition (Oxford, 2006), 194–212; B. Smith, 'Irish politics, 1220–1245', *TCE* 8 (2001), 13–22, at 14–20.

3. D.A. Carpenter, *The Minority of Henry III* (London, 1990), 13–19; idem, *Struggle for Mastery*, 300–3; Clanchy, *England and Its Rulers*, 142–7; *L'histoire de Guillaume le Maréchal, comte de Striguil et de Pembroke, regent d'Angleterre de 1216 à 1219*, ed. P. Meyer, 3 vols (Paris, 1891–1901), ll. 15688–96; D. Crouch, *William the Marshal. Court, Career and Chivalry in the Angevin Empire 1147–1219* (London, 1990), p. 118.

4. *Rogeri de Wendover Chronica sive Flores Historiarum*, ed. H.O. Coxe, 5 vols (London, 1841–4), iv. 2–3.

5. Carpenter, *Minority*, 187–91.

6. J.C. Holt, *Magna Carta*, second edition (Cambridge, 1992), 378–404; R.V. Turner, *Magna Carta* (Harlow, 2003), 80–112.

7. R. Eales, 'The political setting of the Becket translation of 1220', *Studies in Church History* xxx (1993), 127–39.

8. Carpenter, *The Minority*, 389–94.

9. D. Carpenter, 'King, magnates and society. The personal rule of King Henry III, 1234–1258', *Speculum* 60 (1985), 39–70; C. Hillen, 'The minority governments of Henry III, Henry (VII) and Louis IX compared', *TCE* 11 (forthcoming, 2007). The most recent study of des Roches is Vincent, *Peter des Roches*; a new biography of de Burgh remains a desideratum. In the meantime, see Carpenter, *Minority*, 263–300; F.A. Cazel, 'Intertwined careers: Hubert de Burgh and Peter des Roches', *Haskins Society Journal* i (1989) 173–81; C. Ellis, *Hubert de Burgh: a study in constancy* (London, 1952).

10. Vincent, *Peter des Roches*, pp. 114–33.

11. Carpenter, *Minority*, 316–20; idem, 'The fall', 46; Vincent, *Peter des Roches*, pp. 215–27.

12. The role of foreign office holders in England remains a complex and vexed question, which cannot be dealt with in detail here. For a convenient introduction to the subject see C. Egger, 'Henry III's England and the *curia*', *England and Europe in the Reign of Henry III (1216–1272)*, ed. B. Weiler and I.W. Rowlands (Aldershot, 2002), 215–32; H. Ridgway, 'King Henry III and the "aliens" 1236–1272', *TCE* ii (1987), 81–92.

13. Vincent, *Peter des Roches*, 311–20.

14. *Annals of Tewkesbury*, *AM*, I. 86; *RW*, iv. 247–8.

15. *CPR 1232–47*, 28–30.

16. Vincent, *Peter des Roches*, 317.

17. Vincent, *Peter des Roches*, 327.

18. Vincent, *Peter des Roches*, 327.

19. *CCHr 1226–57*, 154–5; *CPR 1232–47*, 7–8; Vincent, *Peter des Roches*, 329.

20. In particular *RW*, iv. 263–4.

21. The exact details of this court case remain complex. For a more detailed treatment see Vincent, *Peter des Roches*, 334–7; N. Denholm-Young, *Richard of Cornwall* (Oxford, 1947), 24–5; R.V. Turner, *The King and his Courts: the role of John and Henry III in the Administration of Justice, 1199–1240* (New York, 1968), 248–51; Stacey, *Politics, Policy*, 38–9.

22. *CR 1231–4*, 187.

23. *Tewkesbury*, *AM*, i. 88; *Dunstable*, *AM*, iii. 136; *RW*, ii. 208.

24. Albrecht von Roßweg, succeeded by Otto von Weiler: F. Battenberg, *Gerichtsschreiberamt und Kanzlei am Reichshofgericht 1235–1451*, Quellen und Forschungen zur höchsten Gerichtsbarkeit im Alten Reich 2 (Cologne and Vienna, 1974), 13–27, 35–9.

25. For a recent, lucid and perceptive survey see Huscroft, *Ruling England*. For more specific case studies for the thirteenth century, see D. Carpenter, 'The English royal chancery in the thirteenth century', *Ecrit et pouvoir dans les chancelleries médiévales. Espace français, espace anglais. Actes du colloque international de Montréal, 7–9 septembre 1995*, ed. K. Fianu and D.J. Guth (Louvain-la-Neuve, 1997), 25–53; and for the early years of Henry III: Stacey, *Politics, Policy*, 1–44.

26. Vincent, *Peter des Roches*, 417–18, especially no. 80; *Anglo-Scottish Relations*, ed. E.L.G. Stones, second edition (Oxford, 1970), 38–53.

27. Vincent, *Peter des Roches*, 409–10.

28. J.R. Maddicott, *Simon de Montfort* (Cambridge, 1994), 7–20. These links and contexts also included trade and the economy: D. Matthew, *Britain and the Continent 1000–1300* (London, 2005); N. Fryde, 'How to get on in Henry III's England – the career of three German merchants', Weiler and Rowlands (eds), *England and Europe*, 207–14.

29. *RW*, iv. 284–5.

30. Stacey, *Politics, Policy*, 38–42.

31. Vincent, *Peter des Roches*, 363–71; Carpenter, *Struggle for Mastery*, 315; for the most convenient overview. C.H. Lawrence, *St Edmund of Abingdon. A Study of Hagiography and History* (Oxford, 1960), 124–37; F.M. Powicke, *King Henry III and the Lord Edward. The Community of the Realm in the Thirteenth Century*, 2 vols (Oxford, 1947), 134–7.

32. Vincent, *Peter des Roches*, pp. 376–7.

33. *CPR 1232–47*, 17.

34. *CR 1231–4*, 310; Vincent, *Peter des Roches*, p. 377.

35. *CR 1231–4*, 168, 179, 275.

36. *CR 1231–4*, 314; Vincent, *Peter des Roches*, p. 378 no. 68, 380–1.

37. *CR 1231–4*, p. 233; *RW*, iv. 268; *CM*, iii. 244–5; Vincent, *Peter des Roches*, pp. 381–2.

38. Vincent, *Peter des Roches*, pp. 386–7; *CPR 1232–47*, 21, 22; *CR 1231–4*, 247, 317–18, 318–19.

39. The following summarises Vincent, *Peter des Roches*, 399–419.

40. Wendover reports that Richard, through his wife, had warned the Marshal against a plot against him (*RW*, iv. 270), but otherwise he seems to have sided with his brother, the king. Denholm-Young, *Richard of Cornwall*, 22–31; Morris, *The Bigod Earls*, 8–12.

41. D. Crouch, 'The last adventure of Richard Siward', *Morgannwg Journal of Glamorgan History* 35 (1991), 7–30.

42. *RW*, iv. 274–5. This is not to say that violations of sanctuary were not tolerated: for a similar incident, but one which received a much more supportive press, see the burning of the Church of St Mary Arches in London, William of Newburgh, *Historia rerum Anglicarum*, in *Chronicles of the Reigns of Stephen, Henry II and Richard I*, ed. R. Howlett, 4 vols (London, 1884–8), vols 1 & 2, iii. 7, v. 20–21; see also J. Gillingham, 'The historian as judge: William Newburgh and Hubert Walter', *EHR* 199 (2004), 1275–87, at 1276–7.

43. Vincent, *Peter des Roches*, 415–16.
44. *RW*, iv. 272; *Annales de Dunstaplia, AM*, iii.134; *CR 1231–4*, 255.
45. Vincent, *Peter des Roches*, 408–11.
46. *RW*, iv. 276. This episode has triggered a rich debate among modern historians: Clanchy, *England and its Rulers*, 220–1; Vincent, *Peter des Roches*, 409–10; Carpenter, *Struggle for Mastery*, 313–14.
47. *CR 1231–4*, 281.
48. Vincent, *Peter des Roches*, 419–23 for the following.
49. Gransden, *Historical Writing*, 356–79 provides what is still the best account of the two and their writings. See also V.H. Galbraith, *Roger of Wendover and Matthew Paris* (Glasgow, 1944), and R. Vaughan, *Matthew Paris* (Cambridge, 1958).
50. *RW*, iv. 295–7; *CM*, iii. 269–71.
51. *CPR 1232–47*, 36; *CR 1231–4*, 371–2, 378, 380. Vincent, *Peter des Roches*, 429–31.
52. Vincent, *Peter des Roches*, 432–3.
53. Vincent, *Peter des Roches*, 435.
54. Vincent, *Peter des Roches*, 443–6.
55. He did, however, continue to play an important role in international affairs: Vincent, *Peter des Roches*, 472–4; Weiler, *King Henry III*, 59–60.
56. Vincent, *Peter des Roches*, 442–3.
57. Vincent, *Peter des Roches*, 438–40.
58. *RW*, iv. 401–8.
59. Smith, 'Irish politics', 14–19.
60. D. Carpenter, 'What happened in 1258?', J. Gillingham and J.C. Holt (ed.), *War and Government in the Middle Ages: Essays in honour of J.O. Prestwich* (Woodbridge, 1984), 106–19; repr. in his *Reign* 183–98.
61. D. Carpenter, 'Simon de Montfort: the first leader of a political movement in English history', *History* 76 (1991), 3–23; Valente, 'Simon de Montfort'; Maddicott, *Simon de Montfort*, 346–70.
62. Carpenter, 'King, Magnates and Society'; Hillen, 'The minority governments'.

3   Rebellion in context

1. C. Valente, 'Simon de Montfort, earl of Leicester, and the utility of sanctity in thirteenth-century England', *JMH* 21 (1995), 27–49.
2. *The Metrical Chronicle of Robert of Gloucester*, ed. W.A. Wright, 2 vols, RS (London, 1886–7), ll. 10735–822.
3. *Vita Edwardi Secundi. The Life of Edward the Second*, ed. and trans. W.R. Childs (Oxford, 2005), 76–7. I am grateful to Phillipp Schofield for this reference.
4. *Vita Gregorii IX*, P. Fabre, L. Duchesne and G. Mollat (eds), *Le 'Liber Censuum' de l'Eglise Romaine*, 3 vols (Paris, 1889–1952), ii. 8–36. See also Tholomaeus of Lucca, following Martinus Polonus, who believed that the king's death had been planned from the beginning: *Die Annalen des Tholomaeus von Lucca in doppelter Fassung nebest Teilen der Gesta Florentinorum und Gesta Lucanorum*, ed. B. Schmeidler, MGH SSrG NS (Berlin, 1930), 127.
5. *Constitutiones 1198–1272*, no. 235; *CM*, iv. 112–19.

6. *Ottokars Österreichische Reimchronik* ed. J. Seemüller, MGH Deutsche Chroniken, 2 vols (Hanover, 1890–3), ll. 22913–20.

7. See, for instance, writing in the fifteenth century, Thomas Ebendorfer, *Chonica Regum Romanorum*, ed. H. Zimmermann, 2 vols, MGH SSrG NS (Hanover, 2003), 464, 769.

8. See, however, C. Valente, *The Theory and Practice of Revolt in Medieval England* (Aldershot, 2003); J.R. Maddicott, ' "1258" and "1297": Some comparisons and contrasts', *TCE* 9 (2003), 1–14, for England; and for a broader European perspective, the essays in *Conflict in Medieval Europe. Changing Perspectives on Society and Culture*, ed. W.C. Brown and P. Gorecki (Aldershot, 2003); J. Rogge, 'Attentate und Schlachten. Beobachtungen zum Verhältnis von Königtum und Gewalt im deutschen Reich während des 13. und 14. Jahrhunderts', M. Kintzinger and J. Rogge (ed.), Königliche Gewalt – Gewalt gegen Könige (Zeitschrift für Historische Forschung, Beiheft 33), (Berlin, 2004), 7–50; D.J. Kagay, 'Structures of Baronial Dissent and Revolt under James I (1213–76)', *Mediaevistik* 1 (1988), 61–85.

9. Colker, 'Margam Chronicle', 134: *sicut factum est tempore regis Iohannis*.

10. *RW*, iv. 264.

11. *RW*, iii. 359–60.

12. *RW*, iv. 276.

13. Bracton, *De Legibus et consuetudinibus Angliae*, ed. George E. Woodbine, 4 vols (New Haven, 1915–42), ii. 110.

14. *CM*, ii. 454–5.

15. *RW*, iii. 139–40.

16. Among contemporary observers outside England, the seditious nature of the English was in fact to become a commonplace and something approximating a national characteristic. *Bibliotheca mundi seu speculi maioris Vincentii Burgundi praesulis Bellovacensis, ordinis praedicatorum, theologi ac doctori eximii, tomus quartus qui Speculum Historiale inscribitur* (Douai, 1624), 1260; *The Historia Occidentalis of Jacques de Vitry*, ed. J.F. Hinnebusch, Spicilegium Friburgense 17 (Fribourg, 1972), 92; *The Chronicle of William de Rishanger of the Barons' War*, ed. J.O. Halliwell, Camden First Series 15 (London, 1840), 17–18.

17. I.S. Robinson, *Henry IV of Germany, 1056–1106* (Cambridge, 1999), 337–44.

18. Otto of St Blasien, *Chronica*, ed. A. Hofmeister, MGH SSrG sep. ed. (Hanover and Leipzig, 1912), 39–41; *Arnoldi Chronica Slavorum*, ed. J.M. Lappenberg, MGH SSrG sep. ed. (Hanover, 1868), 87–90; *La Chronique de Gislebert de Mons*, ed. L. Vanderkindere, Receuil de Textes pour servir a l'étude de l'histoire de Belgique (Brussels, 1904), 155–60.

19. *RW*, iv. 240–2.

20. *CM*, iii. 317.

21. *CM*, iii. 481–5.

22. *De Antiquis Legibus*, 116.

23. *CRR Henry III 7–9*, nos. 1034, 1079; *11–14*, no. 2786.

24. Matthew Paris, for instance, was uncharacteristically fulsome in his praise of Cardinal Otto, partly because Otto reconciled the king to so many of his nobles, including some erstwhile supporters of the Marshal *CM*, iii. 403–4. This is highly speculative, but could be contextualised by an entry in the much later annals of Oseney claiming that, during the Marshal's rebellion, Oxford had sided with the king: *Annales de Oseneia*, *AM*, iv. 77.

25. Which was important, though its significance should not be exaggerated. See, for instance, *CM*, iii. 227.

26. P.J. Geary and J.B. Freed, 'Literacy and violence in twelfth-century Bavaria. The "murder letter" of Count Siboto IV', *Viator* 25 (1994), 15–29.

27. P. Csendes, *Philip von Schwaben. Ein Staufer im Kampf um die Macht* (Darmstadt, 2003), 189–92.

28. *Annales Elwangenses*, MGH SS x, 20.

29. *Continuatio Casuum Sancti Galli. Conradi de Fabaria Continuatio Casuum Sancti Galli*, ed. G. Meyer von Knonau, St Gallische Geschichtsquellen IV, Mittheilungen zur Vaterländischen Geschichte des Historischen Vereins von St Gallen, New Series 7 (St Gall, 1879), 244–5.

30. A. Patschowsky, 'Zur Ketzerverfolgung Konrads von Marburg', *DA* 37 (1981), 641–93; M. Fischer, 'Konrad von Marburg und die Anfänge der Inquisition in Deutschland', *Jahrbuch der Hessischen kirchengeschichtlichen Vereinigung in Hessen und Nassau* 55 (2004), 161–95.

31. *Chronicon Wormatiense*, 169–70. Not quite as supportive of the killing, but still hostile towards Conrad: *Gesta Treverorum Continuatio IV*, 400–2.

32. *Annales Erphordenses fratrum praedicatorum*, in: *Monumenta Erphesfurtensia saeculi xii., xiii., xiv.*, ed. O. Holder-Egger, MGH SSrG sep. ed. (Hanover and Leipzig, 1899), 86.

33. J. Lothmann, *Erzbischof Engelbert I. von Köln (1216–1225): Graf von Berg, Erzbischof und Herzog, Reichsverweser*, Cologne 1993; B. Fischer, 'Engelbert von Berg (1185–1225), Kirchenfürst und Staatsmann. Mit einer Gegenüberstellung zu Thomas Becket (1118–1170)', *Zeitschrift des Bergischen Geschichtsvereins* 94 (1989–90), 1–47. The *Vita*, by Caesarius of Heisterbach, is reprinted in *Die Wundergeschichten des Caesarius von Heisterbach*, ed. A. Hilka, 3 vols (Bonn, 1933–7), vol. 3.

34. There also were rumours that Frederick II had been involved in the murder of Duke Louis of Bavaria: Conradus de Fabaria, *Continuatio Casuum Sancti Galli*, 243–4.

35. See also the introductory remarks to *Violence*, ed. Brown and Gorecki, and S.K. Cohn, *Lust for Liberty: The Politics of Social Revolt in Medieval Europe, 1200–1425* (Cambridge/Mass., 2006).

36. B. Weiler, 'The king as judge: Frederick Barbarossa and Henry II as seen by their contemporaries', *Texts, Histories and Historiographies. Essays in Honour of Timothy Reuter*, ed. P.J. Skinner (Turnhout, forthcoming).

37. C. Burt, 'The demise of the general eyre in the reign of Edward I', *EHR* 120 (2005), 1–14; P. Hyams, 'Nastiness and wrong, rancor and reconciliation', *Conflict in Medieval Europe*, ed. Brown and Gorecki, 195–218; idem, *Rancor and Reconciliation in Medieval England* (Ithaca, 2003), 242–65.

38. *Annals of Oseney*, AM, iv. 81.

39. Weiler, 'King as judge'.

40. Hyams, 'Nastiness and wrong'.

41. *Ottonis de Sancto blasio Chronica*, 72–3.

42. T. Holzapfel, *Papst Innozenz III., Philipp II. August, König von Frankreich und die englisch-welfische Verbindung 1198–1216* (Frankfurt am Main, 1991).

43. W. Hechberger, 'Die Vorstellung vom staufisch-welfischen Gegensatz im 12. Jhdt. Zur Analyse und Kritik einer Deutung', *Heinrich der Löwe: Herrschaft und Repräsentation*, ed. J. Fried and O.G. Oexle (Stuttgart, 2003), 381–426.

44. *Recueil des Historiens* xvi, 643–8.
45. *Constitutiones 1198–1272*, no. 322.
46. J.A. Green, *Henry I. King of England and Duke of Normandy* (Cambridge, 2005), 215–6.
47. J.C. Holt, 'King John and Arthur of Brittany', *Nottingham Medieval Studies* 44 (2000), 82–103.
48. C.T. Wood, 'The Mise of Amiens and Saint-Louis' theory of kingship', *French Historical Studies* 6 (1970), 300–10; R.F. Treharne, 'The Mise of Amiens, 23 January 1264', *Studies in Medieval History, Presented to Frederick Maurice Powicke*, ed. R.W. Hunt (Oxford, 1948), 223–39; J. le Goff, *Saint Louis* (Paris, 1996), 264–7; Maddicott, *Simon de Montfort*, 256–70; Denholm-Young, *Richard of Cornwall*, 118–24. For a more whiggish view see Valente, 'The provisions'.
49. Stürner, *Friedrich II.*, i. 137–41; B.U. Hucker, *Otto IV. Der wiederentdeckte Kaiser* (Frankfurt am Main, 2003), 339–47, 356–63.
50. *Constitutiones et Acta Publica Imperatorum et Regum, 1273–98*, ed. J. Schwalm (Hanover, 1903), nos. 620–1. See also, J. Goll, 'Zu Brunos von Olmütz Bericht an Papst Gregor X. (1273)', *Mitteilungen des Instituts für Österreichische Geschichtsforschung*, xxiii (1902), 487–90; J.K. Hoensch, *Premysl Otakar II. von Böhmen. Der goldene König* (Graz, 1989), 200–12; B. Weiler, 'Image and "Reality" in Richard of Cornwall's German career', *EHR* 113 (1998), 1111–42, at 1132–3; B. Roberg, *Das Zweite Konzil von Lyon [1274]* (Paderborn, 1990), 95–101.
51. Rogge, 'Attentate und Schlachten', passim.
52. That this was a by no means peculiarly German development is evident from the works by S.D. White, 'From Peace to Power: The Study of Disputes in Medieval France,' E. Cohen and M. de Jong, eds, *Medieval Transformations* (Leiden: Brill, 2000), 203–18; 'Feuding and Peace-Making in the Touraine around the Year 1100', *Traditio* 42 (1986), 195–63; ' "Pactum … Legem Vincit et Amor Judicium"*: The Settlement of Disputes by Compromise in Eleventh-Century Western France,' *American Journal of Legal History* 22 (1979), 291–309; F.L. Cheyette, 'Some Reflections on Violence, Reconciliation, and the "Feudal Revolution" ', *Conflict in Medieval Europe*, ed. Brown and Gorecki, 243–64; and the work of W.I. Miller, *Bloodtaking and Peacmeaking. Feud, Law, and Society in Medieval Iceland* (Chicago, 1990).
53. Although we should take notice, for instance, of Henry III's warning to Richard Siward that he should exile himself from court, as Henry might not be able to protect him against the earl of Cornwall's wrath. *Annals of Oseney, AM*, iv. 81.

Part II The ideals and norms of politics

1. J.T. Rosenthal, 'The king's "wicked advisers" and medieval baronial rebellions', *Political Science Quarterly* 82 (1967), 595–618; Valente, *Theory and Practice*.
2. Vincent, 'Conclusion'; idem, *Holy Blood*, 188–96; 'The pilgrimages'.
3. See, Reuter, 'Modern mentalities'.

4. W. Koch, 'Die Edition der Urkunden Kaiser Friedrichs II', *Das Staunen der Welt. Kaiser Friedrich II. von Hohenstaufen, 1194–1250*, Schriften zur Staufischen Geschichte und Kunst 15 (Göppingen, 1996), 40–70.
5. A convenient survey is provided by: G. Althoff, *Macht der Rituale*; idem, *Inszenierte Herrschaft. Geschichtsschreibung und politisches Handeln im Mittelalter* (Darmstadt, 2003); idem (ed.), *Zeichen – Werte – Rituale. Internationales Kooloquium des Sonderforschungsbereichs 496 an der Westfälischen Wilhelms-Universität Münster* (Münster, 2004); H. Keller, *Ottonische Königsherrschaft. Organisation und Legitimation königlicher Macht* (Darmstadt, 2002); *Die Welt der Rituale von der Antike bis heute*, ed. C. Ambos, S. Hotz, G. Schwedler and S. Weinfurter (Darmstadt, 2005).
6. Vincent, 'Pilgrimages', 40.
7. This builds on some of the observations and examples outlined in B. Weiler, 'Henry III through European eyes – communication and historical writing in thirteenth-century Europe', Weiler with Rowlands, *England and Europe*, 137–61.
8. C. Given-Wilson, *Chronicles. The Writing of History in Medieval England* (London, 2004), 65–9.
9. *CM*, v. 617.
10. *Chronica Regia Coloniensis*, 267.

4   Loyalty, justice and honour: Henry (VII) and Frederick II

1. *Constitutiones 1198–1272*, no. 322
2. *ad consilium principum et magnatum pro pace et tranquilitate patrie reformanda.*
3. S. Reynolds, *Kingdoms and Communities in Western Europe 900–1300* (Oxford, 1984), 262–302.
4. *nisi meliorum et maiorum terre consensus primitus habeatur Constitutiones 1198–1272*, no. 305, *HD*, iii. 461. See, however, the difficulties similar principles, a generation later, were to cause de Montfort in England: Maddicott, *Simon de Montfort*, 166–7; and the same principle being implicitly invoked in Bracton, *De Legibus*, iv. 218–23.
5. Arnold, 'Frederick II', which seeks to explain this as a recognition of inevitable difficulty.
6. W. Stürner, 'König Heinrich (VII.). Rebell oder Sachwalter staufischer Interessen?', *Der Staufer Heinrich (VII.). Ein König im Schatten seines kaiserlichen Vaters* (Göppingen, 2001), 12–41. See also the relevant clause in the *Sachsenspiegel: Landrecht*, ed. K.A. Eckhardt (Göttingen, 1955), iii. 52 §2, p. 237.
7. *Constitutiones 1198–1272*, no. 316.
8. *HD* iv. 473–6 (Gregory IX); *Acta Imperii Selecta*, no. 303 (Frederick II).
9. *honorem nostrum, quem de gratia Dei omnipotentis et sua habere dinoscimur.*
10. K. Görich, *Die Ehre*, 12–57. The reading here is, however, more closely related to that proposed by Timothy Reuter, 'Assembly politics in the West from the eight century to the twelfth', *The Medieval World*, ed. Peter Linehan and Janet Nelson (London, 2001), 432–50 [repr. in his *Medieval Polities* at 436–60].
11. *Constitutiones 1198–1272*, no. 193.
12. *iuxta consilium principum, qui tunc aderant, et in eorum presencia. Constitutiones 1198–1272*, no. 193.

13. *precipue principes nostros specialia diligeret et prosequeretur honore, fidelibus nostris generaliter iusticiam observando.*
14. Broekmann, *Rigor Iustitiae*, 306–19.
15. *Ryccardi de Sancto Germano Notarii Chronica*, ed. C.A. Carufi, RIS NS (Bologna, 1936–8), p. 190; *Annales Erphordenses fratrum praedicatorum*, p. 89.
16. Weiler, 'Reasserting power', 261–70.
17. *Continuatio Eberbacensis*, 348.
18. *HD*, iv. 527–30.
19. *HD*, iv. 945–7.
20. *Preterea quia rex filius noster, recedentibus omnibus ab eo post adventum nostrum quos invitos ad se traxerat.*
21. Clauses 15–19; *Constitutiones 1198–1272*, no. 196.
22. *Chronica Regia Coloniensis*, p. 267.
23. H. Beumann, 'Friedrich II. und die heilige Elisabeth. Zum Besuch des Kaisers in Marburg am 1. Mai 1236', *Sankt Elisabeth. Fürstin, Dienerin, Heilige* (Sigmaringen, 1981), pp. 151–66.
24. D. Henniges, 'Vita Sanctae Elisabeth, Landgraviae Thuringiae auctore anonymo nunc primum in lucem edita', *Archivum Franciscanum Historicum* 2 (1909), 240–68 at 267–8.
25. *Constitutiones 1198–1272*, no. 193.
26. One of the reasons for Duke Frederick's deposition in 1235–6, for instance, had been that he took hostages from his nobles [*Urkundenbuch Babenberger*, no. 1198], and in the twelfth century some of those hostile to Henry the Lion had claimed that he had forced hostages from his nobles [*Annales S. Petri Maiores, in: Monumenta Erphesfurtensia*, 66–7].
27. See also, for a broader European perspective, A.J. Kosto, 'Hostages and the habit of representation in thirteenth-century Occitania', *The Experience of Power in medieval Europe, 950–1150*, ed. R.F. Berkhofer III, A. Cooper and A.J. Kosto (Aldershot, 2005), 183–93.
28. *Acta Imperii Selecta*, no. 303.
29. *Constitutiones 1198–1272*, no. 171; T. Struve, *Die Entwicklung der organologischen Staatsauffassung im Mittelalter* (Stuttgart, 1978).
30. *Constitutiones 1198–1272*, no. 196.
31. *Constiutiones 1198–1272*, no. 197; E. Boshof, 'Die Entstehung des Herzogtums Braunschweig-Lüneburg', *Heinrich der Löwe*, ed. W. Mohrmann (Göttingen, 1980), 249–74.
32. Weiler, 'Reasserting power', 263–8; Boshof, 'Reich und Reichsfürsten', 10–13.
33. *Constitutiones 1198–1272*, no. 201; the following will draw on *Urkundenbuch Babenberger*, no. 1198, largely because of the more extensive critical apparatus provided there.
34. *contra honorem nostrum et imperii dignitatem.*
35. *contra honorem nostrum et imperii.*
36. *offensas nostras et imperii per eum attemptatas.*
37. *deum timere debeat et nos et imperium teneatur modis omnibus revereri.*
38. *Urkundenbuch Babenberger*, no. 1193.
39. The duke's treatment of widows may, however, not be entirely fictional. In 1255, for instance, Ottokar of Bohemia restored a property which Duke Frederick (+1246) had seized from a widow. Whether the dispossession had taken place pre-1236 is, of course, a different matter. *Quellen zur Geschichte*

der Stadt Wien. Erste Abtheilung: Regesten aus in-und ausländischen Archive mit Ausnahme des Archivs der Stadt Wien. Erster Band, ed. A. Mayer (Vienna, 1895), no. 722.

40. *Constitutiones 1198–1272*, no. 197. This may contain an allusion to the less than peaceful relationship between Otto's forebears (including Henry the Lion) and those of Frederick II, as well as rumours that, in 1228–9, Otto had been approached about becoming anti-king in competition with Frederick and Henry. Frech, 'Ein Plan'; Weiler, *Henry III*, 40–3.

41. *HD*, iv. 507.

42. *HD*, iv. 527.

43. *Acta Imperii Selecta*, no. 303.

44. *Urkundenbuch der Stadt Erfurt*, ed. C. Beyer, Geschichtsquellen der Provinz Sachsen und angrenzender Gebiete 23, 2 vols (Halle, 1889–97), i, no. 112.

45. *Constitutiones 1198–1272*, no. 154; see also, for a more extensive critical apparatus, *Codex Diplomaticus et Epistolaris Regni Bohemiae*, ed. G. Friedrich *et al.*, 9 vols (Prague, 1904–93), iii, no. 11.

46. In fact, Henry (VII), similarly confirmed the citizens of Frankfurt half the income of the royal mint at Frankfurt because of their loyalty, which it was his duty to reward. *Codex Moenofrancofurtanus. Urkundenbuch der Reichsstadt Frankfurt*, ed. J.F. Böhmer, 2 vols (Frankfurt/Main, 1901–5), i, no. 107. This formula was, however, noticeably absent from a privilege given to the citizens of Oppenheim in September 1234: ibid., no. 104.

47. *HD*, iv. 529, *honorem nostrum et imperii*.

48. *HD*, iv. 527, *imperiale nomen exceperistis et honorem*.

49. *Urkundenbuch Babenberger*, no. 1198.

50. *HD*, iv. 528.

51. *Urkundenbuch der Stadt Worms*, ed. H. Boos, 2 vols (Berlin, 1886–8), i, no. 193; this included the very privileges granted by Frederick in 1236: ibid., no. 182.

52. F. Hausmann, 'Kaiser Friedrich II. und Österreich', J. Fleckenstein (ed.), *Probleme um Friedrich II* (Sigmaringen, 1974), 225–308, at 268–74.

5   Justice, loyalty and the absence of honour: Frederick II and Henry (VII) as seen by their contemporaries

1. *Annales Moguntini*, MGH SS 17, 2; *Annales Sancti Trudberti* MGH SS 17, 293 (which does not mention Sicily, but simply has Henry taken captive and sent *in exilium*, as do the *Annales Maiores Zwifaltenses*, MGH SS 10, 59); *Annales Sancti Georgii in Silva Nigra*, MGH SS 17, 297; *Continuatio Sancrucensis II*, MGH SS 9, 638; *Annales Ottoburani Minores*, MGH SS 17, 317; *Annales Stadenses Auctore Alberto*, MGH SS 16, 362; *Continuatio Lambacenses*, MGH SS 9, 558; *Annales Sancti Rudberi Salisburgenses*, MGH SS 9, 786.

2. *Chronica S Petri Erfordensis Moderna*, in: *Monumenta Erphesfurtensia*, 232.

3. *Annales Erphordenses fratrum Praedicatorum*, in: *Monumenta Erphesfurtensia*, 89.

4. Görich, *Honor imperii*, 331–62; idem, 'Geld und "honor". Friedrich Barbarossa in Italien', in *Formen symbolischer Kommunikation*, ed. Althoff, 177–200; H. Stehkämper, 'Geld bei deutschen Königswahlen im 13. Jahrhundert', J. Schneider (ed.), *Wirtschaftskräfte und Wirtschaftswege: Festschrift Hermann Kellenbenz*, 4 vols (Stuttgart, 1978), i. 83–115.

5. *Chronica Regia Coloniensis*, 266.
6. *Annales Scheftlarienses Maiores*, MGH SS 17, 340.
7. *Annales Wormatienses*, in: *Quellen zur Geschichte der Stadt Worms*, H. Boos (ed.), 3 vols (Berlin, 1886–93), ii. 146.
8. Henniges, 'Vita Sanctae Elisabeth', 267.
9. *Annales Scheftlarienses*, 340; *Continuatio Sancrucensis II*, 638.
10. *Continuatio Praedicatorum Vindobonensium*, 727.
11. *Continuatio Sancrucensis II*, 638.
12. *Hermanni Altahensis Annales*, MGH SS 17, 392.
13. *Acta Imperii Inedita*, nos. 470, 642; *Acta Imperii Selecta*, no. 334.
14. Including those like the Capetian kings of France, whose advances had previously been spurned in the 1220s (when there had been plans for Henry to marry a Capetian princess), and who might have felt threatened by the emperor's Plantagenet marriage. See Weiler, *King Henry III*, 33–46.
15. *Annales Marbacenses*, 96–7. On the text see also: V. Huth, *Staufische 'Reichshistoriographie' und scholastische Intellektualitat: das elsassische Augustinerchorherrenstift Marbach im Spannungsfeld von regionaler Uberlieferung und universalem Horizont* (Ostfildern, 2004).
16. Almost identical points were made in the Chronicle of Ebersheim, another text from thirteenth-century Alsace, but while the *Annals of Marbach* put the beginning of Henry's uprising and tyranny after Frederick announced his visit, in the Chronicle's account it preceded Frederick's visit: the emperor had intended to come and set right the many crimes committed by his son. *Chronicon Ebersheimense*, MGH SS 23, 453.
17. *RI*, nos. 4375, 4378, 4379.
18. *RI*, no. 2115a.
19. His credibility has sometimes been questioned, most recently by Stürner, *Friedrich II*, ii. 304–5 no. 80, and largely because of the elephants and dromedaries mentioned in this account. For a more positive view, centring on this point in particular, see Weiler, 'Reasserting power', 249–50.
20. *Continuatio Eberbacensis*, 348.
21. *Annales Wormatienses*, 146, 148.
22. *Annales Wormatienses*, 146–8.
23. *Urkundenbuch Worms*, ii, no. 175.
24. Ibid., nos. 160, 163–6, 172.
25. Ibid., 182.
26. *Chronicon Wormatiense*, 172.
27. *Chronicon Wormatiense*, 173–4.
28. *Chronicon Wormatiense*, ii. 175.
29. *Chronicon Wormatiense*, ii. 174.
30. In fact, much of the *Chronicon* is taken up with describing the further injustices inflicted on the prelate, and his ultimate reconciliation with the emperor. *Chronicon Wormatiense*, ii. 175–8.
31. *Chroncion Wormatiense*, ii. 178.
32. *Chronicon Wormatiense*, ii. 177–8.
33. *Chronicon Wormatiesne*, ii. 176–7.
34. Broekmann, *Rigor Justitiae*, 297–306.
35. For the text: U. Müller, *Untersuchungen zur politischen Lyrik des deutschen Mittelalters*, Göppinger Arbeiten zur Germanistik (Göppingen, 1974), 65.

36. *Politische Lyrik des Deutschen Mittelalters. Texte I: Von Friedrich II bis Ludwig von Bayern*, ed. U. Müller, Göppinger Arbeiten zur Germanistik (Göppingen, 1972), p. 5.
37. *Politische Lyrik I*, p. 5
38. Müller, *Politische Lyrik*, ii. P. 65
39. *Politische Lyrik*, I, p. 5 (138, ll. 1–6).
40. Daz Riche was vil sere siech,/ sin stimme was vor clage tunkel, heise unde riech,/ rot waren im diu augen/diu oren toup, erstummet waz ez ouch. *Politische Lyrik*, I, p. 6 (no. 140, ll. 1–3).
41. Henniges, 'Vita', 267.
42. Müller, *Politische Lyrik*, ii. 88.
43. Müller, *Politische Lyrik*, I, 34, I, l. 3.
44. Müller, *Politische Lyrik*, ii. 91.
45. Müller, *Politische Lyrik*, i. 35–6, x.
46. Müller, *Politische Lyrik*, i. 34–5, xlviii ll. 4–9.
47. Müller, *Politische Lyrik*, I, 39, lxxv ll. 2–10.
48. Müller, *Politische Lyrik*, I, 39–40; ii. 100.
49. Müller, *Politische Lyrik*, i. 35, 13:1; ii. 90–1.
50. This interpretation builds on and elaborates that proposed by Müller, *Politische Lyrik*, ii. 90–1.
51. *Erste (Bairische) Forstetzung*, p. 405, ll. 616–18. This was an important topos: T. Reuter, 'Die Unsicherheit auf den Straßen im europäischen Früh- und Hochmittelalter: Täter, Opfer und ihre mittelalterlichen und modernen Betrachter', *Träger und Funktionen des Friedens im hohen und späten Mittelalter*, ed. J. Fried, Vorträge und Forschungen xliii (Sigmaringen, 1996), 169–202 (transl. and repr. in his *Medieval Polities*).
52. *Die Kaiserchronik eines Regensburger Geistlichen*, ed. E. Schröder, MGH Deutsche Chroniken (Hanover, 1892), ll. 764–5: *Der chaiser uebel hete getan/ daz er den son also vertraip*.
53. p. 406, ll. 623–48.
54. pp. 406–7, ll. 659–708.
55. *Constitutiones 1198–1272*, no. 196.
56. K. Görich, 'Ehre als Ordnungsfaktor. Anerkennung und Stabilisierung von Herrschaft unter Friedrich Barbarossa und Friedrich II.', *Ordnungskonfigurationen im hohen Mittelalter*, ed. B. Schneidmüller und S. Weinfurter (Ostfildern, 2006), 59–92.
57. A concept central to the work of Knut Görich, who has successfully rescued an otherwise often unjustly neglected subject. See also Broekmann, *Rigor Iustitiae*, 272–350; and, for the twelfth century, Krieg, *Herrscherdarstellung*, 139–290.
58. Conradus de Fabaria, *Continuatio*, 237–9.
59. A. Sommerlechner, *Stupor mundi? Kaiser Friedrich II. und die mittelalterliche Geschichtsschreibung* (Vienna, 1999), 428–34.
60. O. Engels, 'Friedrich Barbarossa im Urteil seiner Zeitgenossen', *Stauferstudien. Beiträge zur Geschichte der Staufer im 12. Jahrhundert*, ed. E. Meuthen and S. Weinfurter (Sigmaringen, 1996), 225–45.
61. In lieu of a very rich literature see M. Blattmann, '"Ein Unglück für sein Volk". Der Zusammenhang zwischen Fehlverhalten des Königs und Volkswohl in Quellen des 7.–12. Jahrhunderts', *Frühmittelalterliche Studien* 30

(1996), 80–102; R. Meens, 'Politics, mirrors of princes and the bible: sins, kings and the well-being of the realm', *Early Medieval Europe*, 7 (1998), 345–57.

6 Loyalties true and false: political values in England

1. M.L. Colker, 'The "Margam Chronicle" in a Dublin manuscript', *Journal of the Haskins Society* iv (1992), 123–48.
2. A. Gransden, *Historical Writing in England, c. 550–c. 1307* (London, 1974), 377–8.
3. *The Metrical Chronicle of Robert of Gloucester*, ed. W.A. Wright, 2 vols, RS (London, 1886–7), i. ll. 10735–822.
4. Gransden, *Historical Writing*, 346–55.
5. *The Deeds of the Normans in Ireland. La Geste des Engleis en Yrlande. A new edition of the chronicle formerly known as The Song of Dermot and the Earl*, ed. E. Mullally (Dublin, 2002), 35–6, who is, however, critical of this theory on the grounds that Isabella Marshal, the suggested patron, was not known to have commissioned other texts. I am grateful to Nicholas Vincent for this reference.
6. The mandate has been edited in Vincent, *Peter des Roches*, 388–9, n. 120.
7. J.R. Maddicott, ' "An infinite multitude of nobles": quality, quantity and politics in the pre-reform Parliaments of Henry III', TCE 7 (1999), 17–46; idem, 'The county community and the making of public opinion', TRHS 5th series 28 (1978), 27–44. Weiler, 'Symbolism', 19–23.
8. J. Gillingham, 'Royal newsletters, forgeries and English historians: some links between court and history in the reign of Richard I', in Martin Aurell (ed.), *La cour Plantagenêt (1154–1204). Actes du Colloque tenu à Thouars du 30 avril au 2 mai 1999* (Poitiers, 2000), 171–86.
9. In previous cases, the appearance of an armed escort had been the first step towards open rebellion: in 1215, for instance, the barons approaching the king to demand a confirmation of the laws of Edward the Confessor had approached him in full armour. That the Marshal arrived with an armed retinue pointed in a similar direction and echoes a prohibition against tournaments, decreed just over a week after this mandate. *CPR 1232–47*, 67–8.
10. *RW*, iv. 275–7.
11. Vincent, *Peter des Roches*, 408–10.
12. *RW*, iv. 270–1.
13. On this encounter see also Vincent, *Peter des Roches*, 425–7. On Agnellus also *Tractatus de aduentu fratrum minorum in Angliam*, ed. A.G. Little (Manchester, 1951), 76.
14. *RW*, iv. 282–3.
15. *CPR 1232–47*, 48–9. See also *CR 1231–4*, 442 (3 June 1234) for Gilbert Basset, 'veniendo versus curiam nostrum ad misericordiam nostrum petendum'.
16. See also G. Althoff, 'Huld. Überlegungen zu einem Zentralbegriff der mittelalterlichen Herrschaftsordnung', *Frühmittelalterliche Studien* 25 (1991), 259–82; idem 'Das Privileg der deditio. Formen gütlicher Konfliktbeendigung in der mittelalterlichen Adelsgesellschaft', *Spielregeln*, 99–125.

17. See also Turner, *The King*, 180–201; 73–93. A similar view was voiced by Frederick II in the 1235 *Reichslandfrieden* (which decreed the appointment of an imperial justiciar who should decide cases on the emperor's behalf, but whose decisions could be overturned by Frederick).

18. The similarity with the arguments used against Duke Frederick should be noted, who, among others, had been put on trial for allying himself with the Lombards (*Urkundenbuch Babenberger*, no. 1198).

19. *RW*, iv. 263–4.

20. *RW*, iv. 265.

21. *RW*, iv. 269–70.

22. *RW*, iv. 275–6.

23. *Malo enim rex fatuus reputari ac remissus, quam crudelis et tyrannus. RW*, iv. 257. This echoed previous remarks about the king: when, in 1231, Richard Marshal had been accused by Hubert de Burgh of plotting against the king, Henry, fearing for the tranquillity of the realm, forgave the earl and invested him with his inheritance. *RW*, iv. 225.

24. *RW*, iv. 264.

25. *Thomas Wykes Annales, Annales Monastici*, iv. 77

26. See the comment of the *Chronicon Roskildense*, in: *Scriptores Minores Historiae Danicae*, ed. M.Cl. Geertz, 2 vols (Copenhagen 1917–23) I, 25, concerning King Nicholas, who was *vir mansuetudus et simplex, minime rector*.

27. Purgatory, Canto VIII; Salimbene de Adam, *Cronica*, ed. G. Scalia, 2 vols (Bari, 1966), i. 444–5.

28. *RW*, iv. 294–7, 299.

29. *RW*, iv. 309–10.

30. *RW*, iv. 309.

31. *Gesta Regis Henrici Secundi Benedicti Abbatis*, ed. W. Stubbs, 2 vols, RS (London, 1867–8), i. 14.

32. *RW*, iv. 309.

33. *RW*, iv. 283.

34. *RW*, iv. 298–9.

35. *RW*, iv. 247–8.

36. *RW*, iv. 268.

37. *RW*, iv. 272.

38. *RW*, iv. 274–5.

39. *RW*, iv. 292–3.

40. Colker, *Margam Chronicle*, 133.

41. Colker, *Margam Chronicle*, 138.

42. Colker, *Margam Chronicle*, 139.

43. Colker, *Margam Chronicle*, 134.

44. *RW*, ed. Henry Richards Luard, 3 vols, RS (London, 1890), ii. 208–9.

45. *RW*, ii. 212–13.

46. *Annales de Theokesberia, AM*, i. 90–3.

47. *Annales de Wintonia, AM*, ii. 86–7.

48. *Annales de Waverleia, AM*, ii. 313–15.

49. C.H. Lawrence, *St Edmund of Abingdon. A study of hagiography and history* (Oxford, 1960), 240–1 (chapter 19 of the *vita*).

50. *Annales Prioratus de Dunstaplia, AM*, iii. 137. See also *Annales Cestrienses. Chronicle of the Abbey of S. Werburg, at Chester*, ed. R.C. Christie (Chester,

1887), 58, which laconically but significantly describe this as a war between the king and the earl; and the *Annals of Southwark and Merton*, which unusually view the conflict with de Burgha and Marshal as two separate affairs: M. Tyson, 'The Annals of Southwark and Merton', *Sussex Archaeological Collections* 36 (1925), 24–57, at 56–7.

51. P. Buc, *L'ambiguïté du Livre: prince, pouvoir, et people dans le commentaries de la Bible au Moyen Age* (Paris, 1994), 246–60; idem 'Principes gentium dominantur eorum: Princely Power Between Legitimacy and Illegitimacy in Twelfth-Century Exegesis', *Cultures of Power*, ed. Bisson, 310–28; idem, 'Pouvoir royal et commentaires de la Bible (1150–1350)', *Annales Économies, Sociétés, Civilisations* 44 (1989), 691–714.

52. Rosenthal, 'The king's wicked advisors'.

53. Carpenter, 'Kings, magnates', passim.

54. *Les Gestes de Chiprois*, ed. G. Reynard (Paris, 1887) chap. 330–8, 172–7; The song against the King of Almain', *Political Songs of England from the Reign of John to that of Edward II*, ed. T. Wright, Camden Society (London, 1839); repr. with a new introduction by P. Coss (Cambridge, 1996), 69–71.

55. This also was a key theme in later images of William Rufus, for instance, King Stephen or King John. E. Mason, 'William Rufus: myth and reality', *Journal of Medieval History*, iii (1977), 1–20; T. Callahan Jr., 'The making of a monster: the historical image of William Rufus', *Journal of Medieval History*, vii (1981), 175–86; B. Weiler, William of Malmesbury on kingship', *History* 87 (2005), 3–22.

56. Walter Map, *De Nugis Curialium. Courtiers' Trifles*, ed. and transl. M.R. James, revised by C.N.L. Brooke and R.A.B. Mynors (Oxford, 1983), v. 6, 484–5.

57. *RW*, iv. 265.

58. *RW*, iv. 269–71, 275.

59. *RW*, iv. 279.

60. *RW*, iv. 278.

61. *RW*, iv. 285–6.

62. Similarly, when warned that the king had requested a papal legate to be sent to England, the Marshal welcomed the opportunity to lay before the pope's representative his grievances against the king's ministers. *RW*, iv. 288.

63. See also Vincent, *Peter des Roches*, 438–41; Smith, 'Irish politics'; 14–19.

64. *RW*, iv. 302.

65. *RW*, iv. 304: *sed melius est mihi mori cum honore pro cause justitiae, quam campum per fugam deserere et probra militiae in perpretuum obtinere.*

66. *RW*, iv. 305–8.

67. *RW*, ii. 208–9.

68. *Annales de Waverleia, Annales Monastici*, ii. 313.

69. *Annales de Waverleia, Annales Monastici*, ii. 313–14. See also, similarly, the *Annales de Duntsaplia, Annales Monastici*, iii. 136–7.

70. *Annales de Oseneia, Annales Monastici*, iv. 79–80.

71. To one Cistercian chronicler from Herefordshire it even outshone the rebellion itself. The *Annales Dorenses* barely touch on the Marshal's role. They simply report that he waged war on the king because of the aliens, and then spend most of a rather short entry on outlining the severity of de Burgh's imprisonment (including that he had been put in fetters), and that

the Marshal had sent an armed band to free him. Richard's death is not mentioned. *Annales Dorenses*, MGH SS 27, 528.

72. *RW*, iv. 225.
73. *RW*, iv. 257: *Hubertus a pueritia prius avunculo meo regi Richardo, et postea regi Johanni patri meo, satis servivit fideliter, ut audivi, qui, is contra me male egerit, nunquam per me iniqua morta morietur;...*
74. *CM*, iii. 227–8.
75. *Annales de Waverleia*, *AM*, ii. 311.
76. *Annales de Theokesberia*, *AM*, i. 88; *Annales de Waverleia*, *AM*, ii. 311; Colker, *Margam Chronicle*, 134.
77. William of Malmesbury, *Historia Novella. The Contemporary History*, ed. and transl. E. King and K.R. Potter (Oxford, 1998), iii. 44, 86–7 for King Stephen. In fact, when Richard the Lionheart had been imprisoned by Emperor Henry VI, much energy had been spent by the English court that the king would not be kept in chains, but that he would be kept honourably and as befitted his status [Görich, 'Richard Löwenherz']. Similarly, when reporting Henry (VII)'s demise, one of the aspects of the king's treatment that stood out to Matthew Paris were that the emperor kept his own son in fetters [*CM*, iii. 323–4; see also Broekmann, *Rigor Iustitiae*, 352–67].
78. *CM*, iii. 229. K. Schreiner, 'Gregor VIII., nackt auf einem Esel. Entehrende Entblößung und schandbares Reiten im Spiegel einer Miniatur der Sächsischen Weltchronik', *Ecclesia et Regnum. Beiträge zur Geschichte von Kirche, Recht und Staat im Mittelalter. Festschrift für Franz-Josef Schmale zu seinem 65. Geburtstag* (Bochum, 1989), 155–202. That this was deemed unbecoming was not limited to those opposing the king: in fact, a papal mandate was procured that Hubert was to be freed from his chains. *CR 1231–4*, 274, 325–6.
79. *RW*, iv. 258.
80. *RW*, iv. 253.
81. *RW*, iv. 273–4.
82. *RW*, iv. 274–5; on Becket: *RW*, ii. 360–2.
83. *Annales de Theokesberia*, *AM*, i. 87.
84. Colker, *Margam Chronicle*, 135. See also F.A. Cazel, 'Religious motivation in the biography of Hubert de Burgh', *Studies in Church History* 15 (1978), 109–19.
85. Colker, *Margam Chronicle*, 136. Psalms 34:12 and 37:21.
86. Colker, *Margam Chronicle*, 137–8.
87. *RW*, iv. 312.
88. *RW*, iv. 313–14.
89. Vincent, *Peter des Roches*, 446–55.
90. *RW*, iv. 248.
91. *RW*, iv. 249.
92. *RW*, iv. 312–4.
93. *RW*, iv. 264. This was a recurrent theme with the St Albans historians, and one that was by no means limited to the years of des Roches' ascendancy. See, for instance, *CM*, iv. 628.
94. *Continuatio Praedicatorum Vindobonensium*, 727.
95. Peter de Rivallis, one of his chief allies, was described as the bishop's son. *RW*, iv. 264; Colker, *Margam Chronicle*, 134; Vincent, *Peter des Roches*, 263.

96. *Österreichische Chronik von den 95 Herrschaften*, 106–7.
97. Colker, *Margam Chronicle*, 134.
98. *RW*, iv. 264.
99. *RW*, iv. 265–6.
100. *RW*, iv. 284–5.
101. *Flores Historiarum*, ii. 207.
102. *RW*, iv. 227.
103. *RW*, iv. 243–4.
104. *RW*, iv. 273.
105. See, for instance, *CM*, iii. 476; 478–9; 485; *RW*, ii. 213.
106. *RW*, iv. 277.
107. *RW*, iv. 302.
108. *RW*, iv. 304.
109. *restituit eos in integrum, hoc est, ad famam, terras et possessiones universas*, *Annales de Dunstaplia*, *AM*, iii. 137.
110. *RW*, iv. 287.
111. *RW*, iv. 288.
112. *Annales de Dunstapliae*, *AM*, iii. 136–7.
113. *RW*, iv. 256–8.
114. *RW*, iv. 271–2.
115. *RW*, iv. 244.
116. *RW*, iv. 283–4, 286.
117. *RW*, ii. 208–9; *Annales de Waverleia*, *AM*, ii. 313.
118. *CLR 1226–40*, 255. E.H. Kantorowicz, *Laudes Regiae. A study in liturgical acclamations and mediaeval ruler worship* (Berkeley, 1946), 175–7.
119. D.A. Carpenter, 'Henry III and the cult of Edward the Confessor', *EHR* (forthcoming).
120. Weiler, 'Re-asserting power', 261–70.
121. *CR 1231–4*, 321.
122. *Annales Monasterii de Theokesberia*, *AM*, i. 91.
123. In fact, with the exception of the *Annales Marbacenses*, most German chroniclers (unlike their Italian counterparts) did not even report that Henry had sought to forge an alliance with the Lombards and Capetians. That information survives almost exclusively in the Italian sources: *Placentini Gibellini*, MGH SS 18, 470; *Annales Bergomates*, MGH SS 18, 810; *Magistri Tolosani Chronicon Faventinum*, ed. G. Rossini, RIS NS (Bologna, 1936–9), 135.
124. L.E. Scales, 'At the Margin of Community: Germans in Pre-Hussite Bohemia', *TRHS* 6th series 9 (1999), 327–52.

Part III   The ways and means of politics

1. *CR 1234–7*, 271 (28 May 1236).
2. *CR 1234–7*, 18 (27 November 1234).
3. C.R. Brühl, *Fodrum, Gistum, Servitium regis. Studien zu den wirtschaftlichen Grundlagen des Königtums im Frankenreich und in den fränkischen Nachfolgestaaten Deutschland, Frankreich und Italien vom 6. bis zur Mitte des 14. Jahrhunderts* (Cologne, 1968); B. Arnold, *Power and Property in Medieval Germany. Economic and social change c. 900–c. 1300* (Oxford, 2004), 75–116.

4. Reuter, 'Assemblies and assembly politics'; see also, for the wider perspective (though with an early medieval focus, the essays collected in *Political Assemblies in the Earlier Middle Ages*, ed. P.S. Barnwell and M. Mostert (Turnhoult, 2003).

7   Creating a public

1. Methodologically, the following is indebted to B. Thum, 'Öffentlichkeit und Kommunikation im Mittelalter. Zur Herstellung von Öffentlichkeit im Bezugsfeld elementarer Kommunikationsformen im 13. Jahrhundert', *Höfische Repräsentation. Das Zeremoniell und die Zeichen*, ed. H. Ragotzky and H. Wenzel (Tübingen, 1990), 65–87.
2. *RW*, iv. 100; Carpenter, *Minority*, 382–8; idem, *Struggle for Mastery*, 314–16.
3. *Chronica Regia Coloniensis*, 267.
4. Imperial charters, for instance, regularly refer to the fact that a grant was based on a charter that had been read before the assembled court, or that it was the result of a public consultative process. *Codex Diplomaticus et epistolarius regni Bohemiae*, ed. G. Friedrich *et al.*, 9 vols (Prague, 1904–93), iii, no. 11; *Urkundenbuch Worms*, ed. Boos, i, no. 193.
5. *Tiroler Urkundenbuch. Erste Abteilung: Die Urkunden zur Geschichte des Deutschen Etschlandes und des Vintschgaus*, ed. F. Huter *et al.*, 3 vols (Innsbruck, 1937–57), iii, no. 1004.
6. *CR 1231–4*, 321.
7. See also the still very much relevant points made by M.T. Clanchy, *From Memory to Written Record. England 1066–1307*, second edition (Oxford, 1993), 253–94.
8. Gillingham, 'Royal newsletters'.
9. These are discussed in more detail in B. Weiler, 'Matthew Paris, Richard of Cornwall's candidacy for the German throne, and the Sicilian Business', *JMH* 26 (2000), 71–92.
10. This concept, although developed in an early medieval context, has been taken from Reuter, 'Assembles and assembly politics'; see also: Reynolds, 'Kingdoms and communities', Powicke, *King Henry III*.
11. For other examples see Weiler, 'Henry III through foreign eyes', passim.
12. *Chronique de Gislebert de Mons*, 157–60.
13. W. Rösener, 'Die ritterlich-höfische Kultur des Mittelalters und ihre wirtschaftlichen Grundlagen', *Rittertum und höfische Kultur der Stauferzeit*, ed. J. Laudage and Y. Leiverkus (Cologne, Weimar and Vienna, 2006), 111–35.
14. *RI*, no. 3966a.
15. *RI*, no. 3978a.
16. *Chronica Regia*, 266.
17. *Gotfredi Continutio Eberbacensis*, 348.
18. *Annales Marbacenses*, 97.
19. *Sermo de Translatione Beate Elyzabeth*, in: *Die Wundergeschichten des Caesarius von Heisterbach*, iii. 386–7; *Chronica Regia Coloniensis*, p. 268.
20. S.D. Church, 'The royal itinerary in the twelfth century', *TCE* 11 (forthcoming, 2007), 31–45.
21. *CLR 1226–40*, 247. As does the order for twenty salted hinds to be ready for Christmas, issued that same month: ibid., 248.

22. *CLR 1226–40*, 287.
23. Roger of Wendover, for instance, pointed out how the July 1233 parliament at Westminster was attended not only by the earls and barons of England, but also by their large armed entourage. *RW*, iv. 270. While writing in the late twelfth century, Walter Map's descriptions of the English royal court similarly point to the number of attendants and hangers on: Map, *De Nugis Curialium*, 438–9, 470–3.
24. *Annales de Dunstaplia, AM*, iii, 127.
25. Vincent, *Peter des Roches*, 280–3.
26. *CM*, iv. 590.
27. *Chronique de Gislebert de Mons*, 155–60; H. Wolter, 'Der Mainzer Hoftag von 1184 als politisches Fest', *Feste und Feiern im Mittelalter. Paderborner Symposion des Mediävistenverbandes*, ed. D. Altenburg, J. Jarnut, H.-H. Steinhoff (Sigmaringen, 1991), 193–9.
28. The most detailed account is provided by Matthew Paris: *CM*, iii. 327.
29. *Chronica Regia Coloniensis*, 267–8.
30. *Chronica Regia Coloniensis*, 267.
31. *Urkundenbuch* Babenberger, no. 1198. This may also contextualise the reference, in the charter confirming Otto of Brunswick's enfeoffment with his duchy at Mainz in 1235, to the meeting having been held specifically to deal with the reform of the realm [*Constitutiones 1198–1272*, no. 197], and to which the princes had been called collectively and individually (*communaliter et specialiter* [*Constitutiones 1198–1272*, no. 201]). Some of the fuzzy terminology thus certainly reflected the circumstances of Frederick's visit, but also his rare presence. Some of the twelfth-century accounts of Henry II returning to England, for instance, could just as easily have been written about Frederick II in 1235 [*Gesta Regis Henrici Secundi Benedicti Abbatis*, ed. W. Stubbs, 2 vols, RS (London, 1867–8), i. 4, 138–9, 207–8], and similar passages relate to Henry III and his family before or after their forays onto the mainland [*De Antiquis legibus*, 22–3, 42; *Wendover*, iv. 334–5. *CM*, v. 623; *Wykes, AM*, iv. 106–7; 122]. *De Antiquis legibus*, 22–3, 42; *Wendover*, iv. 334–5. *CM*, v. 623; *Wykes, AM*, iv. 106–7, 122.
32. *Annales de Dunstaplia, AM*, iii, 84. Cf. also Carpenter, *Minority*, 324–6.
33. *CPR 1232–47*, 67–8, 70.
34. D. Crouch, *Tournament* (London, 2005), 29–30. After all, one of the steps leading up to Runnymede and Magna Carta had been a tournament, called by the rebel barons, and as a means of gathering support and showing military strength. *RW*, iii. 321–2.
35. *Constitutiones 1198–1272*, no. 329.
36. *Annales Marbacenses*, 97; *Chronicon Ebersheimense*, 453; *Gesta Treverorum Continuatio IV*, MGH SSrG 24, 403; *Annales erphordenses fratrum praedicatorum*, 89; *Annales Scheftlarienses Maiores*, 340. G. Wolf, 'Wimpfen, Worms und Heidelberg. Einige Bemerkungen zum Herrschaftsende König Heinrichs', *Zeitschrift für Geschichte des Oberrheins* Neue Folge 98 (1989), pp. 471–86.
37. *RW*, iv. 282–3. It is also reminiscent of the demand made by Edward I of Alexander III of Scotland in 1278, who was ordered to follow the English king to Westminster for his act of homage, as thereby a greater number of

witnesses could be assembled. R.R. Davies, *The First English Empire. Power and Identity in the British Isles 1093–1343* (Oxford, 2000), 22–5.

38. *ibidem honestium cum suis de instantibus negotiis locuturus. CM*, iii. 362–3.
39. *Acta Imperii Selecta*, no. 303.
40. *CM*, iii. 321–2.
41. Weiler, 'Reasserting power', 265.
42. *RW*, iv. 268–9.
43. *RW*, iv. 270–1.
44. *Urkundenbuch Babenberger*, no. 1198.
45. *RW*, iv. 264.
46. *RW*, iv. 272.
47. *RW*, iv. 275–7.
48. The *Flores Historiarum* brings this point home in their description of the 1267 interdict over London: *Flores Historiarum*, iii, 14. For the wider phenomenon in a broader European context see also M.C. Mansfield, *The Humiliation of Sinners: Public Penance in Thirteenth-Century France* (Ithaca, 1995).
49. *Constitutiones 1198–1272*, no. 322.
50. *RI*, no. 2098.
51. H. Kluger, *Hochmeister Hermann von Salza und Kaiser Friedrich II: ein Beitrag zur Frühgeschichte des Deutschen Ordens* (Marburg, 1987). *Annales Marbacenses*, 97; *Chronicon Ebersheimense*, 453; *Gesta Treverorum Continuatio IV*, MGH SSrG 24, 403.
52. *Continuatio Eberbacensis*, 348.
53. *Chronicon Wormatiense*, 174–5.
54. Weiler, 'Reasserting power', 253–6; for a different interpretation see Broekmann, *Rigor Iustitiae*, 297–320.
55. *CM*, iii. 566–7; Maddicott, *Simon de Montfort*, 25.
56. *CM*, iii. 523–4.
57. See, for instance, *CR 1264–8*, 259, 410; *CR 1268–72*, 81, 82, 83; *CLR 1267–72*, no. 850. *Wykes, AM*, iv. 251; *Annales de Twekesbureia*, 93, 115; *Annales de Dunstaplia*, 137; *CM*, iv. 640. See also Weiler, 'Symbolism and politics', 23–4.
58. G. Althoff, 'Colloquium familiare – Colloquium secretum – Colloquium publicum. Beratung im politischen Leben des früheren Mittelalters', *Frühmittelalterliche Studien* 24 (1990), 145–67; see also his, *Friends, Family and Followers. Political and Social Bonds in Early Medieval Europe*, transl. C. Carroll (Cambridge, 2004).
59. *RW*, iv. 283–4.
60. *RW*, iv. 265–6, where, however, Roger also points out that many could hear the king.
61. *RW*, iv. 275–7.
62. *Chronica Regia Coloniensis*, 266.
63. *Annales Scheftlarienses Maiores*, 340.
64. *Urkundenbuch Babenberger*, no. 1198.
65. *Chronica Regia Coloniensis*, 267.
66. *Annales Marbacenses*, 97.
67. *Constitutiones 1198–1272*, no. 196.
68. *CLR 1267–72*, no. 1341.

69. *infinita nobilium multitudo, scilicet regni totalis universitas* – it is almost impossible to translate the claim to universal representation conveyed in the Latin. *CM*, iii. 380.

70. *clericus ac domini regis familiaris, vir quidem discretus et legume terrae peritus, ut quasi mediator inter regem et regni magnates regium propositum et voluntatem in publicum propalaret.*

71. *CM*, iii. 417.

72. *RW*, iv. 275–7.

73. *The Chronicle of Battle Abbey*, ed. and transl. E. Searle (Oxford, 1980), pp. 174–89; *Chronica Jocelini de Brakelonda. The Chronicle of Jocelin de Brakelond*, ed. and transl. H.E. Butler (London, 1949), pp. 20–3; *The Historical Works of Gervase of Canterbury*, ed. W. Stubbs, 2 vols, RS (London, 1879–80), *Chronica*, i. 309–24.

74. *CM*, iii. 381–2.

75. *CM*, iii. 382.

76. Maddicott, 'An infinite multitude', 25–6, no. 46.

77. *vel imperialia vel alia ardua negotia. CM*, iii. 380; Weiler, *King Henry III*, 72–4.

78. *CM* iii. 381: *Et indignanter responderunt se undique et saepe nunc vicesima, nunc tricesima, nunc quinquagesima Gravari promittendo et persolvendo; ... regem tam leviter seducibilem, qui nunquam unum ex inimicis regni, etiam minimum, repulit vel exterruit, nec fines regni unquam ampliavit, sed arctavit et alienis subjugavit.*

79. *secesserunt tandem in locum seorsum secretiorum. CM*, iii. 381.

80. *CM*, iii. 382.

81. *CM*, iii. 383–4. See also Stacey, *Politics, Policy*, 93–131.

82. As suggested by the fact that Gilbert Basset's advice was given *communi audientia*, which may mean either in a way that the other magnates could hear him, or in a general meeting between the king and his magnates.

83. *CM*, iii. 362–4.

84. That Siward was advised to flee the court was perhaps another veiled attack on Henry III (who could not even control his own relatives, and who had only pretended to forgive the rebels of 1233–4).

85. *Annales de Theokesberia, AM*, i. 90.

86. Reuter, 'Assemblies'; Althoff 'Colloquium'.

87. *RW*, iv. 275–6.

88. *RW*, iv. 296–7. See, for comparable accounts, *Flores Historiarum*, ii. 208–9; *Annales de Theokesberia, AM*, i. 91, 93; *Annales de Waverleia, AM*, ii. 315.

89. *CM*, iii. 478.

90. Note the parallel with Bracton, *De Legibus*, ii. 109.

91. *darent ... regi sanum et salubre regno consilium. CM*, iii. 383.

92. *RW*, iv. 247, 255.

93. This is, however, also a somewhat foreshortened perspective. See Carpenter, *Struggle for Mastery*, 369–75; idem, 'Chancellor Ralph de Neville and plans of political reform, 1215–1258', *TCE* 2 (1988), 69–80; 'King, Magnates and Society'.

94. N. Denholm-Young, 'The "Paper Constitution" attributed to 1244', *EHR* 50 (1943), 401–23; C.R. Cheney, 'The "paper constitution" conserved by Matthew Paris', *EHR* 65 (1950), 213–21.

95. *Annales Marbacenses*, 97.

96. *Acta Imperii Selecta*, no. 303.

97. D.A. Carpenter, 'The beginnings of parliament', in his *Reign of Henry III*, 381–408.

98. *Constitutiones 1198–1272*, no. 105.

99. H. Appelt, *Privilegium Minus. Das staufische Kaisertum und die Babenberger in Österreich*, second revised edition (Vienna, Graz and Cologne, 1976).

100. *Chronica Regia Coloniensis*, p. 271; *Constitutiones 1198–1272*, no. 329.

101. Weiler, 'Reasserting power', 269–71.

102. *Chronica Regia Coloniensis*, p. 271; *Constitutiones 1198–1272*, no. 329; Boshof, 'Reich und Reichsfürsten', 10–11.

103. *Historia Welforum*, ed. and transl. E. König, Schwäbische Chroniken der Stauferzeit (Stuttgart, 1938; repr. Sigmaringen, 1978), 66–7; *Ottonis de Sancto Blasio Chronica*, ed. A. Hofmeister, MGH SSrG sep. ed. (Hanover, 1912), 21; *Lamberti Waterloos Annales Cameracenses*, MGH SSrG 16 (Hanover, 1859), 524–5.

104. On Conrad see most recently Fischer, 'Konrad von Marburg'; Patschowsky, 'Zur Ketzerverfolgung'.

105. *Annales Erphordenses*, 85.

106. Similar divisions are implied by Matthew Paris' account of the 1237 parliament (the participants withdrew with their own), and are certainly evident in Matthew's version of the 1238 council convened by the papal legate (while the earl of Lincoln and John fitzGeoffrey withdrew, William Raleigh, as a member of the clergy, remained as the king's representative), as was common in most meetings touching on matters clerical. *CM*, iii. 417.

107. *Annales Erphordenses*, 86.

108. *Annales Erphordenses*, 84–5, 86.

109. *publice et confidenter*.

110. *Annales Erphordenses*, 86–7.

111. *Annales Erphordenses*, 87.

112. William of Newburgh, *Historia Rerum Anglicarum*, in: *Chronicles of the Reigns of Stephen, Henry II., and Richard I.*, ed. R. Howlett, 3 vols, RS (London, 1884–5), ii. 131–4.

113. *rex cum omnibus principibus ac prelates qui aderant … presedit iudicio.*

114. See Maddicott, 'The county community'.

115. *RW*, iii. 318–19.

116. *De Antiquis Legibus Liber*, 19.

117. *De Antiquis Legibus Liber*, 72–3.

118. *De Antiquis Legibus Liber*, 87.

119. *RW*, iv. 309–14.

120. *RW*, iv. 312; *Annales de Twekesbureia, AM*, i. 93; *Annales de Dunstaplia, AM*, iii. 137; *CPR 1232–47*, 48–9.

121. This was a development already evident in the twelfth century. See, for instance, T. Reuter, 'Mandate, privilege, court judgement: techniques of rulership in the Age of Frederick Barbarossa', in his *Medieval Polities*, 413–31.

122. *Continuatio Sancrucensis II*, 638.

123. *Annales Sancti Rudberti Salisburgenses*, 786.

124. Having said this we also should remember that one of the accusations made against Henry (VII) not only by his father but also by numerous chroniclers was that he overruled the advice of his princes. Forceful kingship was welcome, as long as it did not happen too frequently.

8 Addressing the public: rituals, gestures and charters

1. Valente, *Theory and Practice*, provides a good example. This should not, however, distract from the many excellent observations made by Professor Valente.
2. Althoff, *Spielregeln der Politik*; 'Zur Bedeutung symbolischer Kommunikation für das Verständnis des Mittelalters', *Frühmittelalterliche Studien* 31 (1997), 370–89. *Formen und Funktionen*, ed. Althoff; *Zeichen, Rituale, Werte*, ed. Althoff.
3. Some of the most important titles are: K.J. Leyser, *Rule and Conflict in an Early Medieval Society. Ottonian Saxony* (Oxford, 1979); 'Ritual, Zeremonie und Gestik: das ottonische Reich', *Frühmittelalterliche Studien* 27 (1993), 1–26; Althoff, *Spielregeln*; P. Buc, *The Dangers of Ritual* (Princeton, 2001); 'Political rituals and political imagination in the medieval West from the fourth century to the eleventh', *The Medieval World*, ed. Linehan and Nelson, 432–50; 'Rituel politique et imaginaire politique au haut Moyen Âge', *Revue Historique* 306 (2002), 843–83; G. Koziol, *Begging Pardon and Favour. Ritual and Political Order in Early Medieval France* (Ithaca, 1992); *Rituals of Royalty: Power and Ceremonial in Traditional Societies*, ed. D. Cannadine and S. Price (Cambridge, 1987); H.-J. Berbig, 'Zur rechtlichen Relevanz von Ritus und Zeremoniell im römisch-deutschen Imperium', *Zeitschrift für Kirchengeschichte* 92 (1981), 204–49; J.C. Schmitt, *La raison des Gestes dans l'Occident médiéval* (Paris, 1990); *Gestures*, ed. J.C. Schmitt (London, 1984); and the collected articles of Janet Nelson: *Politics and Ritual in Early Medieval Europe* (London, 1984); *Rulers and Ruling Families in Early Medieval Europe* (London, 1999).
4. G. Koziol, 'England, France, and the Problem of Sacrality in Twelfth-Century Ritual', *Cultures of Power*, ed. Bisson, 124–48; C.W. Hollister, 'Anglo-Norman political culture and the Twelfth-Century Renaissance', *Anglo-Norman Political Culture and the 12th-Century Renaissance. Proceedings of the Borchard Conference on Anglo-Norman History, 1995*, ed. C.W. Hollister (Woodbridge, 1997), 1–16; M. Aurell, *L'Empire des Plantagenêt 1154–1224* (Paris, 2003), 123–33; Chaou, *L'ideologie Plantagenêt*.
5. Reuter, 'The Medieval German Sonderweg?'.
6. Nick Vincent, for instance, has pointed to the importance of religious symbolism in the politics of Henry II and Henry III: *The Holy Blood*, 188–96; 'The pilgrimages'; Reuter, '*Velle sibi*'. Klaus van Eickels and Knut Görich have highlighted the significance of friendship rituals and of amorphous concepts such as honour for relations between the kings of England and their neighbours: Görich, 'Verletzte Ehre?'; van Eickels, *Vom inszenierten Konsens*. See also the concluding remarks by Philippe Buc in *Culture Politique des Plantagenêt (1154–1224)*, ed. M. Aurell (Poitiers, 2003), 377–83, and by Nicholas Vincent in *Noblesses de l'espace Plantagenêt*, ed. Aurell. More specifically for the thirteenth century see Weiler, 'Symbolism and politics' and 'Knighting, homage'.
7. Petkov, *The Kiss of Peace*; van Eickels, *Vom symbolischen Konsens*. This has been argued against by C. Garnier, 'Zeichen und Schrift. Symbolische Handlungen und literale Fixierung am Beispiel von Friedensschlüssen des 13. Jahrhunderts', *Frühmittelalterliche Studien* 32 (1998), 263–87, Weiler, 'Knighting, homage'.
8. *RW*, iv. 265.

9. *RW*, iv. 265.
10. *RW*, iv. 276.
11. *RW*, iv. 299.
12. *RW*, iv. 275.
13. *RW*, iv. 303.
14. *RW*, iv. 292–3.
15. The emphasis on appropriate behaviour and speech reflected a broader European trend. See, for instance, dating from the mid-thirteenth century, *The King's Mirror (Speculum regale – Konungs Skuggsjá)*, transl. L.M. Larson (no place, 1917), which contains several chapters about appropriate apparel, language and conversation in the king's presence: caps. 31–4, 40–1, pp. 184–93, 226–34; see also, for a broader overview, T. Behrmann, 'Zum Wandel der öffentlichen Anrede im Spätmittelalter', *Formen und Funktionen*, ed. Althoff, 291–318.
16. *Annales Marbacenses*, 96 (*timens*), 97 (*propter timorem patris*); *Annales Wormatienses*, 146 (*timuit*).
17. *iratus et commotus est supra modum*. *Annales Wormatienses*, 147. See also the similar terminology used in *Gotifredi Continuatio Eberbacensis*, 348 (*turbatus est vehementer*).
18. *Annales Erphordenses*, 89; *Chronicon Ebersheimense*, 453.
19. *intolerabilem superbiam ducis ac stultitiam*. *Annales Erphordenses*, 87.
20. *Hermanni Altahensis Annales*, 392.
21. *Österreichische Chronik von den 95 Herrschaften*, 106–7.
22. *Chronica Regia*, 267.
23. *Continuatio Sancrucensis II*, 638.
24. *Urkundenbuch Erfurt*, i, no. 112
25. *Constitutiones 1198–1272*, no. 322.
26. *Conradus de Fabaria*, 244.
27. *Chronica Regia*, 267.
28. Henniges 'Vita Sancti Elisabethi', 268.
29. This juxtaposition has been admirably theorised by P. Buc, 'Writing Ottonian hegemony. Good rituals and bad rituals in Liutprand of Cremona', *Majestas* 4 (1996), 3–38. I hope I will be forgiven for using this in the context of what, at first sight, may seem like a functionalist approach to ritual.
30. G. Althoff, 'Das Privileg der deditio. Formen gütlicher Konfliktbeendigung in der mittelalterlichen Adelsgesellschaft', *Spielregeln*, 99–125; see, however, idem, *Die Macht der Rituale*, 158–9.
31. This been elaborated in Weiler, 'Reasserting power'.
32. Broekmann, *Rigor Iustitiae*, 352–67.
33. R.R. Davies, *The First English Empire. Power and Identity in the British Isles 1093–1343* (Oxford, 2000), 22–5.
34. *CR 1264–8*, 259; 410; *Wykes, AM*, iv. 251; D. Crouch, *The Image of the Aristocracy in Britain, 1000–1300* (London and New York, 1992), 327–9; Z. Dalewski, 'The knighting of Polish dukes in the Early Middle Ages: ideological and political significance', *Acta Poloniae Historica* 80 (1999), 15–43; Weiler, 'Symbolism and politics', 13–16; 'Knighting, homage', 4–13.
35. *RW*, iv. 310–11.
36. *Annales de Dunstaplia, AM*, iii. 137. For an illustration of the kiss of peace, though one between the monarchs of England and France, see the cover of

this book, taken from Matthew Paris' *Chronica Majora*. Cambridge, Corpus Christi College Parker Library MS 16 fol. 56v.

37. Reuter, 'Velle', passim.
38. *Annales des Theokesbureia, AM,* i. 93.
39. *CM,* iv. 478–9. See K. Schreiner, 'Er küsse mich mit dem Kuß seines Mundes' (Osculetur me oscuto oris sui, Cant 1,1). Metaphorik, kommunikative und herrschaftliche Funktionen einer symbolischen Handlung', *Höfische Kommunikation,* ed. Wenzel and Ragotzky, 89–132.
40. *CM,* iv. 485.
41. When Gilbert Marshal, for instance, had submitted to the king a few years before, his safe conduct had been guaranteed by the archbishop of Canterbury. *CPR 1232–47,* 48–9.
42. *Annales Erphordenses,* 86–7.
43. *Urkundenbuch Worms,* no. 159; *Chronicon Wormatiense,* 171–2.
44. *Urkundenbuch Worms,* no. 160.
45. *Urkundenbuch Worms,* nos. 163 (agreement), 164 (chapter), 165 (Henry (VII)), 166 (the citizens).
46. *Chronicon Wormatiense,* 172–3. When, in August 1235, Frederick II confirmed Otto's enfeoffment with the duchy of Brunswick, he similarly referred to the public ceremonial which accompanied the charter (as well as mentioning that Otto had received his enfeoffment while kneeling before him). *Constitutiones 1198–1272,* no. 197.
47. G. Althoff, 'Beratungen über die Gestaltung zeremonieller und ritueller Verfahren im Mittelalter', *Vormoderne politische Verfahren,* ed. B. Stollberg-Rilinger (Berlin, 2001), 53–71.
48. Görich, *Die Ehre,* 229–57, 291–9.
49. R.M. Haines, 'Canterbury versus York: fluctuating fortunes in a perennial conflict', *Ecclesia Anglicana. Studies in the English Church of the Later Middle Ages* (Toronto, 1989), 69–105.
50. *Early Charters of the Cathedral Church of St Paul, London,* ed. M. Gibbs, Camden 3rd series 58 (1939), no. 182. I am grateful to Nicholas Vincent for this reference.
51. *Tiroler Urkundenbuch,* iii, no. 1004.
52. See also, for the English case Clanchy, *From Memory,* 253–94.
53. Garnier, 'Zeichen und Schrift', passim.
54. As was perhaps most famously the case in the friendship rituals surrounding Anglo-French relations in the twelfth century, studied by Klaus van Eickels, *Vom inszenierten Konsens.*
55. *RW,* iv. 283.
56. *Annales de Dunstaplia, AM,* iii. 137.
57. *misericordiam nostrum petendum. CR 1231–4,* 442; see also *CPR 1232–47,* 45.
58. *CPR 1232–47,* 48.
59. *CPR 1232–47,* 48.
60. *CPR 1232–47,* 48.
61. Even less was promised to Richard Siward: all he received was a pardon for his flight and outlawry, a promise that none of the lands he held by right of his wife or though inheritance would be disseized, and the assurance that he could seek to pursue claims to other lands through the royal courts. *CPR 1232–47,* 49.

62. Vincent, *Peter des Roches*, 440–6.

63. *RW*, iii. 302–11.

64. *RW*, iii. 311–15.

65. *RW*, iii. 315–18.

66. *RW*, iii. 318–19.

67. *Annales de Burton, AM*, i, 439–43, 447–56.

68. See, for instance, *Historia Ecclesie Abingdonensis*, vol. ii, ed. and transl. J. Hudson (Oxford, 2002); Thomas of Marlborough, *History of the Abbey of Evesham*, ed. and transl. J. Sayers and L. Watkins (Oxford, 2003); see also the perceptive remarks made by A. Boureau, 'How law came to the monks: the use of law in English society at the beginning of the thirteenth century', *Past & Present*, 167 (2000), 29–74. I am grateful to Nicholas Vincent for drawing this article to my attention.

69. *Annales de Dunstaplia, AM*, iii. 118.

70. *Annales de Dunstaplia, AM*, iii. 119.

71. *Annales de Dunstaplia, AM*, iii. 120–4.

72. *Die Zwiefalter Chroniken Ortliebs und Bertholds*, ed. and transl. L. Wallach, E. König, and K.O. Müller, Schwäbische Chroniken der Stauferzeit 2 (Stuttgart, 1941; repr. Sigmaringen, 1978) provides a good example.

73. As do, for instance, both the *Annales Scheftlarienses* and those of Heiligenkreuz. *Annales Scheftlarienses*, 340; *Continuatio Sancrucensis II*, 638; *Continuatio Praedicatorum Vindobonensium*, 727; *Hermanni Altahensis Annales*, 392.

74. *Annales Erphordenses*, 87.

75. *Urkundenbuch Erfurt*, nos. 112–14.

76. *Tiroler Urkundenbuch*, iii, no. 1004.

77. *Chronicon Wormatiense*, 170–1.

78. *HD* iv. 499–501

79. *HD* iv. 506–7.

80. *Urkundenbuch Erfurt*, no. 112.

81. *Urkudnenbuch Erfurt*, no. 114.

82. *Urkundenbuch Worms*, nos. 182, 193.

83. *Annales Erphordenses*, 87.

84. *Stürner, Friedrich II*, ii. 266–7.

85. H. Kamp, *Friedensstifter und Vermittler im Mittelalter* (Darmstadt, 2001).

86. *Flores Historiarum*, ii. 208–9; *RW*, iv. 248.

87. *CR 1231–4*, 187.

9   Townsmen, clergy and knights: the public in politics

1. M. Howell, 'Royal women of England and France in the mid-thirteenth century: a gendered perspective', *England and Europe*, ed. Weiler and Rowlands, 163–82; A. Fößel, *Die Königin im mittelalterlichen Reich. Herrschaftsausübung, Herrschaftsrechte, Handlungsspielräume* (Stuttgart, 2000); and the essays collected in *Queens and Queenship in Medieval Europe*, ed. A. Duggan (Woodbridge, 1997).

2. *RW*, iv. 270.

3. *Urkundenbuch Babenberger*, no. 1190.

4. *Urkundenbuch Babenberger*, no. 1198.
5. A possibility which should not be dismissed offhand: S. McGlynn, 'Roger of Wendover and the wars of Henry III, 1216–1234', *England and Europe*, ed. Weiler and Rowlands, 183–206.
6. Which should not be ruled out, as David Carpenter has superbly demonstrated in relation to the events of 1258–65, where he was, however, able to draw on much richer evidence: 'English peasants in politics, 1258–1267', *Past & Present* 136 (1992), 3–42.
7. J.A. Truax, 'Winning over the Londoners: King Stephen, the Empress Matilda and the Politics of Personality', *Haskins Society Journal* 8 (1996), 42–62; C. Barron, *London in the Later Middle Ages. Government and people 1200–1500* (Oxford, 2004), 18–23; Carpenter, *The Struggle*, 392–5; S. Zöller, *Kaiser, Kaufmann und die Macht des Geldes: Gerhard Unmaze von Köln als Finanzier der Reichspolitik und der 'Gute Gerhard' des Rudolf von Ems* (Munich, 1993); M. Groten, *Köln im 13. Jahrhundert: Gesellschaftlicher Wandel und Verfassungsentwicklung* (Cologne, Weimar and Vienna, 1995).
8. E. Miller, 'Rulers of thirteenth-century towns: the cases of York and Newcastle upon Tyne', *TCE* 1 (1985), 128–41.
9. A. Buschmann, 'Der Rheinische Bund von 1254–1257: Landfriede, Städte, Fürsten und Reichsverfassung im 13. Jahrhundert', *Kommunale Bündnisse Oberitaliens und Oberdeutschlands im Vergleich*, ed. H. Maurer (Sigmaringen, 1987), 167–212; M. Kaufhold, *Deutsches Interregnum und europäische Politik. Konfliktlösungen und Entscheidungsstrukturen 1230–1280* (Hanover, 2000), 198–215.
10. T.M. Martin, *Die Städtepolitik Rudolfs von Hapsburg* (Göttingen, 1976).
11. *RW*, iv. 248–9.
12. *CM*, iii. 476.
13. *CM*, iii. 539; M. Prestwich, *Edward I* (London, 1988), 4; M. Howell, *Eleanor of Provence. Queenship in Thirteenth-Century England* (Oxford, 1998), 27–8; *Wykes*, AM, iv. 106–7, 122; *De Antiquis legibus*, 22–3.
14. *RW*, iv. 249–50.
15. *Annales de de Theokesberia*, AM, i. 91.
16. Colker, *Margam Chronicle*, 137.
17. *Annales de Wintonia*, AM, ii. 86–7.
18. *Annales de Oseneia*, AM, iv. 77.
19. *Annales de Wintonia*, AM, ii. 89; *Annales de Dunstaplia*, AM, iii. 162–3.
20. *Annales de Wintonia*, AM, ii. 108. The episode has been treated in more detail in Weiler, 'Symbolism and politics', 34–9.
21. *De Antiquis Legibus*, 6–7.
22. *CM*, iii. 481–4.
23. *Annales de Dunstaplia*, AM, iii. 118–24.
24. *Codex Moenofrancofurtanus*, i, nos. 104, 107.
25. *Chronicon Wormtiense*, 172.
26. As emphasised in the grant to the citizens of Erfurt from July 1234: *Urkundenbuch Erfurt*, i, no. 112.
27. *CM*, iii. 321–3.
28. *Constitutiones 1198–1272*, no. 73.
29. *Constitutiones 1198–1272*, no. 304.
30. *Constitutiones 1198–1272*, no. 171.
31. *Constitutiones 1198–1272*, no. 196.

32. Thorau, 'Sachwalter', deals with these in more detail.
33. *Urkundenbuch*, i, nos. 12–14.
34. *Chronicon Wormatiense*, 171–3; *Urkundenbuch Worms*, i, nos. 154–60, 163–4, 172, 182, 193; Keilmann, *Der Kampf*, 47–106.
35. *Annales Erphordenses*, 87.
36. That the men of Bristol had ships with which they sought to intercept de Burgh does not contradict this image: first of all, it is unlikely that this was a regular fleet (rather than vessels commissioned for the occasion), and, second, such close proximity to Wales probably brought with it an increased awareness of the need for self defence.
37. *Urkundenbuch Worms*, i, nos. 172, 193.
38. He disappeared of the witness lists of Henry (VII) from the autumn of 1234 (*Regesta Archiepiscoporum Maguntinensium. Regesten zur Geschichte der Mainzer Erzbischöfe von Bonifatius bis Heinrich II., 742–1288*, ed. J.F. Böhmer and C. Will, 2 vols (Innsbruck, 1877–86)), that is, roughly around the time when he received several grants from Frederick II (*HD*, iv. 506–7).
39. *Codex Moeno-francofurtanus*, no. 107.
40. *RW*, iv. 247, 250, 253, 264, 268, 272, 274–5, 291, 294–7.
41. *RW*, iv. 267, 272.
42. Matthew Paris' Life of St Edmund in Lawrence, *St Edmund*, 240–3.
43. See the succinct survey by M. Staunton, 'Exile in Eadmer's *Historia Novorum* and *Vita Anselmi*', in: *Saint Anselm, Bishop and Thinker: Papers Read at a Conference Held in the Catholic University of Lublin on 24–26 September 1996*, ed. R. Majeran and E.I. Zielinski (Lublin, 1999), 47–59.
44. *Magna Vita Sancti Hugonis. The Life of St Hugh of Lincoln*, ed. and transl. D.L. Douie and D.H. Farmer, 2 vols (Oxford, 1961–85), i. 68–72. Cory Richards is currently completing his PhD on the hagiography of English bishops, c. 1170–c. 1280, and will deal with these themes in greater detail.
45. B. Weiler, 'William of Malmesbury on kingship', *History* 87 (2005), 3–22, at 18–20.
46. D. d'Avray, ' "Magna carta": its background in Stephen Langton's academic Biblical exegesis and its episcopal reception', *Studi Medievali* 3rd series 38 (1997), 423–38, at p. 428 for the role of the clergy. I am grateful to Professor d'Avray for providing me with a copy of this article, and for drawing my attention more generally to the quite unusual role played by bishops in thirteenth-century English politics. See also M. Kaufhold, 'Die gelehrten Erzbischöfe von Canterbury und die Magna Carta', in *Politische Reflexion in der Welt des späten Mittelalters/ Political Thought in the Age of Schoalsticism. Essays in honour of Jürgen Miethke*, ed. M. Kaufhold (Leiden and Boston, 2004), 43–64 (I am grateful to Phillipp Schofield for this reference).
47. d'Avray, *Magna Carta*, 430.
48. F.M. Powicke, *Stephen Langton* (Oxford, 1928), 95, 109; J.C. Holt, *Magna Carta*, second edition (Cambridge, 1992), 269–82; M.T. Clanchy, *England*, 194.
49. This being the key argument of d'Avray, *Magna Carta*, 432–4, but see also Carpenter, *The Minority*, 296–7, 382–3; Carpenter, *Struggle*, 314–16, 339–40, 348–9; Valente, *Theory and Practice*, 110–5; Clanchy, *England and its rulers*, 192–8, 251–2; Turner, *Magna Carta*, 80–111; Lawrence, *St Edmund*, 130–8; *Councils and Synods with Other Documents Relating to the English Church: II: 1205–1303*, ed. F.M. Powicke and C.R. Cheney (Oxford, 1964), i. 138,

159. See also Matthew Paris' fragment of a *Vita* of Stephen Langton: 'Vita Sancti Stephani archiepiscopi Cantuariensis', *Ungedruckte Anglo-Normannische Geschichtsquellen*, ed. F. Liebermann (Strasbourg, 1879), 318–29, which, however, ends with the archbishop's role in the translation of Becket in 1220; on the text: B. Bolton, *'Pastor Bonus:* Matthew Paris' *Life* of Stephen Langton, archbishop of Canterbury (1207–28)', *Nederlands Archief voor Kerkgeschiedenis* 84 (2004), 57–70.

50. J.W. Baldwin, *Masters, Princes and Merchants: The Social Views of Peter the Chanter and His Circle*, 2 vols (Princeton, 1970); Buc, *L'ambiguïté du Livre*, 193–7.

51. *Annales Scheftlarienses*, 341; *Hermanni Altahensis Annales*, 391–2.

52. *Gestorum Treverorum Continuatio IV*, MGH SS 25, 403.

53. *Annales Marbacenses*, 97; *Gotifredi Viterbensis Continuatio*, 348.

54. *Chronicon Wormatiense*, 174–5.

55. *Gestorum Treverorum Continuatio IV*, provides a good example.

56. *Vita Sancti Engelberti*, in: *Die Wundergeschichten des Caesarius von Heisterbach*. See also: J. Jung, 'From Jericho to Jerusalem. The violent transformation of Archbishop Engelbert of Cologne', *Last things. Death and the Apocalypse in the Middle Ages*, ed. C. Walker Bynum and P. Freedman (Philadelphia, 2000), 60–92, 283–92; Fischer, 'Engelbert von Berg'.

57. *Acta Imperii Selecta*, no. 303.

58. J.A. Watt, 'The theory of papal monarchy in the thirteenth century: the contribution of the canonists', *Traditio* 20 (1964) 178–317; idem, 'Spiritual and temporal powers', *The Cambridge History of Medieval Political Thought, c. 350–c. 1450*, ed. J.H. Burns (Cambridge, 1988), 367–423.

59. *Vita Gregorii*, 17, 22, 26.

60. *CM*, iv. 104–5, 553; v. 37, 121.

61. A.G. Little, *Studies in English Franciscan History* (Manchester, 1917), 33–5; J. Röhrkasten, *The Mendicant Houses of Medieval London 1221–1539* (Münster, 2004), 340–8, 381–94; idem, 'Die englischen Dominikaner und ihre Beziehungen zur Krone im 13. Jahrhundert', *Vita Religiosa im Mittelalter. Festschrift für Kaspar Elm zum 70. Geburtstag* (Berlin, 1999), 483–502; C.H. Lawrence, 'The letters of Adam Marsh and the Franciscan school at Oxford', *Journal of Ecclesiastical History* 42 (1991), 218–38; J.R. Maddicott, *Simon de Montfort* (Cambridge, 1994), 80–4, 117–18; J.W. Hinnebusch, *The Early English Friars Preachers* (Rome, 1951), 462–6; idem, 'Diplomatic activities of the English Dominicans in the thirteenth century', *Catholic Historical Review* 28 (1942), 309–39.

62. See also *Tractatus de aduentu*, 76.

63. *RW*, iv. 268–9.

64. *CLR 1226–40*, 234.

65. *Flores Historiarum*, ii. 208–9.

66. *Annales de Theokesberia*, *AM*, i. 92.

67. W.R. Thomson, 'The image of the Mendicants in the chronicles of Matthew Paris', *Archivum franciscanum historicum* 70 (1977), 3–34.

68. Röhrkasten, *Mendicant Houses*, 341–2, 343, 381–2, 391.

69. *Acta Imperii Inedita*, no. 338. See also D. Berg, 'Staufische Herrschaftsideologie und Mendikantenspiritualität', *Wissenschaft und Weisheit* 51 (1988), 26–51, 185–209.

70. Freed, *Friars*, 161–7; F. Graus, 'Premisl Otakar II. – sein Ruhm und sein Nachleben. Ein Beitrag zur Geschichte der politischen Propaganda und Chronistik', *Mitteilungen des Instituts für Österreichische Geschichtsforschung* 79 (1971), 57–108.

71. Goll, 'Zu Brunos von Olmütz', 487–90.

72. The best general account remains that by H. Kluger, *Hochmeister Hermann von Salza und Kaiser Friedrich II: ein Beitrag zur Frühgeschichte des Deutschen Ordens* (Marburg, 1987).

73. P. Hilsch, 'Der Deutsche Ritterorden im südlichen Libanon: zur Topographie der Kreuzfahrerstaaten in Sidon und Beirut', *Zeitschrift des deutschen Palästina-Vereins* 96 (1980), 174–89.

74. J.M. Powell, 'Frederick II, the Hohenstaufens, and the Teutonic Order in the kingdom of Sicily', *The Military Orders: fighting for the faith and caring for the sick*, ed. Malcolm Barber (Aldershot, 1994), 236–44.

75. H. Nicholson, 'The military orders and the kings of England in the twelfth and thirteenth centuries', *From Clermont to Jerusalem. The Crusades and Crusader Societies (1095–1500). Selected Proceedings of the International Medieval Congress, University of Leeds (10–13 July 1995)*, ed. Alan V. Murray (Turnhout, 1998), 203–17; M.L. Bulst-Thiele, 'Templer in königlichen und päpstlichen Diensten' *Festschrift Percy Ernst Schramm zu seinem siebzigsten Geburtstag*, ed. in P. Classen and P. Seibert, 2 vols (Wiesbaden, 1964), 289–308.

76. *RW*, iv. 256–8.

77. Weiler, *King Henry III*, 62 no. 123.

78. H. Köppen, 'Die englische Rente für den deutschen Orden', *Festschrift Herman Heimpel* (Göttingen, 1977), 402–21.

79. Kluger, *Hochmeister*, passim. *Acta imperii inedita*, no. 25, *Annales Erphordenses*, 98.

80. A theme elaborated further, for instance, in the Zwettl Vita of St Elisabeth. Weiler, 'Reasserting power', 261–5.

81. Boshof, 'Die Entstehung', 249–74.

82. *RW*, iv. 258.

83. Morris, *Bigod Earls*, 8–13.

84. Vincent, *Peter des Roches*, 418–27.

85. *Acta Imperii Inedita*, no. 470.

86. Borchardt, 'Der sogenannte Aufstand', 53–119.

87. *Urkundenbuch Babenberger*, no. 1198.

88. *Continuatio Garstensis*, 596; *Continuatio Lambacenses*, 559.

89. This follows and elaborates on: Vincent, *Peter des Roches*, 409–10.

Conclusion

1. This is not to say that these uses were the only ones: Frederick II's demonstrative emphasis on peace making for instance, when entering Germany in 1235 (Weiler, 'Reasserting power'), or the elaborate confirmatory processes we have witnessed in the reconciliation between Cardinal Otto and the men of Oxford, should warn us against applying too rigid a distinction.

2. For the lack of interest see Weiler, 'Henry III through European eyes', 139–41, and for the tyranny, in this case of Henry II, Gislebert of Mons, *Chonique*, 85.
3. *Diplomatic Documents Preserved in the Public Record Office 1101–1272*, ed. P. Chaplais (London, 1964), no. 163; Wykes, *AM*, iv. 222–5.
4. See Weiler, 'Rebellious sons'.
5. H.-E. Hilpert, *Kaiser- und Papstbriefe in den Chronica Majora des Matthaeus Paris* (Stuttgart, 1981).
6. A point that Timothy Reuter, in particular, has made repeatedly, perhaps most strongly in his 'Modern mentalities'. See also, from an Anglo-French perspective, Vincent, 'Conclusion'.
7. Cohn, *Lust for Liberty*.
8. Reuter, 'Assembly politics', 449.
9. Reuter, 'Assembly politics', 449–50.

Bibliography

Primary sources

Acta Imperii Inedita saeculi XIII et XIV. Urkunden und Briefe zur Geschichte des Kaiserreichs und des Königreichs Sizilien, ed. E. Winkelmann, 2 vols (Innsbruck, 1880–5; repr. 1964).

Acta Imperii Selecta. Urkunden deutscher Könige und Kaiser. Mit einem Anhange von Reichssachen, ed. J.F. Böhmer (Innsbruck, 1870).

Anglo-Scottish relations, 1174–1328: some selected documents, ed. and transl. E.L.G. Stones (Oxford, 1970).

Annales Bergomates, MGH SS 31 (Hanover, 1903).

Annales Cestrienses. Chronicle of the Abbey of S. Werburg, at Chester, ed. R.C. Christie (Chester, 1887).

Annales Cremonenses, MGH SS 31 (Hanover, 1903).

Annales Dorenses, MGH SS 27 (Hanover, 1885).

Annales Elwangenses, MGH SS 10 (Hanover, 1852).

Annales Erphordenses fratrum praedicatorum, in: *Monumenta Erphesfurtensia*, Hahn.

Annales Londonienses de tempore Henrici III, in: *Chronicles of the Reigns of Edward I and Edward II*, ed. W. Stubbs, 2 vols, RS (1882–3).

Annales Marbacenses Qui Dicuntur (Cronica Hohenburgensis cum Continuatione et Additamentis Neoburgensibus), ed. H. Bloch, MGH SSrG sep. ed. (Hanover and Leipzig, 1907).

Annales Moguntini MGH SS 17 (Hanover, 1861).

Annales Ottenburani Minores MGH SS 17 (Hanover, 1861).

Annales Maiores Zwifaltenses MGH SS 10 (Hanover, 1852).

Annales Monastici, ed. H.R. Luard, 5 vols, RS (London, 1864–9).

Annales de Margam, Annales Monastici, ed. H.R. Luard, 5 vols, RS (London, 1864–9), vol. I (London, 1864).

Annales Monasterii de Burton, Annales Monastici, ed. H.R. Luard, 5 vols, RS (London, 1864–9), vol. I (London, 1864).

Annales Monasterii de Waverleia, Annales Monastici, ed. H.R. Luard, 5 vols, RS (London, 1864–9), vol. II (London, 1864).

Annales Monasterii de Wintonia, Annales Monastici, ed. H.R. Luard, 5 vols, RS (London, 1864–9), vol. II (London, 1864).

Annales Monasterii de Theokesberia, Annales Monastici, ed. H.R. Luard, 5 vols, RS (London, 1864–9), vol. I (London, 1864).

Annales de Oseneia, Annales Monastici, ed. H.R. Luard, 5 vols, RS (London, 1864-9), vol. iv (London, 1869).

Annales Prioratus de Dunstaplia, Annales Monastici, ed. H.R. Luard, 5 vols, RS, (London, 1864–9), vol. 3 (London, 1866).

Thomae Wykes Annales, Annales Monastici, ed. H.R. Luard, 5 vols, RS (London, 1864–9), vol. iv (London, 1869).

Annales Neresheimenses MGH SS 10 (Hanover, 1852).

Annales Placentini Gibellini MGH SS 18 (Hanover, 1863).

Annales Placentini Guelfi MGH SS 18 (Hanover, 1863).
Annales Sancti Rudberti Salisburgenses MGH SS 9 (Hanover, 1851).
Annales Scheftlarienses Maiores MGH SS 17 (Hanover, 1861).
Annales Sancti Georgii in Silva Nigra MGH SS 17 (Hanover, 1861).
Annales Sancti Trudberti MGH SS 17 (Hanover, 1861).
Annales Stadenses Auctore Alberto, MGH SS 16 (Hanover, 1859).
Annales Wormatienses, in: *Quellen zur Geschichte der Stadt Worms,* ed. Heinrich Boos, 3 vols (Berlin, 1886–93).
The Annals of Loch Ce. A Chronicle of Irish Affairs, ed. and transl. W.M. Hennessy, 2 vols RS (London, 1871).
Arnoldi Chronica Slavorum, ed. J.M. Lappenberg, MGH SSrG sep. ed. (Hanover, 1868).
Bracton, *De Legibus et consuetudinibus Angliae,* ed. George E. Woodbine, 4 vols (New Haven, 1915–42).
Brut Y Tywysogyon or The Chronicle of the Princes. Peniarth MS. 20 Version, transl. T. Jones (Cardiff, 1952).
Calendar of the Charter Rolls Preserved in the Public Record Office, 6 vols (London, 1903–27).
Calendar of Liberate Rolls for the Reign of Henry III, 6 vols (London, 1916–64).
Calendar of Patent Rolls of the Reign of Henry III Preserved in the Public Record Office, 6 vols (London, 1901–13).
Chronica Jocelini de Brakelonda. The Chronicle of Jocelin de Brakelond, ed. and transl. H.E. Butler (London, 1949).
Chronica de Mailros e Codice Unico in Bibliotheca Cottoniana servato, nunc iterum in lucem edita, ed. J. Stevenson, Bannatyne Club (Edinburgh, 1835).
Chronica Regia Coloniensis Continuatio IV, in: *Chronica Regia Coloniensis (Annales Maximi Colonienses) cum Continuationibus in Monasterio S. Pantaleonis Scriptis Aliisque Historiae Coloniensis Monumentis,* ed. Georg Waitz, MGH SSrG sep. ed. (Hanover, 1880).
Cronica S Petri Erfordensis Moderna, in: *Monumenta Erphesfurtensia saeculi xii., xiii., xiv.,* ed. O. Holder-Egger, MGH SSrG sep. ed. (Hanover and Leipzig, 1899).
The Chronicle of Battle Abbey, ed. and transl. E. Searle (Oxford, 1980).
Chronicon Albrici Trium Fontium MGH SS 23 (Hanover, 1874).
Chronicon Ebersheimense MGH SS 23 (Hanover, 1874).
Chronicon Magni Presbyteri Continuatio MGH SS 17 (Hanover, 1861).
Chronicon Roskildense, in: *Scriptores Minores Historiae Danicae,* ed. M. Cl. Geertz, 2 vols (Copenhagen, 1917–23).
Chronicon Wormatiense saeculi xiii, in: *Quellen zur Geschichte der Stadt Worms,* ed. H. Boos, 3 vols (Berlin, 1886–93).
Die Chronik der Grafen von der Mark von Levold von Northof, ed. Fritz Zschaeck, MGH SS NS (Berlin, 1929).
La Chronique de Gislebert de Mons, ed. L. Vanderkindere, Receuil de Textes pour servir a l'étude de l'histoire de Belgique (Brussels, 1904).
Close Rolls of the Reign of Henry III Preserved in the Public Record Office, 14 vols (London, 1902–38).
Codex Diplomaticus et Epistolaris Regni Bohemiae, ed. G. Friedrich *et al.,* 9 vols (Prague, 1904–93).
Codex Moenofrancofurtanus. Urkundenbuch der Reichsstadt Frankfurt, ed. J.F. Böhmer, 2 vols (Frankfurt/Main, 1901–5).

Colker, M.L. 'The "Margam Chronicle" in a Dublin manuscript', *Journal of the Haskins Society* 4 (1992), 123–48.

Constitutiones et Acta Publica Imperatorum et Regum, 1198–1272, ed. L. Weiland, MGH Leges Sectio IV, 2 (Hanover, 1896).

Constitutiones et Acta Publica Imperatorum et Regum, 1273–98, ed. J. Schwalm, MGH Leges Sectio V, 3 (Hanover, 1903).

Continuatio Casuum Sancti Galli. Conradi de Fabaria Continuatio Casuum Sancti Galli, ed. G. Meyer von Knonau, St Gallische Geschichtsquellen IV, Mittheilungen zur Vaterländischen Geschichte des Historischen Vereins von St Gallen, NS 7 (St Gall, 1879).

Continuatio Claustroneoburgensis tertia MGH SS 9 (Hanover, 1851).

Continuatio Garstensis MGH SS 9 (Hanover, 1851).

Continuatio Lambacensis MGH SS 9 (Hanover, 1851).

Continuatio Praedicatorum Vindobonensium MGH SS 9 (Hanover, 1851).

Continuatio Sancrucensis II MGH SS 9 (Hanover, 1851).

Councils and Synods with Other Documents Relating to the English Church: II: 1205–1303, ed. F.M. Powicke and C.R. Cheney (Oxford, 1964).

The Deeds of the Normans in Ireland. La Geste des Engleis en Yrlande. A new edition of the Chronicle formerly known as the Song of Dermot and the Earl, ed. E. Mullally (Dublin, 2002).

Diplomatic Documents preserved in the Public Record Office 1101–1272, ed. P. Chaplais (London, 1964).

Early Charters of the Cathedral Church of St Paul, London, ed. M. Gibbs, Camden 3rd series 58 (1939).

Flores Historiarum, ed. H.R. Luard, 3 vols, RS (London, 1890).

Gervase of Canterbury, *The Historical Works of Gervase of Canterbury*, ed. William Stubbs, 2 vols, RS (London, 1879–80).

Gesta Regis Henrici Secundi Benedicti Abbatis, ed. W. Stubbs, 2 vols, RS (London, 1867–8).

Les Gestes de Chiprois, ed. G. Reynard (Paris, 1887).

Gestorum Treverorum Continuatio IV MGH SS 25 (Hanover, 1880).

Gotfredi Viterbiensis Gesta Heinrici VI Continuatio Eberbacensis, MGH SS 22 (Hanover, 1872).

Henniges, D., 'Vita Sanctae Elisabeth, Landgraviae Thuringiae auctore anonymo nunc primum in lucem edita', *Archivum Franciscanum Historicum* 2 (1909), 240–68.

Hermanni Altahensis Annales, MGH SS 17 (Hanover, 1861).

Historia Diplomatica Friderici Secundi, ed. A. Huillard-Breholles, 7 vols in 12 (Paris, 1852–61).

Historia Ecclesie Abingdonensis, vol. ii, ed. and transl. J. Hudson (Oxford, 2002).

Historia Welforum, ed. and transl. E. König, Schwäbische Chroniken der Stauferzeit (Stuttgart, 1938; repr. Sigmaringen, 1978).

Jacques de Vitry, *The Historia Occidentalis of Jacques de Vitry*, ed. J.F. Hinnebusch, Spicilegium Friburgense 17 (Fribourg, 1972).

Die Kaiserchronik eines Regensburger Geistlichen, ed. E. Schröder, MGH Deutsche Chroniken (Hanover, 1892).

The King's Mirror (Speculum regale – Konungs Skuggsjá), transl. L.M. Larson (no place, 1917).

Die Konstitutionen Friedrichs II. für das Königreich Sizilien, ed. W. Stürner, MGH Leges (Hanover, 1996).

Lamberti Waterloos Annales Cameracenses, MGH SS 16 (Hanover, 1859).

Lawrence, C.H, *St Edmund of Abingdon. A Study of Hagiography and History* (Oxford, 1960).

Layettes du Tresor de Chartes, ed. H.-F. Laborde and A. Teulet, 4 vols (Paris, 1863–1909).

The Liber Augustalis or Constitutions of Melfi Promulgated by the Emperor Frederick II for the Kingdom of Sicily in 1231, transl. J.M. Powell (Syracuse: Syracuse University Press, 1971).

Magistri Tolosani Chronicon Faventinum, ed. G. Rossini, RIS NS (Bologna, 1936–9).

Magna Vita Sancti Hugonis. The Life of St Hugh of Lincoln, ed. and transl. D.L. Douie and D.H. Farmer, 2 vols (Oxford, 1961–85).

Matthew Paris, *The Chronica Maiora of Matthew Paris*, ed. H.R. Luard, 7 vols, RS (London, 1872–4).

——, 'Vita Sancti Stephani archiepiscopi Cantuariensis', in: *Ungedruckte Anglo-Normannische Geschichtsquellen*, ed. F. Liebermann (Strasbourg, 1879), 318–29.

The Metrical Chronicle of Robert of Gloucester, ed. W.A. Wright, 2 vols, RS (1886–7).

Monumenta Erphesfurtensia saeculi xii., xiii., xiv., ed. O. Holder-Egger, MGH SSrG sep. ed. (Hanover & Leipzig, 1899).

Ottokars Österreichische Reimchronik ed. J. Seemüller, MGH Deutsche Chroniken, 2 vols (Hanover, 1890–3).

Ottonis de Sancto Blasio Chronica, ed. A. Hofmeister, MGH SSrG sep. ed. (Hanover and Leipzig, 1912).

Political songs of England from the reign of John to that of Edward II, ed. T. Wright, Camden Society (London, 1839); repr. with a new introduction by P. Coss (Cambridge, 1996).

Politische Lyrik des Deutschen Mittelalters. Texte I: Von Friedrich II bis Ludwig von Bayern, ed. U. Müller, Göppinger Arbeiten zur Germanistik (Göppingen, 1972).

Quellen zur Geschichte der Stadt Worms, ed. H. Boos, 3 vols (Berlin, 1886–93).

Radulfi de Diceto Decani Lundoniensis Opera Historica, ed. W. Stubbs, 2 vols, RS (London, 1876).

Regesta Archiepiscoporum Maguntinensium. Regesten zur Geschichte der Mainzer Erzbischöfe von Bonifatius bis Heinrich II., 742–1288, ed. J.F. Böhmer and C. Will, 2 vols (Innsbruck, 1877–86).

Regesta Imperii: Die Regesten des Kaiserreiches unter Philipp, Otto IV., Friedrich II., Heinrich (VII.), Conrad IV., Heinrich Raspe, Wilhelm und Richard, 1198–1272, ed. J.F. Böhmer, E. Winkelmann and J. Ficker, 3 vols (Innsbruck, 1881–1901).

Rogeri de Wendover Chronica sive Flores Historiarum, ed. H.O. Coxe, 5 vols, English Historical Society (London, 1841–4).

Ryccardi de Sancto Germano Notarii Chronica, ed. C.A. Garufi, RIS NS 7:2 (Bologna, 1936–8).

Sachsenspiegel: Landrecht, ed. K.A. Eckhardt (Göttingen, 1955).

Salimbene de Adam, *Cronica*, ed. G. Scalia, 2 vols (Bari, 1966).

Thomas Ebendorfer, *Chonica Regum Romanorum*, ed. H. Zimmermann, 2 vols MGH SS NS (Hanover, 2003).

Thomas of Marlborough, *History of the Abbey of Evesham*, ed. and transl. J. Sayers and L. Watkins (Oxford, 2003).

Tiroler Urkundenbuch. Erste Abteilung: Die Urkunden zur Geschichte des Deutschen Etschlandes und des Vintschgaus, ed. F. Huter *et al.*, 3 vols (Innsbruck, 1937–57).

Tractatus de aduentu fratrum minorum in Angliam, ed. A.G. Little (Manchester, 1951).

Tyson, M, 'The Annals of Southwark and Merton', *Sussex Archaeological Collections* 36 (1925), 24–57.

Urkundenbuch der Stadt Erfurt, ed. C. Beyer, Geschichtsquellen der Provinz Sachsen und angrenzender Gebiete 23, 2 vols (Halle, 1889–97).

Urkundenbuch der Reichsstadt Frankfurt, ed. J.F. Böhmer and F. Lau, 2 vols (Frankfurt, 1901–5).

Urkundenbuch der Stadt Friedberg: erster Band, ed. M. Foltz (Marburg, 1904).

Urkundenbuch der Stadt Worms, ed. Heinrich Boos, 2 vols (Berlin, 1886–8).

Urkundenbuch für die Geschichte des Niederrheins oder des Erzstifts Cöln, der Fürstenthümer Jülich und Berg, Geldern, Meurs, Cleve und Mark, und der Reichsstifte Elten, Essen und Werden, ed. T.J. Lacomblet, 4 vols (Düsseldorf, 1840–58).

Urkundenbuch zur Geschichte der Babenberger in Österreich. Vierter Band. Zweiter Halbband. Ergänzende Quellen 1195–1287 ed. O. Freiherr von Mitis, H. Dienst, C. Lackner, H. Hageneder (Vienna and Munich, 1997).

Vincent of Beauvais, *Bibliotheca mundi seu speculi maioris Vincentii Burgundi praesulis Bellovacensis, ordinis praedicatorum, theologi ac doctori eximii, tomus quartus qui Speculum Historiale inscribitur* (Douai, 1624).

Vita Edwardi Secundi. The Life of Edward the Second, ed. and transl. W.R. Childs (Oxford, 2005).

Vita Gregorii IX, P. Fabre, L. Duchesne and G. Mollat (eds), *Le 'Liber Censuum' de l'Eglise Romaine*, 3 vols (Paris, 1889–1952), ii. 8–36.

Walter Map, *De Nugis Curialium. Courtiers' Trifles*, ed. and transl. M.R. James, revised by C.N.L. Brooke and R.A.B. Mynors (Oxford, 1983).

William of Malmesbury, *Historia Novella. The Contemporary History*, ed. and transl. E. King and K.R. Potter (Oxford, 1998).

William Rishanger, *The Chronicle of William de Rishanger of the Barons' War*, ed. J.O. Halliwell, Camden First Series 15 (London, 1840).

Die Wundergeschichten des Caesarius von Heisterbach, ed. A. Hilka, 3 vols (Bonn, 1933–7).

Die Zwiefalter Chroniken Ortliebs und Bertholds, ed. and transl. L. Wallach, E. König, and K.O. Müller, Schwäbische Chroniken der Stauferzeit 2 (Stuttgart, 1941; repr. Sigmaringen, 1978).

Secondary sources

Althoff, G., *Friends, Family and Followers. Political and Social Bonds in Early Medieval Europe*, transl. C. Carroll (Cambridge, 2004).

—— (ed.), *Zeichen – Werte – Rituale. Internationales Kolloquium des Sonderforschungsbereichs 496 an der Westfälischen Wilhelms-Universität Münster* (Münster, 2004).

——, *Die Macht der Rituale. Symbolik und Herrschaft im Mittelalter* (Darmstadt, 2003).

——, *Inszenierte Herrschaft. Geschichtsschreibung und politisches Handeln im Mittelalter* (Darmstadt, 2003).

——, *Spielregeln der Politik im Mittelalter. Kommunikation in Frieden und Fehde* (Darmstadt, 1997).

—— (ed.), *Formen und Funktionen öffentlicher Kommunikation im Mittelalter* (Stuttgart, 2001).

——, 'Beratungen über die Gestaltung zeremonieller und ritueller Verfahren im Mittelalter', in *Vormoderne politische Verfahren*, ed. Barbara Stollberg-Rilinger (Berlin, 2001), 53–71.

——, 'Zur Bedeutung symbolischer Kommunikation für das Verständnis des Mittelalters', *Frühmittelalterliche Studien* 31 (1997), 370–89.

——, 'Das Privileg der deditio. Formen gütlicher Konfliktbeendigung in der mittelalterlichen Adelsgesellschaft', *Spielregeln*, 99–125.

——, 'Huld. Überlegungen zu einem Zentralbegriff der mittelalterlichen Herrschaftsordnung', *Frühmittelalterliche Studien* 25 (1991), 259–82.

——, 'Colloquium familiare – Colloquium secretum – Colloquium publicum. Beratung im politischen Leben des früheren Mittelalters', *Frühmittelalterliche Studien* 24 (1990), 145–67.

Ambos, C., S. Hotz, G. Schwedler and S. Weinfurter (eds), *Die Welt der Rituale von der Antike bis heute* (Darmstadt, 2005).

Appelt, H., *Privilegium Minus. Das staufische Kaisertum und die Babenberger in Österreich*, second revised edition (Vienna, Graz and Cologne, 1976).

Arnold, B., *Power and Property in Medieval Germany. Economic and social change c. 900–c. 1300* (Oxford, 2004).

——, *Medieval Germany, 500–1300. A political interpretation* (London, 1997).

——, *Princes and Territories in Medieval Germany* (Cambridge, 1991).

——, *Medieval German Knighthood, 1050–1300* (Oxford, 1985).

——, 'Emperor Frederick II (1194–1250) and the political particularism of the German princes', *JMH* 26 (2000), 239–52.

Aurell, M., *L'Empire des Plantagenêt 1154–1224* (Paris, 2003).

Aziz, M.A., 'La croisade de l'Empereur Frédéric II et l'Orient Latin', *Autour de la Première Croisade*, ed. M. Balard (Paris, 1996), 373–8.

Baaken, G., 'Die Erhebung Heinrichs, Herzogs von Schwaben, zum Rex Romanorum (1220/1222)', his *Imperium und regnum. Zur Geschichte des 12. und 13. Jahrhunderts. Festschrift zum 70. Geburtstag*, ed. K.-A. Frech and U. Schmidt (Cologne, Weimar and Vienna, 1997), 289–306.

Baldwin, J.W., *Masters, Princes and Merchants: The Social Views of Peter the Chanter and His Circle*, 2 vols (Princeton, 1970).

Barnwell, P.S. and M. Mostert (eds), *Political Assemblies in the Earlier Middle Ages* (Turnhoult, 2003).

Barron, C.M., *London in the Later Middle Ages. Government and people 1200–1500* (Oxford, 2004).

Battenberg, F., *Gerichtsschreiberamt und Kanzlei am Reichshofgericht 1235–1451*, Quellen und Forschungen zur höchsten Gerichtsbarkeit im Alten Reich 2 (Cologne and Vienna, 1974).

Behrmann, T., 'Zum Wandel der öffentlichen Anrede im Spätmittelalter', *Formen und Funktionen*, ed. Althoff, 291–318.

Berbig, H.-J., 'Zur rechtlichen Relevanz von Ritus und Zeremoniell im römisch-deutschen Imperium', *Zeitschrift für Kirchengeschichte* 92 (1981), 204–49.

Beumann, H., 'Friedrich II. und die heilige Elisabeth. Zum Besuch des Kaisers in Marburg am 1. Mai 1236', *Sankt Elisabeth. Fürstin, Dienerin, Heilige* (Sigmaringen, 1981), 151–66.

Blattmann, M. '"Ein Unglück für sein Volk". Der Zusammenhang zwischen Fehlverhalten des Königs und Volkswohl in Quellen des 7. – 12. Jahrhunderts', *Frühmittelalterliche Studien* 30 (1996), 80–102.

Bolton, B., '*Pastor Bonus:* Matthew Paris' *Life* of Stephen Langton, archbishop of Canterbury (1207–28)', *Nederlands Archief voor Kerkgeschiedenis* 84 (2004), 57–70.

Borchardt, K., 'Der sogenannte Aufstand Heinrichs (VII.) in Franken 1234/35', *Forschungen zur bayerischen und fränkischen Geschichte: Festschrift Peter Herde*, ed. K. Borchardt and E. Bünz (Würzburg, 1998), 53–119.

Borgolte, M. (ed.), *Das europäische Mittelalter im Spannungsbogen des Vergleichs: Zwanzig internationale Beiträge zu Praxis, Problemen und Perspektiven der historischen Komparatistik* (Berlin, 2001).

Boshof, E., 'Reich und Reichsfürsten in Herrschaftsverständnis und Politik Kaiser Friedrichs II. nach 1230', *Heinrich Raspe – Landgraf von Thüringen und römischer König (1227–1247)*, ed. M. Werner (Frankfurt am Main *et al.*, 2003), 3–27.

——, 'Die Entstehung des Herzogtums Braunschweig-Lüneburg', *Heinrich der Löwe*, ed. W. Mohrmann (Göttingen, 1980), 249–74.

Boureau, A., 'How law came to the monks: the use of law in English society at the beginning of the thirteenth century', *Past & Present* 167 (2000), 29–74.

Broekmann, T., *Rigor Iustitiae. Herrschaft, Recht und Terror im normannisch-staufischen Süden (1050–1250)* (Darmstadt, 2005).

Brown, W.C. and P. Gorecki (eds), *Conflict in medieval Europe. Changing Perspectives on Society and Culture* (Aldershot, 2003).

Brühl, C.R., *Fodrum, Gistum, Servitium regis. Studien zu den wirtschaftlichen Grundlagen des Königtums im Frankenreich und in den fränkischen Nachfolgestaaten Deutschland, Frankreich und Italien vom 6. bis zur Mitte des 14. Jahrhunderts* (Cologne, 1968).

Buc, P., *The Dangers of Ritual* (Princeton, 2001).

——, *L'ambiguïté du Livre: prince, pouvoir, et people dans le commentaries de la Bible au Moyen Age* (Paris, 1994).

——, 'Résumé', *Culture Politique des Plantagenêt (1154–1224)*, ed. M. Aurell (Poitiers, 2003), 377–83.

——, 'Rituel politique et imaginaire politique au haut Moyen Âge', *Revue Historique* 306 (2002), 843–83.

——, 'Political rituals and political imagination in the medieval West from the fourth century to the eleventh', *The Medieval World*, ed. P. Linehan and J.L. Nelson (London and New York, 2001), 432–50.

——, 'Writing Ottonian hegemony. Good rituals and bad rituals in Liutprand of Cremona', *Majestas* 4 (1996), 3–38.

——, 'Principes gentium dominantur eorum: Princely Power Between Legitimacy and Illegitimacy in Twelfth-Century Exegesis', *Cultures of Power: Lordship, Status and Process in Twelfth Century Europe*, ed. T.N. Bisson (Philadelphia, 1995), 310–28.

——, 'Pouvoir royal et commentaires de la Bible (1150–1350)', *Annales Économies, Sociétés, Civilisations* 44 (1989), 691–714.

Bulst-Thiele, M.L., 'Templer in königlichen und päpstlichen Diensten' *Festschrift Percy Ernst Schramm zu seinem siebzigsten Geburtstag*, ed. P. Classen and P. Seibert, 2 vols (Wiesbaden, 1964), 289–308.

Burt, C., 'The demise of the general eyre in the reign of Edward I', *EHR* 120 (2005), 1–14.

Burton, D.W., 'Requests for prayer and royal propaganda under Edward I', *TCE* 3 (1991), 25–35.

Buschmann, A., 'Landfriede und Verfassung. Zur Bedeutung des Mainzer Reichslandfriedens von 1235 als Verfassungsgesetz', *Aus Österreichs Rechtsleben in Geschichte und Gegenwart. Festschrift Ernst C. Hellbling*, ed. Rechtswissenschaftliche Fakultät der Universität Salzburg (Salzburg, 1971), 449–72.

——, 'Der Rheinische Bund von 1254–1257: Landfriede, Städte, Fürsten und Reichsverfassung im 13. Jahrhundert', *Kommunale Bündnisse Oberitaliens und Oberdeutschlands im Vergleich*, ed. H. Maurer (Sigmaringen, 1987), 167–212.

Callahan Jr. T., 'The Making of a Monster: the Historical Image of William Rufus', *JMH* 7 (1981), 175–86.

Cannadine, D. and S. Price (eds), *Rituals of Royalty: Power and Ceremonial in Traditional Societies* (Cambridge, 1987).

Carpenter, D.A., *The Struggle for Mastery. The Penguin History of Britain 1066–1284* (London, 2003).

——, *The Reign of Henry III* (London, 1996).

——, *The Minority of Henry III* (London, 1990).

——, 'Henry III and the cult of Edward the Confessor', *EHR* (forthcoming).

——, The meetings of King Henry III and Louis IX', *TCE* 10 (2005), 1–31.

——, 'Westminster Abbey in Politics, 1258–1269', *TCE* 8 (1999), 49–58.

——, 'The English royal chancery in the thirteenth century', *Ecrit et pouvoir dans les chancelleries médiévales. Espace français, espace anglais. Actes du colloque international de Montréal, 7–9 septembre 1995*, ed. K. Fianu and D.J. Guth (Louvain-la-Neuve, 1997), 25–53.

——, 'The beginnings of parliament', *Reign of Henry III* (London: Hambledon, 1006), 381–408.

——, 'The burial of Henry III, the *regalia* and royal ideology', *The Reign of Henry III* (London: Hambledon, 1996), 427–59.

——, 'English peasants in politics, 1258–1267', *Past & Present* 136 (1992), 3–42.

——, 'Simon de Montfort: the first leader of a political movement in English history', *History* 76 (1991), 3–23.

——, 'King, Magnates and Society. The Personal Rule of King Henry III, 1234–1258', *Speculum* 60 (1985), 39–70.

——, 'What happened in 1258?', *War and Government in the Middle Ages: Essays in honour of J.O. Prestwich*, ed. J. Gillingham and J. Holt (Woodbridge, 1984), 106–19; repr. *Reign* 183–98.

——, 'The Fall of Hubert de Burgh', *Journal of British Studies* 19 (1980) 1–17; repr. *Reign*, 45–60.

Cazel, F.A., 'Intertwined Careers: Hubert de Burgh and Peter des Roches', *Haskins Society Journal* 1 (1989) 173–81.

——, 'Religious motivation in the biography of Hubert de Burgh', *Studies in Church History* 15 (1978), 109–19.

Chaou, A., *L'ideologie Plantagenêt. Royauté arthurienne et monarchie politique dans l'espace Plantagenêt (xii–xiii siècles)* (Rennes, 2001).

Cheney, C.R., 'The "paper constitution" conserved by Matthew Paris', *EHR* 65 (1950), 213–21.

Cheyette, F.L., 'Some Reflections on Violence, Reconciliation, and the "Feudal Revolution"', *Conflict in Medieval Europe*, ed. Brown and Gorecki, 243–64.

Chiffoleau, J., 'I ghibellini de regno di Arles', *Federico II e le città Italian*, ed. P. Toubert and A. Paravacini Bagliani (Palermo, 1994), 364–88.

Church, S.D., 'The royal itinerary in the twelfth century', *TCE* 11 (2007), 31–45.

Clanchy, M.T. *England and its Rulers, 1066–1307*, third edition (Oxford, 2006).

——, *From Memory to Written Record. England 1066–1307*, second edition (Oxford, 1993).

——, 'Did Henry III have a policy?', *History* 53 (1968), 203–16.

Cohn, S.K., *Lust for Liberty: The Politics of Social Revolt in Medieval Europe, 1200–1425* (Cambridge/Mass., 2006).

Crouch, D., *Tournament* (London, 2005).

——, *The Birth of Nobility: Social Change, 950–1350. Constructing Aristocracy in England and France, 900–1300* (Harlow, 2005).

——, *The Image of the Aristocracy in Britain, 1000–1300* (London and New York, 1992).

——, 'Les historiographies médievales franco-anglaises: le point du départ', *Cahiers de la civilisation médiévale* 48 (2005), 317–25.

Csendes, P., *Philip von Schwaben. Ein Staufer im Kampf um die Macht* (Darmstadt, 2003).

Dalewski, Z., 'The Knighting of Polish dukes in the Early Middle Ages: ideological and political significance', *Acta Poloniae Historica* 80 (1999), 15–43.

Davies, R.R., *Domination and Conquest. The experience of Ireland, Wales and Scotland 1100–1300* (Cambridge, 1990).

——, *The First English Empire. Power and Identity in the British Isles 1093–1343* (Oxford, 2000).

d'Avray, D., ' "Magna Carta": its background in Stephen Langton's academic Biblical exegesis and its episcopal reception', *Studi Medievali* 3rd series 38 (1997), 423–38.

Denholm-Young, N., *Richard of Cornwall* (Oxford, 1947).

——, 'The "Paper Constitution" attributed to 1244', *EHR* 50 (1943), 401–23.

Matthew, D., *Britain and the Continent 1000–1300. The impact of the Norman Conquest* (London, 2005).

Duggan, A. (ed.), *Queens and Queenship in Medieval Europe* (Woodbridge, 1997).

Eales, R., 'The political setting of the Becket translation of 1220', *Studies in Church History* 30 (1993), 127–39.

Egger, C., 'Henry III's England and the *curia*', *England and Europe*, ed. Weiler and Rowlands, 215–32.

Ehlers, J., *Die Deutschen und das europäische Mittelalter. Bd. 3: Das westliche Europa* (Berlin, 2004).

—— (ed.), *Deutschland und der Westen Europas im Mittelalter* (Stuttgart, 2002).

Ellis, C., *Hubert de Burgh: a Study in Constancy* (London, 1952).

Engels, O., 'Friedrich Barbarossa im Urteil seiner Zeitgenossen', *Stauferstudien. Beiträge zur Geschichte der Staufer im 12. Jahrhundert*, ed. E. Meuthen and S. Weinfurter (Sigmaringen, 1996), 225–45.

Fischer, B., 'Engelbert von Berg (1185–1225), Kirchenfürst und Staatsmann. Mit einer Gegenüberstellung zu Thomas Becket (1118–1170)', *Zeitschrift des Bergischen Geschichtsvereins* 94 (1989–90), 1–47.

Fischer, M., 'Konrad von Marburg und die Anfänge der Inquisition in Deutschland', *Jahrbuch der Hessischen kirchengeschichtlichen Vereinigung in Hessen und Nassau* 55 (2004), 161–95.

Flachenecker, H., 'Herzog Ludwig der Kelheimer als Prokurator König Heinrichs (VII.)', *Zeitschrift für Bayerische Landesgeschichte* 59 (1996), 835–48.

Fößel, A., *Die Königin im mittelalterlichen Reich. Herrschaftsausübung, Herrschaftsrechte, Handlungsspielräume* (Stuttgart, 2000).

Frech, K.A., 'Ein Plan zur Absetzung Heinrichs (VII): die gescheiterte Legation Kardinal Ottos in Deutschland 1229–1231', *Von Schwaben bis Jerusalem: Facetten staufischer Geschichte*, ed. S. Lorenz and U. Schmidt (Sigmaringen, 1995), 89–116.

Freed, J.B., *Noble Bondsmen. Ministerial marriages in the archdiocese of Salzburg, 1100–1343* (Ithaca, 1995).

——, *The Friars and German Society in the Thirteenth Century* (Cambridge/Mass., 1977).

Fryde, N., 'How to get on in Henry III's England – the career of three German merchants', *England and Europe*, ed. Weiler and Rowlands (Ashgate: Aldershot, 2002) 207–14.

Galbraith, V.H., *Roger of Wendover and Matthew Paris* (Glasgow, 1944).

Garnier, C., 'Zeichen und Schrift. Symbolische Handlungen und literale Fixierung am Beispiel von Friedensschlüssen des 13. Jahrhunderts', *Frühmittelalterliche Studien* 32 (1998), 263–87.

Geary, P.J., and J.B. Freed, 'Literacy and violence in twelfth-century Bavaria. The "murder letter" of Count Siboto IV', *Viator* 25 (1994), 15–29.

Gillingham, J., 'The historian as judge: William Newburgh and Hubert Walter', *EHR* 199 (2004), 1275–87.

——, 'Civilizing the English? The English Histories of William of Malmesbury and David Hume', *Historical Research*, 74 (2001), 17–43.

——, 'Royal newsletters, forgeries and English historians: some links between court and history in the reign of Richard I', *La cour Plantagenêt (1154–1204). Actes du Colloque tenu à Thouars du 30 avril au 2 mai 1999*, ed. Martin Aurell (Poitiers, 2000), 171–86.

Gilsdorf, S., 'Bishops in the middle: mediatory politics and the episcopacy', *The Bishop: Power and Piety at the First Millenium*, ed. S. Gilsdorf (Münster, 2004), 75–112.

Given, J., *State and Society in Medieval Europe. Gwynedd and Languedoc under Outside Rule* (Ithaca, 1990).

Given-Wilson, C., *Chronicles. The Writing of History in Medieval England* (London, 2004).

Görich, K., *Die Ehre Friedrich Barbarossas. Kommunikation, Konflikt und politisches Handeln im 12. Jahrhundert* (Darmstadt, 2001).

——, 'Ehre als Ordnungsfaktor. Anerkennung und Stabilisierung von Herrschaft unter Friedrich Barbarossa und Friedrich II.', *Ordnungskonfigurationen im hohen Mittelalter*, ed. B. Schneidmüller und S. Weinfurter (Ostfildern, 2006), 59–92.

——, 'Verletzte Ehre? Richard Löwenherz als Gefangener Heinrichs VI.', *Historisches Jahrbuch der Görres-Gesellschaft* 123 (2003), 65–91.

——, 'Geld und "honor". Friedrich Barbarossa in Italien', *Formen symbolischer Kommunikation*, ed. Althoff, 177–200.

Goff, J. le, *Saint Louis* (Paris, 1996).

Goll, J., 'Zu Brunos von Olmütz Bericht an Papst Gregor X. (1273)', *Mitteilungen des Instituts für Österreichische Geschichtsforschung* 23 (1902), 487–90.

Gransden, A., *Historical Writing in England, c. 550–c. 1307* (London, 1974).

Graus, F., 'Premisl Otakar II. – sein Ruhm und sein Nachleben. Ein Beitrag zur Geschichte der politischen Propaganda und Chronistik', *Mitteilungen des Instituts für Österreichische Geschichtsforschung* 79 (1971), 57–108.

Green, J.A., *Henry I. King of England and Duke of Normandy* (Cambridge, 2006).

Groten, M., *Köln im 13. Jahrhundert: Gesellschaftlicher Wandel und Verfassungsentwicklung* (Cologne, Weimar and Vienna, 1995).

Guttenberg, E. Freiherr von, *Das Bistum Bamberg*. *Erster Teil*, Germania Sacra: Zweite Abteilung – Die Bistümer der Kirchenprovinz Mainz 1 (Berlin and Leipzig, 1937).

Haines, R.M., 'Canterbury versus York: fluctuating fortunes in a perennial conflict', *Ecclesia Anglicana*. *Studies in the English Church of the Later Middle Ages* (Toronto, 1989), 69–105.

Hausmann, F., 'Kaiser Friedrich II. und Österreich', *Probleme um Friedrich II.*, ws. J. Flecksenstein (Sigmaringen, 1974), 25–308.

Hechberger, W., 'Die Vorstellung vom staufisch-welfischen Gegensatz im 12. Jhdt. Zur Analyse und Kritik einer Deutung', *Heinrich der Löwe: Herrschaft und Repräsentation*, ed. J. Fried and O.G. Oexle (Stuttgart, 2003), 381–426.

Hechelhammer, B., *Kreuzzug und Herrschaft unter Friedrich II. Handlungsspielräume von Kreuzzugspolitik (1215–1230)* (Ostfildern, 2004).

Hiestand, R., 'Friedrich II. und der Kreuzzug', *Friedrich II: Tagung des deutschen Historischen Instituts in Rom im Gedenkjahr 1994*, ed. A. Esch and N. Kamp (Tübingen, 1996), 128–49.

Hillen, C., *Curia Regis. Untersuchungen zur Hofstruktur Heinrichs (VII.) 1220–1235 nach den Zeugen seiner Urkunden* (Frankfurt am Main, 1999).

——, 'The minority governments of Henry (VII), Henry III and Louis IX compared', *TCE* 11 (Woodbridge, 2007).

——, 'Hof und Herrschaft Heinrichs (VII.). Betrachtungen zum Beraterkreis des Königs', *Der Staufer Heinrich (VII.). Ein König im Schatten seines kaiserlichen Vaters* (Göppingen, 2001), 54–70.

Hilpert, H.-E., *Kaiser- und Papstbriefe in den Chronica Majora des Matthaeus Paris* (Stuttgart, 1981).

Hilsch, P., 'Der Deutsche Ritterorden im südlichen Libanon: zur Topographie der Kreuzfahrerstaaten in Sidon und Beirut', *Zeitschrift des deutschen Palästina-Vereins* 96 (1980), 174–89.

Hinnebusch, J.W., *The Early English Friars Preachers* (Rome, 1951).

——, 'Diplomatic activities of the English Dominicans in the thirteenth century', *Catholic Historical Review* 28 (1942), 309–39.

Hoensch, J.K., *Premysl Otakar II. von Böhmen. Der goldene König* (Graz, 1989).

Hollister, C.W., 'Anglo-Norman political culture and the Twelfth-Century Renaissance', *Anglo-Norman Political Culture and the 12th-Century Renaissance. Proceedings of the Borchard Conference on Anglo-Norman History, 1995*, ed. C.W. Hollister (Woodbridge, 1997), 1–16.

Holt, J.C., *Magna Carta*, second edition (Cambridge, 1992).

——, 'King John and Arthur of Brittany', *Nottingham Medieval Studies* 44 (2000), 82–103.

Holzapfel, T., *Papst Innozenz III., Philipp II. August, König von Frankreich und die englisch-welfische Verbindung 1198–1216* (Frankfurt am Main, 1991).

Howell, M., *Eleanor of Provence. Queenship in Thirteenth-Century England* (Oxford, 1998).

——, 'Royal women of England and France in the mid-thirteenth century: a gendered perspective', *England and Europe*, ed. Weiler and Rowlands, pp. 163–82.

Hucker, B.U., *Otto IV. Der wiederentdeckte Kaiser* (Frankfurt am Main, 2003).

Huffman, J.P., *Family, Commerce and Religion in London and Cologne. Anglo-German Emigrants, c. 1000–c. 1300* (Cambridge, 1998).

——, 'Prosopography and the anglo-imperial connection: a Cologne ministerialis family and its English relations', *Medieval Prosopography* 11 (1990), 53–134.

Huscroft, R., *Ruling England, 1042–1217* (Harlow, 2004).

Huth, V., *Staufische 'Reichshistoriographie' und scholastische Intellektualität: das elsässische Augustinerchorherrenstift Marbach im Spannungsfeld von regionaler Überlieferung und universalem Horizont* (Ostfildern, 2004).

Hyams, P., *Rancor and Reconciliation in Medieval England* (Ithaca, 2003).

——, 'Nastiness and wrong, rancor and reconciliation', *Conflict in Medieval Europe*, ed. Brown and Gorecki, 195–218.

Jobson, A. (ed.), *English Government in the Thirteenth Century* (Woodbridge, 2004).

Jones, M. and M. Vale (eds), *England and her Neighbours 1066–1453: essays in honour of Pierre Chaplais* (London, 1989).

Jordan, W.C., '*Quando fuit natus*: Interpreting the birth of Philip Augustus', *The Work of Jacques LeGoff and the Challenges of Medieval History*, ed. M. Rubin (Woodbridge, 1997), 171–88.

Jung, J., 'From Jericho to Jerusalem. The violent transformation of Archbishop Engelbert of Cologne', *Last Things. Death and the Apocalypse in the Middle Ages*, ed. C. Walker Bynum and P. Freedman (Philadelphia, 2000), 60–92, 283–92.

Kagay, D.J., 'The line between history and memoir: James I of Aragon and the *Llibre del feyts*', *Mediterranean Historical Review* 11 (1996), 165–76.

——, 'Structures of baronial dissent and revolt under James I (1213–76)', *Mediaevistik* 1 (1988), 61–85.

Kamp, H., *Friedensstifter und Vermittler im Mittelalter* (Darmstadt, 2001).

Kantorowicz, E.H., *Laudes Regiae. A Study in Liturgical Acclamations and Mediaeval Ruler Worship* (Berkeley, 1946).

Kaufhold, M., *Deutsches Interregnum und europäische Politik. Konfliktlösungen und Entscheidungsstrukturen 1230–1280* (Hanover 2000).

——, 'Die gelehrten Erzbischöfe von Canterbury und die Magna Carta', *Politische Reflexion in der Welt des späten Mittelalters/Political Thought in the Age of Scholasticism. Essays in honour of Jürgen Miethke*, ed. M. Kaufhold (Leiden and Boston, 2004), 43–64.

Keilmann. B., *Der Kampf um die Stadtherrschaft in Worms während des 13. Jahrhunderts*, Quellen und Forschungen zur hessischen Geschichte 50 (Darmstadt and Marburg, 1985).

Keller, H., *Ottonische Königsherrschaft. Organisation und Legitimation königlicher Macht* (Darmstadt, 2002).

Kennedy, H., I. Alonso and J. Escalano (eds), *Building Legitimacy. Political Discourses and Forms of Legitimacy in Medieval Societies* (Leiden, 2004).

Kluger, H., *Hochmeister Hermann von Salza und Kaiser Friedrich II: ein Beitrag zur Frühgeschichte des Deutschen Ordens* (Marburg, 1987).

Köppen, H., 'Die englische Rente für den deutschen Orden', *Festschrift Herman Heimpel*, ed. Max-Planck Institut für Geschichte (Göttingen, 1972), 402–21.

Kosto, A.J., 'Hostages and the habit of representation in thirteenth-century Occitania', *The Experience of Power in Medieval Europe, 950–1150*, ed. R.F. Berkhofer III, A. Cooper and A.J. Kosto (Aldershot, 2005), 183–93.

Koziol, G., *Begging Pardon and Favour. Ritual and Political Order in Early Medieval France* (Ithaca, 1992).

——, 'England, France, and the Problem of Sacrality in Twelfth-Century Ritual', *Cultures of Power. Lordship, Status, and Process in Twelfth-Century Europe*, ed. T.N. Bisson (Philadelphia, 1995), 124–48.

Krieg, H., *Herrscherdarstellung in der Stauferzeit. Friedrich Barbarossa im Spiegel seiner Urkunden und der staufischen Geschichtsschreibung* (Ostfildern, 2003).

Lawrence, C.H., *St Edmund of Abingdon. A Study of Hagiography and History* (Oxford, 1960).

——, 'The letters of Adam Marsh and the Franciscan school at Oxford', *Journal of Ecclesiastical History* 42 (1991), 218–38.

Leyser, K.J., *Rule and Conflict in an Early Medieval Society. Ottonian Saxony* (Oxford, 1979).

——, 'Ritual, Zeremonie und Gestik: das ottonische Reich', *Frühmittelalterliche Studien* 27 (1993), 1–26.

Little, A.G., *Studies in English Franciscan History* (Manchester, 1917).

Lothmann, J., *Erzbischof Engelbert I. von Köln (1216–1225): Graf von Berg, Erzbischof und Herzog, Reichsverweser* (Cologne, 1993).

Lower, M., *The Barons' Crusade. A Call to Arms and Its Consequences* (Philadelphia, 2005).

Maddicott, J.R., *Simon de Montfort* (Cambridge, 1994).

——, ' "1258" and "1297": Some comparisons and contrasts', *TCE* 9 (2003), 1–14.

——, ' "An infinite multitude of nobles": quality, quantity and politics in the pre-reform Parliaments of Henry III', *TCE* 7 (1999), 17–46.

——, 'The county community and the making of public opinion', *TRHS* 5th series 28 (1978), 27–44.

Mansfield, M.C., *The Humiliation of Sinners: Public Penance in Thirteenth-century France* (Ithaca, 1995).

Martin, T.M., *Die Städtepolitik Rudolfs von Hapsburg* (Göttingen, 1976).

Mason, E., 'William Rufus: myth and reality', *Journal of Medieval History* 3 (1977), 1–20.

Matthew, D., *Britain and the Continent 1000–1300* (London, 2005).

McGlynn, S., 'Roger of Wendover and the wars of Henry III, 1216–1234', *England and Europe*, ed. Weiler and Rowlands, 183–206.

Meens, R., 'Politics, mirrors of princes and the Bible: sins, Kings and the well-being of the realm', *Early Medieval Europe* 7 (1998), 345–57.

Miller, E., 'Rulers of thirteenth-century towns: the cases of York and Newcastle upon Tyne', *TCE* 1 (1985), 128–41.

Miller, W.I., *Bloodtaking and Peacemaking. Feud, Law, and Society in Medieval Iceland* (Chicago, 1990).

Morris, M., *The Bigod earls of Norfolk in the Thirteenth Century* (Woodbridge, 2005).

Müller, U., *Untersuchungen zur politischen Lyrik des deutschen Mittelalters*, Göppinger Arbeiten zur Germanistik (Göppingen, 1974).

Nicholson, H., 'The military orders and the kings of England in the twelfth and thirteenth centuries', *From Clermont to Jerusalem. The Crusades and Crusader Societies 1095–1500. Selected Proceedings of the International Medieval Congress, University of Leeds (10–13 July 1995)*, ed. A.V. Murray (Turnhout, 1998), 203–17.

Nelson, J.L., *Rulers and Ruling Families in Early Medieval Europe* (London, 1999).

——, *Politics and Ritual in Early Medieval Europe* (London, 1984).

Patschowsky, A., 'Zur Ketzerverfolgung Konrads von Marburg', *DA* 37 (1981), 641–93.

Petkov, K., *The Kiss of Peace. Ritual, Self, and Society in the High and Late Medieval West* (Leiden and Boston, 2003).

Powell, J.M., 'Frederick II, the Hohenstaufens, and the Teutonic order in the kingdom of Sicily', *The Military Orders: Fighting for the Faith and Caring for the Sick*, ed. M. Barber (Aldershot, 1994), 236–44.

Powicke, F.M., *King Henry III and the Lord Edward. The Community of the Realm in the Thirteenth Century*, 2 vols (Oxford, 1947).

——, *Stephen Langton* (Oxford, 1928).

Prestwich, M., *Edward I* (London, 1988).

Ragotzky, H. and H. Wenzel (eds), *Höfische Repräsentation. Das Zeremoniell und die Zeichen* (Tübingen, 1990).

Reuter, T., *Medieval Polities and Modern Mentalities*, ed. J.L. Nelson (Cambridge, 2006).

——, 'Modern mentalities and medieval polities', *Medieval Polities* (Cambridge: Cambridge University Press, 2006), 3–18.

——, 'Mandate, privilege, court judgement: techniques of rulership in the Age of Frederick Barbarossa', *Medieval Polities*, 413–31.

——, 'Assembly politics in the West from the eight century to the twelfth', *The Medieval World*, ed. P. Linehan and J. Nelson (London, 2001), 432–50; repr. *Medieval Polities*, 193–216.

——, '*Velle Sibi Fieri in forma hac.* Symbolisches Handeln im Becketstreit', *Formen und Funktionen*, ed. Althoff, 201–25; repr. and transl. in his *Medieval Polities*, 167–91.

——, 'The making of England and Germany, 850–1050: points of comparison and difference', *Medieval Europeans. Studies in Ethnic Identity and National Perspectives in Medieval Europe*, ed. A.P. Smyth (London, 1998), 53–70; repr. *Medieval Polities*, 284–99.

——, 'Die Unsicherheit auf den Straßen im europäischen Früh- und Hochmittelalter: Täter, Opfer und ihre mittelalterlichen und modernen Betrachter', *Träger und Funktionen des Friedens im hohen und späten Mittelalter*, ed. J. Fried (Sigmaringen, 1996), 169–202; repr. and transl. *Medieval Polities*, 38–71.

——, 'The medieval German Sonderweg? the empire and its rulers in the high middle ages', *Kings and Kingship* ed. Duggan, 297–325; repr. *Medieval Polities*, 388–412.

——, 'Unruhestiftung, Fehde, Rebellion, Widerstand: Gewalt und Frieden in der Politik der Salierzeit', *Die Salier und das Reich. Gesellschaftlicher und ideengeschichtlicher Wandel im Reich der Salier*, ed. S. Weinfurter, 3 vols (Sigmaringen, 1992), iii, 297–325; repr. and transl. *Medieval Polities*, 355–87.

Rexroth, Frank 'Tyrannen und Taugenichtse. Beobachtungen zur Ritualität europäischer Königsabsetzungen im späten Mittelalter', *HZ* 278 (2004), 27–53.

Reynolds, S., *Kingdoms and Communities in Western Europe 900–1300* (Oxford, 1984).

——, 'How different was England?', *TCE* 7 (1999), 1–16.

Ridgway, H., 'King Henry III and the "aliens" 1236–1272', *TCE* 2 (1987), 81–92.

Roberg, B., *Das Zweite Konzil von Lyon [1274]* (Paderborn, 1990).

Robinson, I.S., *Henry IV of Germany, 1056–1106* (Cambridge, 1999).

Röhrkasten, J., *The Mendicant Houses of Medieval London 1221–1539* (Münster, 2004).

——, 'Die englischen Dominikaner und ihre Beziehungen zur Krone im 13. Jahrhundert', *Vita Religiosa im Mittelalter. Festschrift für Kaspar Elm zum 70. Geburtstag*, ed. F.J. Felten, N. Jaspert and S. Haarländer (Berlin, 1999), 483–502.

——, 'Londoners and London mendicants in the late midde ages', *Journal of Ecclesiastical History* 47 (1996), 446–77.

Rösener, W., 'Die ritterlich-höfische Kultur des Mittelalters und ihre wirtschaftlichen Grundlagen', *Rittertum und höfische Kultur der Stauferzeit*, ed. J. Laudage and Y. Leiverkus (Cologne, Weimar and Vienna, 2006), 111–35.

Rogge, J., 'Attentate und Schlachten. Beobachtungen zum Verhältnis von Königtum und Gewalt im deutschen Reich während des 13. und 14. Jahrhunderts', *Königliche Gewalt – Gewalt gegen Könige*, ed. M. Kintzinger and J. Rogge (Zeitschrift für Historische Forschung, Beiheft 33), (Berlin, 2004), 7–50.

Rosenthal, J.T., 'The king's "wicked advisers" and medieval baronial rebellions', *Political Science Quarterly* 82 (1967), 595–618.

Scales, L.E., 'At the margin of community: Germans in Pre-Hussite Bohemia', *TRHS* 6th series 9 (1999), 327–52.

Schaller, H.M., 'Die Frömmigkeit Kaiser Friedrichs II', *Das Staunen der Welt: Kaiser Friedrich II. von Hohenstaufen 1194–1250, Schriften zur staufischen Geschichte und Kunst* xv, (Göppingen, 1996), 128–51.

Schmidt, U., *Königswahl und Thronfolge im 12. Jahrhundert* (Cologne, Weimar and Vienna, 1987).

Schmitt, J.C., *La raison des Gestes dans l'Occident médiéval* (Paris, 1990).

——, (ed.), *Gestures* (London, 1984).

Schreiner, K., ' "Er küsse mich mit dem Kuß seines Mundes" (Osculetur me oscuto oris sui, Cant 1,1). Metaphorik, kommunikative und herrschaftliche Funktionen einer symbolischen Handlung', *Höfische Kommunikation*, ed. Wenzel and Ragotzky, 89–132.

——, 'Gregor VIII., nackt auf einem Esel. Entehrende Entblößung und schandbares Reiten im Spiegel einer Miniatur der Sächsischen Weltchronik', *Ecclesia et Regnum. Beiträge zur Geschichte von Kirche, Recht und Staat im Mittelalter. Festschrift für Franz-Josef Schmale zu seinem 65. Geburtstag*, ed. D. Berg and H.-W. Goetz (Bochum, 1989), 155–202.

Schwarz, J., *Herrscher- und Reichstitel bei Kaisertum und Papsttum im 12. und 13. Jahrhundert* (Cologne and Vienna, 2003).

Shepard, L., *Courting Power: Persuasion and Politics in the Early Thirteenth Century* (New York, 1999).

Smith, B., 'Irish politics, 1220–1245', *TCE* 8 (2001), 13–22.

Stacey, R.C., *Politics, Policy and Finance under Henry III 1216–1245* (Oxford, 1987).

Staniland, K., 'The nuptials of Alexander III of Scotland and Margaret Plantagenet', *Nottingham Medieval Studies* 30 (1986), 20–45.

Staunton, M., 'Exile in Eadmer's *Historia Novorum* and *Vita Anselmi*', *Saint Anselm, Bishop and Thinker: Papers Read at a Conference Held in the Catholic University of Lublin on 24–26 September 1996*, ed. R. Majeran and E.I. Zielinski (Lublin, 1999), 47–59.

Stehkämper, H., 'Geld bei deutschen Königswahlen im 13. Jahrhundert', *Wirtschaftskräfte und Wirtschaftswege: Festschrift Hermann Kellenbenz*, ed. J. Schneider, 4 vols (Stuttgart, 1978), i. 83–115.

Struve, T., *Die Entwicklung der organologischen Staatsauffassung im Mittelalter* (Stuttgart, 1978).

Stürner, W., *Friedrich II.*, 2 vols (Darmstadt, 1994–2000).

——, 'König Heinrich (VII.). Rebell oder Sachwalter staufischer Interessen?', *Der Staufer Heinrich (VII.). Ein König im Schatten seines kaiserlichen Vaters* (Göppingen, 2001), 12–41.

——, 'Der Staufer Heinrich (VII.) (1211–1242): Lebensstationen eines gescheiterten Königs', *Zeitschrift für Württembergische Landesgeschichte* 52 (1993) 13–33.

Thirteenth Century England, ed. P. Coss and S.D. Lloyd (1983–93); R.H. Britnell, R. Frame and M.C. Prestwich (1995–2005); J. Burton, P.R. Schofield and B. Weiler (2007–).

Thomson, W.R., 'The image of the Mendicants in the chronicles of Matthew Paris', *Archivum franciscanum historicum* 70 (1977), 3–34.

Thorau, P., *König Heinrich (VII.), das Reich und die Territorien. Untersuchungen zur Phase der Minderjährigkeit und der 'Regentschaften' Erzbischof Engelberts I. von Köln und Herzog Ludwigs I. von Bayern (1211) 1220–38*, Jahrbücher der Deutschen Geschichte: Jahrbücher des Deutschen Reichs unter Heinrich (VII.), Teil I (Berlin, 1998).

——, 'Die erste Bewährungsprobe Heinrichs (VII.)', *Der Staufer Heinrich (VII.). Ein König im Schatten seines kaiserlichen Vaters* (Göppingen, 2001), 43–52.

Thum, B., 'Öffentlichkeit und Kommunikation im Mittelalter. Zur Herstellung von Öffentlichkeit im Bezugsfeld elementarer Kommunikationsformen im 13. Jahrhundert', *Höfische Repräsentation*, ed. Ragotzky and Wenzel, 65–87.

Treharne, R.F., 'The Mise of Amiens, 23 January 1264', *Studies in medieval history, presented to Frederick Maurice Powicke*, ed. R.W. Hunt (Oxford, 1948), 223–39.

Truax, J.A., 'Winning over the Londoners: King Stephen, the Empress Matilda and the politics of personality', *Haskins Society Journal* 8 (1996), 42–62.

Turner, R.V., *Magna Carta* (Harlow, 2003).

——, *The King and his Courts. The Role of John and Henry III in the Administration of Justice, 1199–1240* (Ithaca, 1968).

Valente, C., *The Theory and Practice of Revolt in Medieval England* (Aldershot, 2003).

——, 'The Provisions of Oxford: assessing/assigning authority in time of unrest', *The Experience of Power in Medieval Europe, 950–1350*, ed. R.F. Berkhofer III, A. Cooper and A.J. Kosto (Aldershot, 2005), 25–42.

——, 'Simon de Montfort, earl of Leicester, and the utility of sanctity in thirteenth-century England', *JMH* 21 (1995), 27–49.

van Eickels, K., *Vom inszenierten Konsens zum systematisierten Konflikt. Die englisch-französischen Beziehungen und ihre Wahrnehmung an der Wende vom Hoch- zum Spätmittelalter* (Stuttgart, 2002).

Vaughan, R., *Matthew Paris* (Cambridge, 1958).

Vincent, N., *Peter des Roches. An alien in English politics 1205–1238* (Cambridge, 1996).

——, *The Holy Blood. King Henry III and the Westminster Blood Relic* (Cambridge, 2001).

——, 'The pilgrimages of the Angevin kings of England, 1154–1272', *Pilgrimage. The English experience from Becket to Bunyan*, ed. C. Morris and P. Roberts (Cambridge, 2002), 12–45.

——, 'Conclusion', *Noblesses de l'espace Plantagenêt (1154–1224)*, ed. M. Aurell (Poitiers, 2001), 207–14.

Watt, J.A., 'The theory of papal monarchy in the thirteenth century: the contribution of the canonists', *Traditio* 20 (1964) 178–317.

——, 'Spiritual and temporal powers', *The Cambridge History of Medieval Political Thought, c. 350-c. 1450*, ed. J.H. Burns (Cambridge, 1988), 367–423.

Weiler, B., *King Henry III of England and the Staufen Empire, 1216–1272* (Woodbridge, 2006).

——, 'The king as judge: Henry II and Frederick Barbarossa as seen by their contemporaries', *Texts, Histories and Historiographies. Essays in memory of Timothy Reuter*, ed. P.J. Skinner (Turnhout, forthcoming).

——, 'Kings and sons: rebellious princes and the structures of revolt in Western Europe, 1170–c. 1280', *Historical Research* (forthcoming).

——, 'Knighting, homage and the meaning of ritual: the kings of England and their neighbors in the thirteenth century', *Viator* 37 (2006), 275–300.

——, 'Reasserting power: Frederick II in Germany (1235–6)', *Representations of Power in Medieval Germany, 700–1500*, ed. S. MacLean and B. Weiler (Turnhout, 2006), 241–70.

——, 'William of Malmesbury on kingship', *History* 87 (2005), 3–22.

——, 'Symbolism and Politics in the Reign of Henry III', *TCE* 9 (2003), 15–41.

——, 'Henry III through European eyes – communication and historical writing in thirteenth-century Europe', *England and Europe*, ed. Weiler and Rowlands (Ashgate: Aldershot, 2002), 137–61.

——, 'Frederick II, Gregory IX and the liberation of the Holy Land 1231–9', *Studies in Church History* 35 (2000), 192–206.

——, 'Image and reality in Richard of Cornwall's German career', *English Historical Review* 113 (1998), 1111–42.

—— with Ifor Rowlands (ed.), *England and Europe in the Reign of Henry III (1216–1272)* (Aldershot, 2002).

Wendehorst, A., *Das Bistum Würzburg. Teil 1: Die Bischofsreihe bis 1254*, Germania Sacra Neue Folge 1: Die der Kirchenprovinz Mainz (Berlin, 1962).

White, S.D., 'From Peace to Power: The Study of Disputes in Medieval France,' E. Cohen and M. de Jong, eds, *Medieval Transformations* (Leiden: Brill, 2000), 203–18.

——, 'Feuding and Peace-Making in the Touraine around the Year 1100', *Traditio* 42 (1986), 195–63.

——, ' "*Pactum ... Legem Vincit et Amor Judicium*": The Settlement of Disputes by Compromise in Eleventh-Century Western France', *American Journal of Legal History* 22 (1979), 291–309.

Wolf, G., 'Wimpfen, Worms und Heidelberg. Einige Bemerkungen zum Herrschaftsende König Heinrichs', *Zeitschrift für Geschichte des Oberrheins* Neue Folge 98 (1989), 471–86.

Wood, C.T., 'The Mise of Amiens and Saint-Louis' theory of kingship', *French Historical Studies* 6 (1970), 300–10.

Zöller, S., *Kaiser, Kaufmann und die Macht des Geldes: Gerhard Unmaze von Köln als Finanzier der Reichspolitik und der 'Gute Gerhard' des Rudolf von Ems* (Munich, 1993).

Index